D1507398

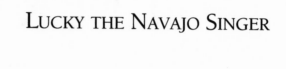

LUCKY THE NAVAJO SINGER

LUCKY THE

RECORDED BY
ALEXANDER H. LEIGHTON
AND DOROTHEA C. LEIGHTON

NAVAJO SINGER

EDITED AND ANNOTATED BY
JOYCE J. GRIFFEN

FOREWORD BY
ALEXANDER H. LEIGHTON

UNIVERSITY OF NEW MEXICO PRESS
ALBUQUERQUE

First edition

Library of Congress Cataloging–in–Publication Data

Leighton, Alexander H. (Alexander H.), 1908–

Lucky, the Navajo singer / recorded by Alexander H. Leighton and
Dorothea C. Leighton ; edited and annotated by Joyce J. Griffen ;
foreword by Alexander H. Leighton.

p.   cm.

Includes bibliographical references and index.

ISBN 0-8263-1374-4 :

1. Navajo Indians—Biography.   2. Navajo Indians—Social life
and customs.   3. Ramah (N.M.)—Biography.   4. Ramah (N.M.)—
Social life and customs.   I. Leighton, Dorothea Cross, 1908–   .
II. Griffen, Joyce.   III. Title.

E99.N3L546   1992

978.9′83—dc20

[B]

92–9027

CIP

Designed by
Linda Mae Tratechaud

For the Navajo—as for any other minority group with a clear sense of identity—there exists another form of responsibility in resisting any kind of engulfment. This time the responsibility is not only to its own self but also toward the larger nation-state of which it is a member. Being different—preserving their own cultural identity—the Navajo are enriching the country, the nation-state, and also the rest of mankind, with their own heritage, world view, beliefs, values, language, traditions, symbols, and art. Truly, no national greatness may ever exist if it deprives others (and, as a consequence, deprives itself) of the possibility of achieving a unity of essentially human purposes within a variety of cultural traditions—faces and hearts which are not identical.

Navajo greatness—the real meaning of the cultural core of the *Diné,* "The People"—is in this way inevitably linked to the national greatness of the United States of America: *E Pluribus Unum.* I trust in the will and courage of the Navajo people and in the capacity of the Anglos and other Americans to understand and to realize that, in this case, as in many others, national greatness will be enriched by those who choose to develop on the basis of their own cultural identity.

—Miguel León-Portilla, "Aztecs and Navajos: A Reflection on the Right of Not Being Engulfed" (1975:24)

Contents

ILLUSTRATIONS

FOREWORD

In the late thirties and early forties, the question of how culture and personality relate to each other was of considerable interest to a number of leading anthropologists, sociologists, psychologists, and psychiatrists. A list of names would include Edward Sapir, Ruth Benedict, Margaret Mead, Ralph Linton, Clyde Kluckhohn, W.I. Thomas, Leo Simmons, Gordon Allport, Harry Stack Sullivan, William Alanson White, Abram Kardiner, and Adolf Meyer. Even though written some years later, the following quotation from the introduction to *Personality in Nature, Society and Culture,* edited by Kluckhohn and Murray, illustrates the kind of issues discussed:

> Is there a connection between the mental illnesses characteristic of a given group and the social norms that this group enforces with special severity? Does a people's way of bringing up their children make a particular type of personality unusually common in that society? Why do certain kinds of delinquency appear most frequently among the children of certain social classes? How much of an individual's personality is fixed by his biological constitution? How much is personal life style influenced by the society's traditional designs for living (its "cul-

ture")? Why are ways of behaving that are punished by one group rewarded, or at any rate tolerated, by another? Is individual deviance culturally defined, or are there absolute standards of psychological abnormality? What is the role of outstanding personalities and of other individuals in social change? (Kluckhohn and Murray 1948:xi)

Such interest in culture and personality seems to have emerged in the twenties among Sapir and his students at Chicago. In 1933 the sociologist, W.I. Thomas, also at Chicago, submitted an influential report to the Social Science Research Council entitled, "On the Organization of a Program in the Field of Personality and Culture." Benedict's classic and beautifully written *Patterns of Culture* appeared in 1934, attracting wide attention to a theory in which culture had a dominant influence in shaping personality.

Theory development through speculation rather than empirical studies came to be the center of interest for most of those concerned about culture and personality, following the mode already established in psychoanalytic literature. Particularly intriguing was the possibility of bringing about a synthesis of cultural theory and psychoanalysis.

There were, however, individuals who took exception to this emphasis on "Big Theory," among whom was Adolf Meyer, chief of the Department of Psychiatry at John's Hopkins Medical School. Although he believed that the questions being raised were of first order importance, he considered the preoccupation with speculative schemes to be premature and apt to generate and popularize notions that had little evidence to support them. In his view basic factual information regarding both culture and personality was as yet insufficient, and this made it desirable for contemporary studies to emphasize systematic observation and description followed by comparative analysis based on the obtained data. W.I. Thomas, who with Florian Znaniecki had produced the monumental *Polish Peasant* (1927), was among those who held similar views.

My entry into this exciting arena came in 1937 or 1938 while I was in psychiatric training under Meyer. The point of departure for me was puzzlement over how "normal" people (i.e. not mentally ill) handled those inner conflicts and difficult interpersonal relationships that appeared to play such a destructive role in the lives of the patients I was seeing daily and trying to help. It seemed self-evident that such conflicts and difficult relations were by no means confined to the mentally ill. Were there differences in how "normals" managed them?

An attempt to find answers to this question revealed that very few comparative studies of ill and well personalities had ever been made. So far as I could see, most of the ideas in psychiatry about normality were inferences based on the investigation of abnormal persons. To one like myself with a background in natural history and neurophysiology, this absence appeared to be a serious scientific defect—an impression which was strengthened when I realized that psychiatry was the only branch of clinical medicine based almost exclusively on the study of pathology. In all the others studies of pathological conditions were complemented by studies of normal functioning.

Out of these considerations came the notion that there might be a lot to gain from a descriptive study of normal personalities in their normal settings. With encouragement from Meyer, Dorothea Leighton (who was also a psychiatric resident at Hopkins) and I began exploring ways and means. The technique of investigation that lay most readily at hand was Meyer's system for conducting personality studies, a technique in which we were already trained. It was the standard approach employed by Meyer and his colleagues (and by most other academic psychiatrists in North America at this time) for understanding the origins, present status, and modifiability of mental and emotional disorders. Despite its diagnostic and healing purpose, we found the method fairly easy to adapt for the study of nonpatients. This may have been due in part to the fact that Meyer, as he once told me, had originally developed the personality study so as to better understand himself.

I was strongly persuaded that to comprehend a personality you must also understand his or her context. This was, again, doubtless due to the naturalist training that included researches in animal behavior, and to a sense of deprivation in having very little direct access to this kind of information when working with patients. But it was also in the orientation of the personality study itself, as well as in Meyer's views regarding the information needed in order to comprehend the functioning of a personality, whether ill or well. Our first research notion, therefore, envisioned taking a sample of individuals in a given community and studying both sample and community. The sample members would be investigated by an adaptation of the personality study, and the community by techniques and concepts that we expected to obtain from anthropology and sociology.

This way of structuring the research idea led to extensive reading and consultation regarding communities and the techniques for investigating them. This in turn brought the concept of culture to the fore. As Malinowski told us, with characteristic firmness and flare, we were too much immersed in our own culture to be adequate observers. Thus it was with guidance by Clyde Kluckhohn and Ralph Linton, with backing from Meyer, and a grant from the Social Science Research Council, that we arrived at a snow-covered "Kainti" early in January of 1940. Kluckhohn introduced us to "Bill Sage."

Our goals were two: to probe the feasibility of making systematic personality studies in this nonclinical setting, and to learn about Navajo culture by observing it through the personality studies and in the daily life going on around us.

By the end of May, data for six studies had been gathered plus several additional biographic sketches.

In the course of this work three impressions led to additional goals. The first had to do with the fact that the major component in the personality study consisted of a life history. In telling their histories, our subjects would report on numerous specific cultural sentiments and practices in terms that showed their meaning to him or her, and, very often, the later consequences and outcomes. This presentation was very different from the generalizations about Navajo culture one commonly heard from anthropologists or read in the literature. The life history consisted of descriptions of particular events in the course of a life and of how particular cultural elements played a part in what transpired. Thus the researcher could sometimes see the same interpersonal event, ceremonial, or cultural idea from more than one angle.

This perspective was not limited to Navajo culture; it also included bits and pieces of Anglo, Spanish, and Zuni culture that touched the lives of our autobiographers, that interacted with the Navajo elements and with events more situational than cultural, such as "small pox" and "the big snow." The life histories gave a picture of Navajo persons wending through life, experiencing many different kinds of influences, but with "the Navajo Way" always making up large stretches of the path they trod.

The second impression was of marked differences among Navajo individuals, in how they interpreted and utilized cultural elements. There was also variation in the elements each mentioned and in the degree of credence and importance attached. This turned our attention to the differences of cultural expression from person to person and to why these differences might occur. It seemed likely that variations in temperament and cognitive abilities, together with chance life experiences, created differences in how people absorbed and utilized the envelope of Navajo culture in which each had lived and was still living.

These observations and impressions suggested that while the ethnographic approach is sensitive to commonalities that make up a culture, the life-history approach is by contrast sensitive to individual variations in meaning and expression. It seemed evident that both would be required if there were to be progress toward understanding the nature of the relationships between culture and personality. When I expressed such thoughts to Kluckhohn, he told me that Sapir had once said that every individual lives in a culture that is different from that of every other individual.

The third impression gathered at Kainti was that when you make personality studies of persons who are members of the same community, their lives touch and sometimes entwine so that each study illuminates and is illuminated by each of the other studies. This not only provides information about intracultural variation and differences of viewpoints, but it also provides information about how the community functions as a societal system.

These three impressions generated by the fieldwork led to three goals beyond the original pair. The first was to explore the different ways Navajo cultural patterns functioned in the individuals' lives. The second was to explore the possible use of a set of personality studies as a method in community study, and to formulate how such data might be integrated with ethnographic and sociological types of information. The third goal, some of it developed later in the course of analyzing the data, consisted in trying to design a replicable and systematic method for making a personality study of a normal person. This included specifications about what kind of data to collect, how to organize them, and how to conduct analysis. The focus was on noting the person's dominant patterns of behavior and common expressions of sentiment and on describing how these functioned in the basic process of life: gaining subsistence, negotiating interpersonal relationships, managing sex and reproduction, and coping with feelings about supernatural forces. It seemed to me that this could pave the way for developing methods for classifying personalities and their component subpatterns thereby opening the door to quantification and the establishment of at least some scientifically based probability—such as degree and kinds of variations among personalities, and when and how cultural patterns exert an influence. In sum we decided to see if we could embark on a taxonomy of personalities and personality patterns.

The monograph, *Gregorio, the Hand-Trembler* (Leighton and Leighton 1949), describes and illustrates these ideas. Supplemental information may also be found in an *American Anthropologist* article, "Some Types of Uneasiness and Fear in a Navajo Indian Community" (Leighton and Leighton 1942:194–209).

It was our hope that we could follow *Gregorio* with similar monographs based on each of the other Navajo personality studies and studies obtained later the same year from Yupik people on St. Lawrence Island in Alaska, and then perhaps a final volume synthesizing the whole. World War II brought interruptions so that *Gregorio* was not completed until 1949. In the years that followed, academic interest in culture and in personality began to pull away from each other, so that culture-personality as a multidisciplinary field became attenuated and at a distance from the main stream in both the social sciences and psychiatry. Furthermore the areas of culture and personality each became even more preoccupied with the construction of theories while growing less interested in empirical observation and description. Under these circumstances it seemed best to wait and publish in a more favorable climate, and Dorothea Leighton ultimately placed the fieldnotes where they might be available to others at a later date.

It is to be noted, however, that concern with the study of life histories as such has never altogether died out, and may be again increasing, as witnessed by the current vigor of the Life History Society. Advances towards more systematic methods may also be taking place in accordance with the needs stressed by Langness and Frank (1981). In some respects the earlier students of how personality and culture affect each other may now have been replaced by investigators conducting long term population studies. A number of these have been gathering data on individuals for almost half a century. Examples include the Terman study (Terman and Oden 1959) and the Oakland growth study (Block 1971; Eichhorn et. al. 1981) on the West Coast, and the Harvard Medical School study of adult development (Monks 1957; Glueck and Glueck 1968; Valliant 1983; Valliant 1977) on the East Coast, which now subsumes the Glueck study of the Harvard Law School and the Bock and Heath study of the Harvard University Health Services. John Clausen in the West and George E. Valliant in the East may be mentioned as current leaders in the analyses of these data. Additional programs include the follow-up investigations of Lee Robins and her associates at Washington University in St. Louis (Robins 1966), the Lundby study headed by Ölle Hagnell in Sweden (Hagnell 1980), and the Stirling County study in Atlantic Canada (Leighton 1986:111–127; Murphy 1980: 390–96).

Against this background it is most pleasing to see the publication of Lucky's story. I am exceedingly grateful to Joyce Griffen for her initiative in undertaking the task and for carrying it out so splendidly. Although I cannot claim to be an objective evaluator—the re-reading of the notes raises too many deeply moving recollections—this portrait is Lucky as I knew him. The original material is enormously enriched by Joyce's insightful organization and supplemental explanations.

We see here briefly a Navajo picked out on the vast stage of the Southwest as he and it were more than fifty years ago.

Alexander H. Leighton
December 1991

REFERENCES

Benedict, Ruth
1934 Patterns of Culture. New York: Houghton-Mifflin.

Block, J.
1971 Lives Through Time. Berkeley: Bancroft Books.

Eichhorn, D., J. Clausen, N. Haan, M. Honzik, and P. Mussen, eds.
1981 Present and Past in Middle Life. New York: Academic Press.

Glueck, S., and E. Glueck
1968 Delinquents and Non-Delinquents in Perspective. Cambridge, Massachusetts: Harvard University Press.

Hagnell, Ö.
1980 The Lundby Study on Psychiatric Morbidity (Sweden). In Prospective Longitudinal Research: An Empirical Basis for the Primary Prevention of Psychosocial Disorders. S.A. Mednick and A.E. Baert, eds. Oxford: Oxford University Press.

Kluckhohn, Clyde, and H.A. Murray, eds.
1948 Introduction. In Personality in Nature, Society and Culture. New York: Alfred A. Knopf.

Langness L.L., and G. Frank
1981 Lives: An Anthropological Approach to Biography. Novato, California: Chandler and Sharp.

Leighton, A.H.
1986 The Initial Frame of Reference of the Stirling County Study: Main Questions Asked and Reasons for Them. In Mental Disorders in the Community, Progress and Challenges. J. Barrett and R. Rose, eds. New York: Guilford Press. Pp. 111–127.

Leighton, Alexander H., and Dorothea C. Leighton
1942 Some Types of Uneasiness and Fear in a Navajo Indian Community. American Anthropologist 44 (2): 194–209.
1949 Gregorio, The Hand-Trembler: A Psychobiological Personality Study of a Navajo Indian. Cambridge, Massachusetts: The Peabody Museum of American Archaeology and Ethnology, Harvard University.

Monks, J.P.
1957 College Men at War. Boston: American Academy of Arts and Sciences.

Murphy, J.M.
1980 Depression in the Community: Findings from the Stirling County Study. Canadian Journal of Psychiatry 35 (5): 390–396.

Robins, L.
1966 Deviant Children Grow Up. Baltimore: Williams and Wilkins.

Terman, L.M., and M.H. Oden
1959 The Gifted Group at Midlife. Stanford: Stanford University Press.

Thomas, W.I., and Florian Znaniecki
1927 The Polish Peasant in Europe and America. New York: Alfred A. Knopf.

Valliant, G.E.
1977 Adaptation to Life. Boston, Massachusetts: Little Brown.
1983 The Natural History of Alcoholism. Cambridge, Massachusetts: Harvard University Press.

PREFACE

Lucky's life history was recorded more than fifty years ago. During that elapsed half-century many of the people involved in this book have died, including Lucky himself, and fashions in writing about the American Southwest have come and gone. Humanistic anthropology has gained legitimacy and professional interest in life histories has increased, while the Navajo protagonists of a series of novels have brought Navajo culture for the first time to the attention of many readers.

The number of published life histories of Native Americans is woefully small, however, and only a handful of them are Navajo. The first book-length Navajo life history was Dyk's *Son of Old Man Hat: A Navaho Autobiography*, published in 1938; *Gregorio, the Hand-Trembler*, recorded by the Leightons, appeared in 1949.[1]

After the publication of *Gregorio*, almost three decades passed before additional Navajo biographies appeared. Bennett's *Kaibah, Recollection of a Navajo Childhood* appeared in 1974, Frisbie was senior editor of *Navajo Blessingway Singer: The Autobiography of Frank Mitchell*, published in 1978, and two other life history volumes were published in 1980: Irene Stewart's

A Voice in Her Tribe: A Navajo Woman's Own Story and the Dyks' *Left Handed: A Navajo Autobiography,* the sequel to *Old Man Hat.* Regarding the life history approach, Langness and Frank's *Lives: An Anthropological Approach to Biography* (1981) is highly recommended, as is Geertz's *Works and Lives: The Anthropologist as Author* (1988).

That the life history dictated by Lucky the Navajo Singer, translated by Bill Sage and recorded for the most part by Alexander H. Leighton, is now appearing involves not only the passage of a half-century but some unlikely juxtapositions. I had collected life histories of Navajo women employed in Flagstaff, Arizona, and met Dorothea Leighton when I organized a session on Navajo women for a meeting of the American Anthropological Association (the papers presented there were later published as vol. 6, nos. 1 and 2, of the *American Indian Quarterly*). I was struck by the fact that several early and eminent Navajo scholars had been women, and I sought and was granted interviews with four of them, including Dorothea Leighton.[2] The quotes and comments cited herein as D. C. Leighton, p.c. (personal communication), are from the interview with her that I recorded in Berkeley on March 10 and 11, 1982. Later that same year the Alexander H. Leighton and Dorothea C. Leighton Collection, which contains the typescripts of Lucky's life history, was given to the Special Collections Library of Northern Arizona University.[3]

Two versions of Lucky's life history exist in typescript in the collection; the earlier is labeled LUCKY on the cover of the black binding and is headed merely "Life Story" on the first page of the manuscript. The edited version used here, titled "Lucky the Navajo Singer," was prepared by Dorothea C. Leighton in 1981 and 1982. While the less-polished English of the LUCKY version carries a certain immediacy it is more difficult to read smoothly, and it makes Lucky appear to be speaking a kind of pidgin English although his words must have been spoken smoothly and at times poetically,[4] and Bill as translator put those words into his best English.

The Leighton's field notes were sorted under various headings and later summarized. I have cited them either as Summary of a specific topic (social relations, for example) or as the topic itself (Social Relations). Parentheses within these quotations refer to the field notes of other workers. Quotations cited by date and page number are also Leighton field notes, which are also typed under subject headings. However, they were never edited for anonymity, so in them I have supplied the required pseudonyms. Parentheses, except in the Introduction, are as they appear in the original manuscript, and where, late in Lucky's story, "Abbreviated" and "Verbatim" indicate switching back and forth between summary and full descriptions. Brackets indicate variant wording from an earlier version of Lucky's story (see below) and I have used { and } for my own in-text insertions. Navajo names for ceremonies and prayers have been capitalized but not otherwise set off, and I have italicized Navajo nouns only on their first appearance.

Lucky should be the star of his life history, and I have tried to present it so that those concerned with it alone may read it with a minimum number of interruptions. Quotations are therefore indented and can be readily skipped, as can the end notes. These contain the usual editorial miscellany, and they are followed by bibliographic information on the references I have used. Within the manuscript there are no natural breaks that suggest conventional chapters, so I have added subheadings which I hope will make some of the events of Lucky's life easier to locate.

I deeply regret that Dorothea is not alive to see this book; she died in August 1989. Her friendship was important to me, and I am grateful to have known her. I am grateful also to my friends Charlotte Beyal, Franklin Denipah, and Ida Mae Provorse, and to the Navajo women who spoke with me in 1979 and 1980; to Northern Arizona University for the Organized Research Grant which supported two summers of that activity and for a sabbatical devoted to gathering data on some consequences of the forced relocation of Navajos from the former Joint-Use Area of the reservation. I am grateful also to other women who are Navajo scholars; thank you, Jennie R. Joe, Ann Hedlund, Susan Kent, Louise Lamphere, Ann Metcalf, Nancy Parezo, Mary Shepardson, Katherine Spencer, and Anne Wright, and, most especially, Charlotte Frisbie. My thanks go also to Navajo scholars David F. Aberle, David Brugge, and John Farella, and to my first professor of anthropology, Omer C. Stewart. Dr. Alexander H. Leighton has been both interested and helpful as the work progressed, and I am grateful to him for permission to use pictures taken in 1940 and to quote from the field notes in the Leighton Collection. I wish also to thank Jennifer White and Virginia Wallace for hospitality at several stages of the work. Librarians always are due many thank-yous; mine go especially to Octavia Fellin of the Gallup Public Library for her efforts to track down some of the events alluded to by Lucky; to those most valuable reference librarians Muriel Coil and Dana Cole at Northern Arizona University; and to the staff of NAU's Special Collections Library.

I wish also to thank Bill's daughter Marie, who not only carried on her father's helpfulness to *belaganas*—Anglos—but also has communicated to me her sense of the vivid richness of the Navajo lives of a half-century ago in the northwestern New Mexico. The opportunity to know her, her sisters, and other family members has been a rare privilege. I am glad I met her father, if belatedly, and I am grateful to him for speaking for the Leightons to Lucky and for his faithful translation and patience with the long hours the project required. I am grateful to Lucky for those, too, and for his care in setting forth for the Leightons, with what seems to be complete honesty, almost untinged with fear, a life history that can only enrich us.

I know that all of you have enriched my life, and I am grateful. As for my husband Bill: once again, thank you, more than words can say.

Joyce J. Griffen

INTRODUCTION:
PEOPLE, PLACE, AND TIME

"LUCKY" AND "BILL"

The voices of many people resonate in this book; despite the title, it is more an opera than it is a performance by Lucky alone.[1] Lucky himself would not have been heard beyond a small area of the American Southwest but for his friend and translator Bill Sage. (Lucky and Bill are pseudonyms, as are the names of most of the people and several of the places in this book, as required by the terms of use of the Dorothea C. Leighton and Alexander H. Leighton Collection.) Bill has been of substantial importance in anthropology, for it was on his goodwill and on his numerous skills that Clyde Kluckhohn and many others depended through years of research in northwestern New Mexico. The dependence lasted quite some time, for Bill "began working with Kluckhohn as an interpreter back in the thirties [and] has hosted so many field workers that he and his family once built a special hogan 'for the anthropologists'" (Blanchard 1971:4). In turn, Bill's daughter remembers that wages paid by Kluckhohn and others were very important to the Sage family during the Depression years, when employment in the area was almost nonexistent (p.c., Nov. 9, 1989).

Clyde Kluckhohn

Clyde Kluckhohn was seriously ill as a teenager, and he journeyed to New Mexico with the hope that he would recover there. In his book *To the Foot of the Rainbow,* published when he was twenty-two, he writes of the beginnings of his acquaintance with the people who became his lifelong focus—the Diné, the Navajo people. He had special ties with families in the Ramah area, where Bill Sage was born, and in Kainti, where Bill moved when he married, for in the Navajo way a husband moves to his wife's area. Thus it was that, in 1940, Kluckhohn directed the doctors Leighton to the Sage household in Kainti.

Kainti

Kainti is a pseudonym for the area where the Sages and Lucky, a clan relative of Bill's wife Ellen, lived, and where he told his story to the Leightons. Kainti is, even now, spatially and socially distinct from Ramah, although the term "Ramah studies" is well recognized as a shorthand term for the very large research effort spearheaded by Kluckhohn. As Blanchard wrote, lumping in Kainti as usual,

> Approximately 1,250 Navajos live in the Ramah area of New Mexico, 505 square miles some 50 miles south of Gallup on the western border of the state. The Ramah Navajos, because of the intensity of social science research in the region, have become an anthropological tradition, being one of the most studied groups of people in the world (1975:44).

Because of Clyde Kluckhohn's openhandedness a great many people ultimately took part in Ramah area research. Dorothea Leighton remembered (p.c., Mar. 10, 1982) that

> Clyde was very enthusiastic always to have people of any old discipline go out to his Indians because, he always said, he always learned something from these incursions that he'd never noticed before. And I can see how that would really happen; everybody who came had a somewhat different background from him, probably, different interests to some extent, and so

on. And the only thing he ever asked anybody to do, really, beside often talking to him, was to give him a set of their field notes.

It was not just that Kluckhohn was generous; he was intellectually broad as well:

> To the fundamental idea of charting the fortunes of individuals and their culture through time were added the principles of multiple observation by different persons and of multiple approaches by individuals who had received their training in various disciplines. We felt that in this way some progress could be made toward factoring out the distortions due both to the personal equation and to the stereotyped fashions prevalent in each intellectual field at particular time-points (Kluckhohn 1949: v–vi).

Immediately before this last quotation Kluckhohn wrote that it was just this conception of the Ramah project that had crystallized during his discussions with Alexander and Dorothea Leighton.

ALEXANDER H. LEIGHTON AND DOROTHEA CROSS LEIGHTON

These two young physicians had married after graduation from medical school and just before beginning their psychiatric residencies at the Phipps Clinic in Baltimore, a psychiatric clinic attached to the School of Medicine of Johns Hopkins University, from which both had received their M.D. degrees.

Dorothea Cross had enrolled in medical school with the goal of becoming a general practitioner (and "I think I would have been rather good at it, too"), but, she declared,

> When I decided to get married I decided also that you can't be a GP, married. *I* couldn't have been a GP, married, because I'd like to have a family and you didn't really look to your husband to help much with the children in those days, even though they were improving—a little. And so I decided I would do whatever he was going to do, was about the way I thought. And he had decided that he was going into psychiatry. Well I hadn't any

particular aversion to psychiatry; you know, it has something to do with being a GP after all. But I wouldn't have chosen it myself (D.C. Leighton, p.c., Mar. 10, 1982).

Alexander H. Leighton's enthusiasm for psychiatry is thoroughly understandable; at the time, Johns Hopkins was at the forefront of psychiatric training, in large part because of one extraordinary person, Dr. Meyer.

ADOLF MEYER

His is an unlikely voice here. He was born in 1866 in Switzerland, and his grandfather had been visited on the family's farm by Goethe and Pestalozzi. His father was a Zwinglian minister, one uncle was a physician (Meyer "once suggested that his uncle and father represented body and mind, the division which he had to resolve" [Lidz 1966:323]), and his mother at one time had suffered from depression and from the delusion that her emigrant son was dead.

Adolf Meyer became a physician like his uncle, but left Switzerland to pursue postgraduate work in Edinburgh and London, where he was introduced to the writings of Huxley and to his biological orientation. The doctorate completed, Meyer emigrated to the United States where he was introduced to

> the writings of Charles Peirce and William James . . . and became friends with John Dewey, and later with George H. Mead and Charles Cooley. He found himself caught up in one of the most exciting phases of American intellectual history (Lidz 1966:324).

From a melding of all these influences, Dr. Meyer came to the conclusion that

> The life stories of patients seemed to make sense; their experiences seemed to clarify why they were disturbed and suggested ways of helping them. Bolstered by [the American philosophy of] pragmatism, he could cease looking for "something else" to explain their mental disorders. As a neuroanatomist and

neuropathologist, he knew that what he found in a brain might explain disorganization of thought and behavior, but it could never explain a life story or show how to remedy it" (Lidz 1966:326).

Furthermore, Dr. Meyer strongly encouraged his students to write their own life histories, and he stressed the importance of gaining a knowledge of other cultures.

> By the 1930s many psychiatrists were aware of the potential use-fulness of the cross-cultural laboratory, and such eminent figures as Harry Stack Sullivan, Abram Kardiner, and Eric [sic] Erikson were among the psychiatrists and psychoanalysts working with anthropologists and pointing out the need for a cultural dimension in the study of individual psychodynamics (Kennedy 1973:1120).

No less a personage than the early cultural anthropologist Bronislaw Malinowski had urged Alexander Leighton toward field work:

> [Y]ou are too close to American culture. . . . To prepare yourself for the research you want to do you must go and study another culture first, then you can return equipped to study your own (Leighton 1984:189–190).

KARDINER AND LINTON

At Columbia University the psychiatrist Abram Kardiner and the anthropologist Ralph Linton had teamed up to offer a seminar which, Dorothea Leighton later said, "was an experiment to see what a psychiatrist could deduce about the personalities to be found in a particular group from descriptions of the group's culture" (Griffen 1988:232). In the seminar a series of anthropologists presented "their people" for discussion and analysis.[2]

During the winter of 1938–39 the Leightons commuted weekly, their travel financed by Dr. Meyer, from Baltimore to Columbia University in New York City to attend the Kardiner–Linton seminar. That spring they were awarded a twelve-month grant from the Social Science Research Council to enable them to attend Columbia University during the fall of 1939 in order to audit all the anthropology courses they could, including, again, this seminar.[3] The remainder of their research year was to be spent in collecting life histories in the field.

An earlier long-distance introduction to Clyde Kluckhohn was involved in the decision to work with Navajos. Dorothea Leighton recalled that (p.c., Mar. 10, 1982)

> when we got the idea that it would be interesting to try anthropology to see what it had to offer to psychiatry, we asked around at the Phipps Clinic, where we were, if they knew an anthropologist—we didn't. One fellow raised his hand, and that was Norman Cameron, and he said yeah, he knew an anthropologist, he used to be in college with him, at the University of Wisconsin, so we asked him who he was and where he was, and he gave us Kluckhohn's name and address, and so we wrote to him. Well, he was the first one we ever talked to, and I guess it was mostly by mail for quite a while. I don't remember when we first met him, actually. I really don't remember that.

Alexander Leighton (1984:190) credited Kluckhohn with having been "an enormously helpful coach and mentor" once the Navajo and the Yupik Eskimo had been chosen for life-history collection because they were contrastive, non-Anglo cultures.

So after medical school and a seminar-style introduction to anthropology, and armed with interdisciplinary and cross-cultural perspectives, the Leightons set out for the field. In January 1940, they drove to New Mexico, met the Sages, and rented a nearby hogan, probably the one "built for the anthropologists." Ellen Sage, Bill's wife, was pregnant during that spring, and when a daughter was born she was named Dorothea. On January 21, 1940, soon after their arrival, the Leightons were introduced by Bill Sage to Lucky, whose life history they began recording on April 1, 1940.

The Setting, in Place and Time

It is a trap to assume that the past is the same as the present, only less so. The area of New Mexico into which Lucky was born and where the Leightons recorded his life story was not that of Tonto and the Lone Ranger, nor was it one of Indian raids and general alarums. It was still, however, in many very real aspects, the frontier.

The Hispanics living in the area were descendants of the Spanish who in 1692 settled permanently in what is now New Mexico, and for the most part they were unquestioningly and almost exclusively Roman Catholic. A very different religion was practiced by the Mormons, members of the Church of Jesus Christ of Latter-day Saints, a southeastern offshoot of that group's expansion into Utah. Originally named Navajo, Ramah was founded, deserted, then founded again several times between 1877 and 1883 by the Saints, whose struggling bands had been charged by the church hierarchy with converting and educating the Lamanites, the Mormon term for Native Americans. Interest in this endeavor quickly waned, however, and in 1900 they were formally released from their "Indian mission" (Telling n.d.: 17).

The isolation of both Hispanics and Mormons in northwestern New Mexico had shaped lives that, viewed through the eyes of an eastern establishment observer, could only be seen as exotic. To describe them in *To the Foot of the Rainbow,* Kluckhohn (1927:8) quoted Evon Vogt, another Anglo well known in the area, who also had been sent from the university to the Southwest for his health (Vogt had been threatened with tuberculosis and had spent several weeks in a sanatorium):

> There are many curious, unknown phases of American life in this Southwest of ours, of which the Penitente brotherhood [which was exclusively Hispanic] is merely the most fantastic; the cramped, meager existence of the Mormon community at Ramah is almost equally surprising in this day and age.

The Navajo Indians, the area's third major social group, also inhabited a frontier, for they were geographically isolated from the main body of the Navajo reservation and had been politically isolated from both tribal and federal agencies. It was not until 1927 that this group of Navajos was placed under the jurisdiction of the newly established Eastern Navajo Agency in

Crownpoint, New Mexico (Blanchard 1971:28), and Kluck-hohn wrote that, even so,

> prior to May, 1940, there was no sustained supervision from the Indian Service. The first government school in the area was built in 1943. Contact with missionaries hardly began until 1944. Finally, the Ramah Navaho were geographically isolated from the other Navaho groups. There was no question as to where the social system began or ended (1949:v).

He might well have noted, as did Blanchard (1971:25), that where the social system was concerned the Navajos

> were little concerned with matters beyond their own immediate household needs. . . . [V]ery little, if any, sense of political unity transcending traditional kinship ties existed in the everyday affairs.

It was just this out-of-the-mainstream situation of the three groups—Navajo, Hispanic, and Anglo—that so strongly recommended the area to Clyde Kluckhohn as a locale to study.

The Kainti area is almost equidistant from the transportation and trade hub of Gallup ("Indian Capitol of the World") to the north, and Ramah, New Mexico, to the south. Gallup is a creature of the railroad, its tracks once proudly traveled twice a day by the famed Super Chief, and of Route 66, the transcontinental highway, now Interstate 40, which closely parallels the railroad tracks.

Kainti exists because Navajos already lived there and so, in the 1880s and 1890s, traders came to fill the interface between them and the eastern markets that were newly accessible because of the railroad. The area appears less than prosperous today, so it is well to recall the earlier Navajo economy as it existed before a half-century of overgrazing and the federally mandated stock-reduction program of the 1930s. As Kluck-hohn first described the area (1927:151),

> In this paradise the only wholly self-supporting tribe of Indians in the southwest live a happy and industrious life. They

are extremely prosperous and are a valuable economic asset to the country. In 1923 it is estimated that they marketed products to the value of four million dollars.[4]

KAINTI

During Lucky's lifetime—and, in fact, it is not all that different today—Kainti was not identifiable as a cluster of dwellings around a crossroads or as a town in its own right. Rather, in Lucky's time it was an area where members of families traded at a particular post and where activities (many of them described by Lucky) drew participants from those who could travel that far, by horseback or horse-drawn wagon or on foot, in order to attend. Lucky's groundedness in place comes through clearly in his story and is reflected also in statistics. Kainti, Gallup, Zuni, and Manuelito are each mentioned more than ten times as often as is Ramah, which appears in this book under a pseudonym.

It is well to remember that, in the area's isolation, the traditional Navajo healing ceremonies performed by Lucky did not suffer in comparison with the medical practices of his neighbors. Telling reports that during a major outbreak of typhoid fever the Ramah Mormons anointed the sick with blessed oil and

> turned to doctors only as a final expedient. In the Ramah area, the typhoid epidemic began in June 1908, for example, and medical assistance was not sought until September.

Bishop Lewis, the Morman leader,

> does not depreciate the science of medicine and believes that much good is done and pain relieved by same; but he puts more confidence in the word of the Lord, than in that of a Doctor (Telling n.d.: 55, quoting Book E, 141).

LUCKY HIMSELF

On first meeting him, the Leightons described Lucky as "a stout party, rather solemn looking" (Jan. 21, 1930:3); in March,

Dorothea Leighton wrote that Lucky "looked a jovial party in his forties" (Mar. 19, 1940:23). In their summary of him, the Leightons wrote that he

> has apparently been in good health most of his life. He has been in danger of serious injury or death on several occasions but has escaped unharmed or with only minor injuries from the accidents that have been rather frequent in his reckless life. Apparently Lucky does not worry much about his health; however, he is a little fearful that someone may do him harm either directly or by the use of evil supernatural power. He has eight living children and is said to have lost three others. Since he has observed and heard of a good deal of illness, there are many references to injuries and ailments; among the latter are illnesses attributed to witchcraft (Summary of Survival Data 1).
>
> In discussing illnesses he has observed or known about, he refers specifically to such injuries as a broken leg (LS 163, 202), but he speaks of most states of ill health vaguely as "sickness" or describes them by their symptoms. We often find that the headache or sore throat or stomach ache was fatal and must have been but one sign of a serious disease (LS 454, 481, 357–359). He believes that witchcraft is sometimes the cause of disease[5] (LS 25, 49, 61, 431) (Survival Data 6).

The Leightons noted that

> Lucky displays a love of food and drink and seems to have some interest in clothes and jewelry (Summary of Subsistence Data 2). Suitable clothing for his own frequent attendance at Sings and clothing for his large family have undoubtedly been major items of expense. However, we know from Bill's account that the children were ragged and neglected before Lucky became a Singer (Summary of Subsistence Data 14).

Lucky, the Leightons judged, lacked several virtues:

> He frequently shows a certain callousness toward the feelings of others, stealing from those who have befriended him, (See "Subsistence") or playing rough jokes such as taking the meat away from the Zuni herder (LS 290) or forcing the young boy to go

with the Mexican woman and then teasing him about it (LS 424) (Summary of Social Relations 57).

Although "after his marriage, Lucky worked at his wife's place," he still

> spent a good deal of time away from home, doing odd jobs, picking pinyons, working on the railroad or at lumber camps, trading, and attending ceremonials. He did not stay at any one type of work for long at a time, and would leave whenever conditions were unfavorable. He showed little interest in his herds or farm. This roving life with no steady employment did not serve to support his large family adequately. Lucky drank, gambled, and sometimes stole property from his wife and her relatives when he found himself in need of funds (Summary of Subsistence Data 1).

It is extremely important to remember, however, that the matrilineal clan system of the Navajos made such male behavior not only tenable but, indeed, quite common, and that the necessity for men to leave home for extended periods of wage-work is typical in economically marginal communities—Mormon men also have found it necessary to follow this practice:

> When the fields did not yield enough to feed the saints . . . the men were forced to go abroad to supplement the meager returns. The citizens of Ramah continue this practice perforce today (Telling n.d.: 35).

A word is in order about Navajo marriages of a half-century ago. In his life history, Lucky describes the traditional, formal Navajo basket wedding that many couples had; but many couples, probably an equal number, also became married as did Lucky and his wife: they started living together, most probably after several meetings, some of which most probably involved sexual intercourse. Lucky followed another custom common at that time as well as today. Called matrilocality, it meant that at his marriage Lucky took up residence on his wife's land, which also was his wife's mother's land. In fact, without saying that this is what is going on, Lucky gives several instances of the practice of mother-in-law avoidance, which eases to some degree the stress caused by such matrilocal residence. Just as predictable, particularly in the early years of his marriage, were Lucky's absences for varying periods of time, and for a variety of reasons. When he was in residence he was expected to, and did, make himself useful to the extended-family group, particularly with heavier chores such as hauling water and wood.

The Leightons saw almost nothing of Lucky's family. His wife, a grown daughter, and her youngest son came to a sing for Bill, and the Leightons noted that "both women were very quiet," that Lucky's wife "had a worried look," and that "she has apparently felt neglected and badly treated at times and has threatened to divorce him" (Social Relations 39).

The Navajo kinship system is very different from the Anglo system, which considers both the father's and the mother's sides of the family equally important. In the Navajo way, Lucky's children are member not of his clan but of their mother's, a fact that I think correlates with the observable differences in social distance between Lucky and the Sage children, and between Lucky and his own quite numerous progeny. In fact, two children had been born to Lucky's wife before he mentions them at all, and they are mentioned then only because the second one had died. But it is not that Lucky is cold toward children; for with the Sage children, particularly the boys, Lucky interacts with all the affability and warmth of traditional Navajos. These children are members of Ellen Sage's clan (Tábaahá—the central double-*a* is nasalized). This also is Lucky's clan, so Lucky could have spoken of Mrs. Sage as his sister and called her children "son" and "daughter."

> This afternoon at the time Lucky was snapping at Clinton with a rubber band, Clinton came and leaned on Lucky's shoulder and twisted his right ear (Social Relations 4).
>
> Lucky and Harold Sage were playing checkers south of fire with Clinton interfering, and Lucky remonstrating in loud voice with severe tone, belied by his amused look (Social Relations 5).
>
> The Medicine Man (Lucky) came out of hogan and began

spinning lariat. Lassoed Harold Sage's foot at a distance of about four feet (Jan. 21, 1940:3).

Lucky scarcely mentioned where he lived, and this too has to do with Navajo custom. In the Navajo way, dwellings and land are not owned per se, but rather the right to use them passes from mother to daughter: Lucky himself had not so much a home as a dwelling. As from his children, Lucky was rather distanced from it, and the Leightons saw only its exterior:

> After a mile or two we went off the road a little to Lucky's hogan. It is a sloppy affair, made of horizontal boards with little gaps between them. (This is not Lucky's permanent home.—A.L.) A large handsome Indiana wagon to south of hogan, which Bill says Lucky owns. South of this is a corral full of sheep and goats (about 100). Half a dozen little kids skipping and climbing about. (One very small kid ran out of hogan when door was open.)
> Near hogan on north side is a frame and screen, such as Sages use for sorting beans. Lucky's boy nowhere around. Bill says he is out rounding up horses preparatory to going to Kainti (Subsistence 3).

Some two weeks later, the Leightons discovered that Lucky had a second reisdence:

> After Lucky got his groceries we took him to his hogan, not the one we saw before, but one farther west and on the south side of the road. It is larger than the other and made with upright slabs like Bill's hogan, but still in bad need of chinking (Subsistence 5).

The Leightons concluded:

> Lucky is very little concerned with shelter. Although he has lived with various families, he does not describe either their households or his own. We noted that his dwellings are not kept in very good repair. The only aspect of housing which has interested him has been the ceremonial function of the hogan (Summary of Survival Data 1).

LUCKY

Forty-two years after Lucky recounted the story of his life, Dorothea Leighton's recollection (p.c. Mar. 10, 1982) was that

> there was this odd character who was a singer, to some extent, and he wanted to talk to us, tell us his story, I think partly because he just liked to do this but also he was thinking he was going to have to go off to jail pretty quick. According to him, he wanted to leave some money for his wife. I don't know that she ever got any of it, but anyway he came very regularly, very insistently, to spend some more time telling his story. . . . He was kind of a no-good, and he got to be a singer because he spent an awful lot of time going to sings, partly because he just liked it, and he didn't have much of anything else to do, and finally the various people who were disturbed by his lack of accomplishment, you might say lack of industry, asked him why he didn't get to be a singer or make something of it. So he found somebody who wouldn't charge him too much (laughs) and he sort of got the certificate. I don't know how much he was called on to sing, but evidently the singer's character doesn't make so much difference, you know, at least in some contexts; it's what he can do with it if he does it right, and he was evidently smart and he learned things, he kept going to sings and he was very much interested in it, from the first time he ever went to one. But he really told some very bad stories on himself, you know; it was kind of surprising. I suppose he told them because he knew perfectly well that the interpreter knew about it anyhow, that he need not worry about saying anything that Bill wouldn't already know.

After the Leightons left New Mexico, Bill Sage reported to Kluckhohn that, in fact, Lucky did serve time at Ft. Defiance later in the year.

> The judge heard about the quarrel with Barney and Tony and gave him thirty days for drinking. Then he [Lucky] had some time still to serve from the summer before, so no one knew just when he would be back (Social Relations 14).

The field notes of the time strongly suggest that it was Bill Sage who, for whatever reason or reasons, was most concerned to have Lucky recount his life history. Certainly, Bill felt that Lucky was indebted to him:

> Bill Sage says he expects Lucky to sing for him for little or nothing when he needs it, to make up for what Bill contributed. So far he has received nothing in return (Religion 5).

Bill was very explicit about just why Lucky was indebted, and because of this we learn in some detail how Lucky became a singer:

> As Lucky went out after discussing the Sings he had learned, Bill said, "He talks now as if he had made himself a singer, but he wouldn't be a singer yet if it hadn't been for me and the other chapter officers. About five or six years ago he sold five sheep belonging to his wife, and she brought the case before the chapter officers. She run [sic] him away and told him she wanted her sheep back and then she didn't want to see him any more. Could marry anybody else he wanted to. She had had enough; twenty years of it was enough—drinking, gambling, stealing her things, and not giving anything in return. Never knew where he was. He would go off to a Sing for a day and not come back for ten days or a couple of months. The children were all raggy and poor and the Indians around had to help the family all the time. Once he was away for a whole year at Ft. Apache, said he was working, but the men that came back from down there, they said he wasn't doing any work, just gambling." One of Lucky's relatives paid the sheep back to the wife, the same one who paid the horse for him before. Then Bill and the other chapter officers persuaded her to take him back.
>
> They talked over what to do with him, chiefly Bill and another man. They thought since he already knew the songs, the best thing he could do was to become a Singer—that is, arrange to pay a Singer and get the story parts, which he didn't know. He had picked up so much going around to Sings all the time, that it would not be difficult for him to become qualified.
>
> Bill spoke to Lucky along this line, and so did other chap-

ter officers. They all got together and contributed enough feathers and paraphernalia to make up his medicine bag. Bill himself gave deer hide from a deer killed by a mountain lion and some feathers. In that way Lucky got his start. He has behaved much better since then, earning a living and taking better care of his family. He still drinks a lot, but he doesn't go to town so often and so doesn't expose himself to the opportunity (Subsistence 8).

Although she was writing not of Lucky but of Navajo *jish* or medicine bundles, Charlotte Frisbie (1987:82) summed up Lucky's professional qualifications:

With this support, he learned Blessingway, the five-night Ghostway, the two-night Apache Windway, "Hatnilniway," part of Mountainway, part of Navajo Windway, part of the nine-night Nightway, a bit of Featherway, and Coyoteway. His jish was assembled early, after he had learned only the blackening part of Ghostway (Ibid.: 4, 5). Becoming a singer improved his economic and social position and enabled him to assume responsibility for his eight living children, but [Lucky] evidently never became totally dependable. Occasionally he failed to appear when promised, even though the date had been set and his jish had been sent ahead; at other times, he slept while others sang (Frisbie 1987:82).

W. W. Hill (1943:14) is responsible for one, perhaps two, additional reports on Lucky.

Some people do not like to joke if there are women present; others would just as soon. There was a meeting . . . [but] not all the group had arrived. There was a man whose name was [Lucky]. He made many jokes. He did not care if there were women present. He was in the kitchen. We did not know he was there. He made a penis and testicles of dough, hung them on the outside of his pants, walked unconcernedly out before the waiting group, and said "What is going on here?" Some of the women looked the other way and were ashamed. Afterward some of the people said, "Why didn't you put more to it?" [He] said, "I could not find any hair." They said, "It would have been a good one if you could have had that!"

Hill does not identify Lucky as the perpetrator of the second episode, but it fits too well not to be him:

> Once there was a man who was always doing things which were funny. He came to a War Dance. He was very drunk and came into the hogan where the chanter was and wanted to play the drum. They would not let him because he was drunk. They put him out of the hogan. When everyone was eating he sneaked back into the hogan and took the head off the drum and defecated in the pot [which was the body of the drum] and put the head back on. When they began drumming for the swaying singing they began to smell something very bad. Finally they discovered what it was and what the man had done. Some of the people were very angry. It spoiled the ceremony.

LUCKY'S LIFE HISTORY

The chronology of Lucky's recounting of his life history is best set forth in excerpts from the Leighton's field notes (I have made no attempt to specify who wrote which note, although since Alexander Leighton recorded most of Lucky's life history it seems safe to assume that the notes are his):

> {Jan. 21, 1940} We first met Lucky when Bill brought him in to see us. Bill explained that Lucky was a Singer and was on his way to do part of a Night Way where someone was sick. When Lucky told his story, Bill acted as interpreter (Social Relations 26).
>
> {Apr. 1, 1940} Bill again urged us to get Lucky's story while we could. We agreed, believing that a good offer should not be turned down. Bill and Lucky sat in our hogan. D. L. was present for a short time and then went to the large hogan. She asked Bill if he [Lucky] minded her being around. Bill replied, "Oh no, only when he talks about Holy People, and when he comes to that part he will let us know. Lucky began telling his story at about 2:45 in the afternoon (Social Relations 54).

{Apr. 5, 1940} Decided not to go but work here on Lucky's story because, as he says with simplicity, he may not be available after Tuesday at nine, when his and Tony's case comes up. He laughed after saying it.

Lucky was able to continue two days later.

{Apr. 7, 1940} While working on life story this morning, Lucky asks, through Bill, if I would take him to see a man five miles west. Says he will go by horse if I haven't enough gas, but if I can take him, we can work some more on life story this afternoon (Subsistence 12).

{Apr. 8, 1940} Lucky left to go home and {then} return here for the night before going to Dale tomorrow. We gave him our last white shell and wished him luck. He said he would continue his story in two days unless they sent him to jail.

As it turned out, Lucky was not incarcerated at this time,[6] but he absented himself for more than two weeks.

{Apr. 25, 1940} Fortunately, he was able to return. The story was not taken up again in two days, but he appeared from somewhere on the morning of April 25 and plowed a quarter of a field with Harold. Bill came in and reported that Lucky was here and asked if we wanted to go on with the story. We really wanted to continue working on Bill's story but decided we had better take Lucky's while we could get it. Bill assured us that this was wise because Lucky might be called away for Sings; he had sung at a number of places since we had last worked with him April 9.

After lunch Lucky came in, shook hands, sat around for a while, and then went out. A little later he came back with Bill, and we resumed the story at three o'clock (Social Relations 55).

Another April 25 note is that

Lucky says he thinks he will go home tonight and then come back tomorrow. He says he will be here at eight in the morning and wants to work all morning, all afternoon and all evening. I paid him the dollar due for four hours work (Subsistence 12).

Next day,

{Apr. 26, 1940:2} Bill Sage came in with Lucky. Bill said, "He brought me over here and I am just translating what he says. Would you let him have an advance of $3.00." I was putting some hair tonic on my head and Lucky said it smelled good and could he drink it. I talked about the tonic for a while before I made a show of consulting my bank book and then announcing that I couldn't give him that much, $1.50 was all I could afford now. {To which is added in Dorothea Leighton's notes {Apr. 26, 1940: 1–2}, "Lucky seemed grateful for the money and departed."}

Work soon resumed, but it was sporadic

{Apr. 29, 1940:44} On the afternoon of April 29 Lucky asked to be taken to the Kainti store, using the proposition of being able to tell more story as bait. A. L. took him to the store for groceries later in the day (Social Relations 56).

{Apr. 30, 1940} He was away singing somewhere in the middle of April, we were told. An Apache Wind Way that he had just performed was described to us. Then on April 30, Lucky told us that someone had sent for him the night before to come and sing and that he would have to go that afternoon (Summary of Subsistence Data 7).

{Apr. 30, 1940} Lucky has changed his mind about going to the Sing today; will go tomorrow.

{May 6, 1940} Lucky took his pay to date (for giving life story) {a question mark has been penciled in above this insertion} and bought a lot of groceries (Subsistence 5).

{May 8, 1940} Lucky is going to plow this afternoon . . . and then come back tomorrow, to go on with his story (Subsistence 5).

{May 10, 1940} Lucky comes again and says he is going home in a little while; would like to go with us to Ramah tomorrow to get some medicine plants that grow near road at Pescado. I give him the turtle shell and he says, "Thank you, my nephew" (Religion 4).

Finally, on May 11, Alexander Leighton wrote:

> I tried to get Lucky to go medicine hunting on the way down, but he evidently wanted to go to Ramah. On the way back he directed me to drive in toward the Zuni reservoir. There he leaped across the full ditch and looked around but, I think, found nothing. We drove on to the place where the road crosses a ditch just above a cement dam. He got out again, went down in the arroyo below the ditch and was there quite a while. When he came up he had an aromatic somewhat minty plant in his fist, and what looked like a sort of ground pine in his shirt pocket (May 11, 1940:1d).

With this, Lucky disappears from the Leightons' view.[7]

He leaves much as he had entered: he is a healer, he sets forth his credentials and his knowledge of his materials and their uses, and the purposes and qualities of his interactions with the Leightons are finely gauged: he interacted with them as his colleagues and his peers, very much on a basis of equality. Particularly early in the life history he makes several statements about his memory of events and of places so that his youthful recall can be taken into account and, because he also is a healer, he emphasizes his memories of the performances of ceremonies. In recounting his life history to the Leightons, Lucky was concerned to share his professional knowledge with them across cultural boundaries. He told them, I think, what he felt it was important for them, his fellow healers, to know.

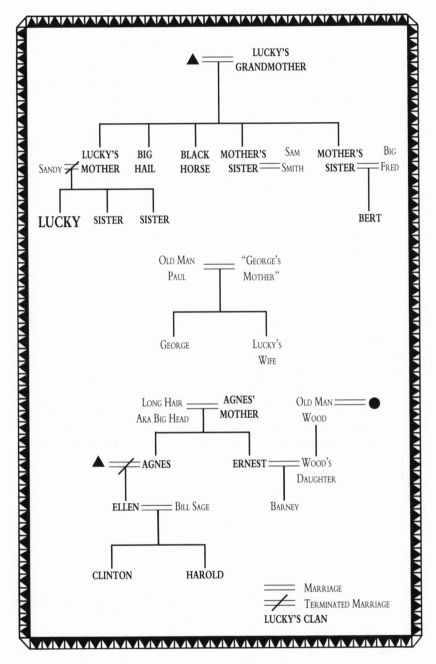

LUCKY'S CLAN

Note: It is not clear whether Ralph, Lucky's half-brother, was born of Lucky's mother's earlier, or Lucky's father's later, marriage. He is not included here, although I think that his going logging with Bert and Lucky argues for the former.

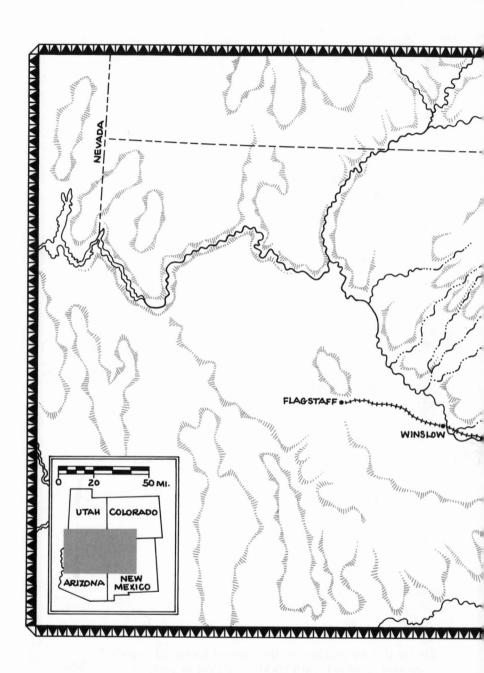

NEVADA

FLAGSTAFF

WINSLOW

0   20   50 MI.

UTAH | COLORADO

ARIZONA | NEW MEXICO

22

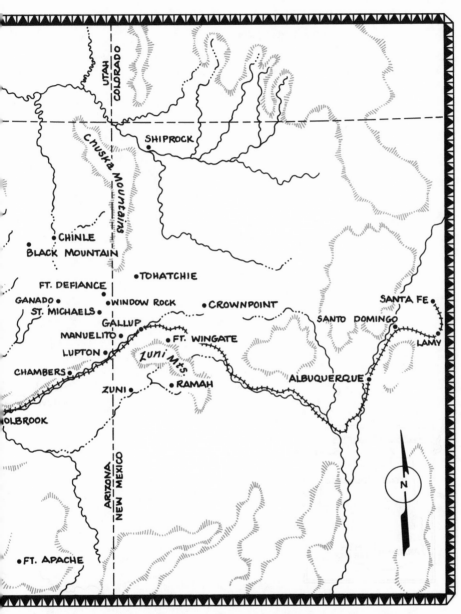

Because they are pseudonyms, the names of Kainti and several other
places mentioned in Lucky's life history do not appear here.

LUCKY

BILL SAGE ON LEFT, LUCKY ON RIGHT. "AT NINE-THIRTY (APRIL 7, 1940) I TOOK A CLOSE-UP OF BILL AND LUCKY. LAST NIGHT LUCKY SAW A PICTURE OF THE OLD MEDICINE MAN IN 'INDIANS AT WORK,' AND SAID HE WANTED A PICTURE JUST LIKE THAT (IN FUN). BILL COMBED HIS HAIR FOR THE OCCASION, LUCKY PUT ON HAROLD SAGE'S GAY BOOTS."

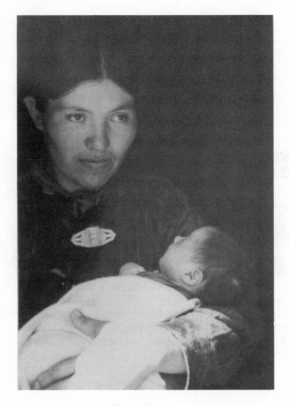

ELLEN SAGE WITH BABY DOROTHEA

MAKING THE CORNCAKE

Old Man Wood

ELLEN SAGE WITH A SPINNING STICK

HAULING WATER

LUCKY THE NAVAJO SINGER

(N.B. THIS MANUSCRIPT HAS BEEN PARTIALLY EDITED ALREADY AND PERSON AND PLACE NAMES CHANGED SYSTEMATICALLY {IN ACCORDANCE WITH PSEUDONYMS ADOPTED IN THE RAMAH STUDIES}. THE ALTERED NAMES ARE RETAINED, AND THE ORIGINALS CAN BE FOUND ON AN ALPHABETIZED LIST.)

LUCKY'S CHILDHOOD

I think I'm about forty years old. At present I am a Singer,[1] but I don't have to talk about that until I get to it in my story.

There is a place down here that we call the XR ranch, and I was between here and that place when my memories begin. I had a mother, I remember, but I didn't get to know her very well before she got sick and died. After she died we moved a little way off to the north.[2]

I had two sisters and a grandmother and grandfather. My grandmother took care of me and started to raise me.[3] She used to carry me on her back, herding our fifteen head of goats.

My grandfather had got very old and was dying and blind. I was able to go a little way from the hogan and I remember I used to lead him when he wanted to go anywhere, like to the store at the XR ranch. Even though he was so old, he wanted to be doing something all the time. We didn't have anyone to do a little work for us around our home. There was water on the east side of the XR store, and that was where we got our water [this was the only place where we got water]. We had a little water jug that the old man would carry on his back. I used to lead him over to the water hole, and we would fill the jug with water and bring it back on his back. [This was only way we can get water for home.] I don't know how long I was doing this, but I got so that I could remember pretty well.

Then I had to herd whatever goats we had by myself. I didn't have very good clothes and most of the time had no shoes. My old lady grandmother was with me most of the time when I was herding, but she was gray-headed. My grandfather used to be a singer and whenever people wanted him to do some medicine for them, I used to lead him to their hogans so that he could doctor the people around there. My two sisters were growing up too [they grow up a little older], and whenever we had time we used to play a lot.

One day my grandmother got sick. I don't know whether she had some sickness or was just too old. One day a Navajo singer whose name means Whirling Water came over to sing for her. He didn't cure her, and finally she died. One day I was out herding by myself and when I came home with the goats, my folks had moved from that home to another place. I found out that they had moved because my grandmother had died.

> Lucky has not stated his attitude toward the various groups who enter his tale. However, it is apparent that his main concern is with Navahos and things Navaho.[4] The doings of other tribes are also reported with a good deal of interest. Mexicans and white men are viewed with a certain indifference, although they are occasionally useful in offering employment, furnishing whiskey, buying livestock, taking jewelry on pawn, and assisting with the burial of the dead (Social Relations 58).

When she died, they sent word to the white man at the store. Two white men came over from there and they buried the old lady and burned the hogan that we had been living in.[5] She had a son who lived quite a way to the west. After she was buried, my folks sent me off to tell the son to come over. I didn't know what way to go to get there, but they told me and I started out and made it.

When I got there the son was away somewhere else. He was married and his young wife wanted to come back home with me while he was away. So we came back together. There were two other sons besides the one I went for, who lived below Kainti.[6] That makes three sons for the old lady. There was one daughter, too, who had some children. We stayed four nights where they burned the hogan. After the four days we moved, but not very far away. We had corn there and we left it all by itself.

One day my grandfather[7] and I started to go out south from there, near the store. Old Man Sage lived there at that time. When we got there, they wanted my grandfather to hold a sing[8] for a girl at her first bleeding.[9] I didn't know anything about a corncake they were making, and I was wondering what it was. The night they had the sing lots of men and women came there. They told me that one of the men who came was my father. When I first saw that man, he picked me up and told me I was his son.[10] My grandfather sang the First Part songs, the Hogan songs, and when he finished them, he let the other people sing.

I went to sleep for some time that night, and my grandfather woke me up. A woman was stirring up yucca root, trying to raise some suds.[11] When she got it ready, the girl came over and washed her head with it. After she washed it, she went outside the hogan and started off running and almost everyone inside the hogan went out and ran a race with the girl.[12] I could hear them hollering as they went off. The girl and all the boys came home, and my grandfather went on singing. After that they brought in a lot of food and everybody got something to eat. Then they combed the girl's hair and wet a little white clay which they rubbed on her face on the side of each cheek. After that they "shaped" the girl outside, then she came in and gave a piece of the cake to each person. I remember she was holding a basket, the first time that I seen one. {This seems unlikely, and the earlier version suggests he is referring to the type of basket used in Navajo ceremonies. It reads "I remember she was holding the basket, and this was the first time that I seen it."} From then on I began to know about the way they did this sing.[13]

My grandfather and I started home. He had a big load of the corncake on his back.[14] When we got back he went to sleep right away.[15] I played with the children outside. First we played near the hogan, then finally I took the children just over the hill. They picked up a lot of little sticks and made a little hogan as I bossed them. I was trying to fix it up so that we could have a sing like the one the night before. We made a little hogan, and I picked one of my sisters to take the girl's part. I was the singer. We brought up a little water and old dishes and mixed up some mud. We dug a pit and built a fire in it and put in some wet mud in place of the cake.[16] When I started singing, everybody sang with me. We picked up some little rocks and made them round for make-believe *naneskadi* (Indian bread).[17] We were all singing, but we didn't know what we were singing about. The girl went out and ran a race. We were going on with it when my aunt came over and stopped us. She said we had no business to do that and chased us all home. We had picked up a wood chip and had cut the mud "cake" with it. She made us carry wood and bring a lot of water after we got home until sundown.

I don't know how long we lived there. Most of the time I was still herding the goats. I had to go barefoot all the time. I had pants and a shirt but they were always raggy. This was summertime and it was pretty hot. There was an old basket, all torn up, that was lying around, not any good any more. When I went out herding I wore the basket for a hat. I had never seen a hat until I went to that sing where some people were wearing hats, and that made me think about wanting to wear a hat. At first the basket wouldn't stay on my head, so I fastened string in two places that would go under my chin and keep it on my head.

I began to know Ned. When he was out herding sheep, he killed some porcupines. Every time he killed one he roasted it in a pit and brought it over to me to help him eat it. He said his children wouldn't eat porcupine, so he brought it to me. I think we were pretty good porcupine eaters!

> Lucky's recollections of his early years are tinged with a feeling of deprivation. He was conscious of being badly clothed (LS 4, 10, 14). In telling of a sing where for twenty-five or fifty cents he could have had some of the medicine, he says that he had no money and that he had no mother or father to buy it for him (LS 244). When Lucky got into trouble over stealing the cattle {this comes later in Lucky's story}, Wood sought to excuse him by introducing this "poor orphan" theme (LS 324) (Summary of Subsistence Data 17–18).

One day I was herding all by myself. I had a blanket that was pretty near all torn to pieces. I was herding in a canyon and I found a cave there. I went into the cave and lay down and went to sleep sometime in the afternoon. I slept all afternoon until after dark. I don't know what time I woke up, but when I looked out it was all dark and I didn't know where I was. I got out and started walking to an open place. There were two or three big rocks standing up, and I could tell from them which way was toward home. I started walking home. Somebody was hollering and I could see lights some places but I didn't pay any attention, just kept going till I got home. There were a few people out looking for me because the goats had come home. They asked me where I had been all that time. I was pretty cold when I got home and they told me it wasn't right to go to sleep when I was herding. I told them I went to sleep in a cave, and they said I mustn't do that anymore.

I found another thing that was good to do: I used to ride one of the big goats pretty nearly all day.

A Murder

One of my uncles, named Black Horse, came over to our place one day. He wanted me to go home with him to take care of a bunch of sheep and horses that he had over there.[18] He took me down to his place along about this time of year (April). He separated the poor sheep out from the herd and I herded them. I would start off pretty early in the morning and come back at night. My uncle would bring me a little lunch at noon. While I was herding my uncle told me he wanted to send me to school at St. Michaels.[19] He said he didn't like the way I was dressed, with no shoes, no pants, no clothes and basket-hatted. He said, "It's going to be hard for you to get along around here. There's no one who can give you any kind of coat or shoes or anything." He told me he would take me there that summer.[20] When I heard that, I got scared. I thought that the time to go would be right away, so one day I ran off to my grandfather's place and left my uncle. While I was there with my grandfather, my uncle came again and wanted to take me home, so he and I went back there. I remember he used to fight with his two wives all the time. I stayed there a few days, then I ran away again.

That uncle never showed up again, but his brother came over one day, crying as he came. He told us that his brother had killed one of his wives. He said that a few days after I left, Black Horse got sick. One of his wives went out and got a medicine man called Big Singer. He didn't know how many days the medicine man stayed there, but he didn't cure the man. He left and went home. Black Horse's first wife was out herding and the sick man was there with his young second wife. Staying there by himself, Black Horse thought he was getting worse and worse and wouldn't get well any more. He began to think he wanted to kill his wife, so he did, he killed her. He had a handsaw. His wife was sitting by him but facing the other way. Either with the handsaw or the rasp, he hit her on the head, broke right through the bone. She fell down right there inside the hogan on the south side.[21]

When the first wife who was herding brought the sheep home and came inside the hogan, she saw all that had happened. I think the dead one hadn't fallen down right away but moved around. The other wife could see the brains hanging all around on the groceries and the dishes.[22]

Black Horse's brother was living just a little way from there. The woman was crying and ran over to the brother's place. Then he started off and came to where I was. He was bringing the news about the trouble that Black Horse had made, and he was going on to the store. He wanted to tell the storekeeper about it and see what he would say about it. He didn't know what was the matter with Black Horse, whether he was just sick in his body or out of his mind half the time. They were kind of afraid that he was near there. Before he came to us, he had gone by the hogan where Black Horse and the dead woman were. He could see that the blanket was off the door, and he thought that Black Horse was still inside.

He went on to the store and gave the whole story to the storekeeper. The man said that he couldn't do anything for the brother, but he wanted him to go right back and talk to Black Horse. He shouldn't talk about the trouble, just tell Black Horse that the storekeeper wanted him to come right away today. "Tell him to come see me, come at once," he said. "I know that man. He used to be a pretty good man and he's one of my good friends around here. He trades here with me all the time. I'd like to know what is wrong with him."

The brother went back to Black Horse's place and found him still inside.[23] He asked him to come out and go over to his hogan. Right away he answered, "All right," and came out and they walked over to the other hogan. After they gave him something to eat, he started to tell his troubles. He said that he knew he had killed his wife and he didn't know what made him do it. He said, "I don't know what happened to my mind, I didn't know a thing in the world, but I did it."

His brother said to him, "We're all sorry about that, but we can't help it now. All I want to tell you is that the storekeeper over there wants you to come down right away. He wants to talk to you. He doesn't want to hurt you in any way. He just wants to see you today." Black Horse asked what the storekeeper wanted to see him about. The brother said, "He asks you to come down and he wants to talk to you very nicely about this. He won't hurt you at all." Black Horse said, "Get me a horse, I'll go over there." There was a horse there, all ready, and they told him he could ride it. Before he started off, he told his brother that he must take care of the sheep and horses while he's gone. He had about seven hundred head of sheep and pretty close to a hundred head of horses. And he went off to the store.

Nobody went with him, he went to the store all by himself. A few days later the storekeeper told the family, "When Black Horse came to me, his brother was there and gave me the story of what he did. After he finished, I asked Black Horse first if he meant to do it. He said 'I didn't mean to do it.' Well, I harnessed up my team and told him, 'Let's go to Gallup.' He said all right, so we got in the buggy and went to town. We told the court, there in town." This storekeeper spoke Navajo pretty well. His Indian name meant "Mr. Stock"; I don't remember his English name.

He said that when he brought Black Horse into town he told the court what he had done to his wife, and that right after he killed his wife he tried to hang himself, but he had failed in that and just sat inside the hogan. His brother brought the storekeeper word, and the storekeeper asked to have Black

Horse come to the store. Black Horse came over by himself, just as requested. The storekeeper told the court, "These people are very good people. I've known them for many years. I wouldn't have thought this man could have done such a thing. He has always been good to people and tried to get along with them. I don't know what happened to him." They kept Black Horse and told him they were going to keep him for ten years. They would send him to Santa Fe right away.[24]

This was what the storekeeper told the family when he got back. He said they had turned loose the horse that Black Horse rode to the store and kept the saddle at the store. So right at the point where I was to go to school, that trouble came, so I didn't go, I just kept herding.

(What did the people say to each other about the man who killed the woman?) I remember that they were talking about it this way: When Black Horse got sick, the medicine man they got gave him some kind of medicine that put him out of his mind. People said that back in the old days they used to do that. The old people used to know how to use it, but they have all died. They think that, in this way, the medicine man caused Black Horse to do that. They talked about a bad kind of medicine man who does this to rich people—they make them sick, then tell them they have the medicine to make them better. When they decide they've gotten enough money, then they cure the person with the right kind of medicine. That's the way they talked about it.

(Did anyone think that the woman might have been harming the man?) The first wife was fighting Black Horse all the time about the younger wife. The first wife was the mother of the one that got killed.[25]

(Did anyone think that Black Horse believed the young wife was making him sick?) They didn't think that the one that was killed had harmed him at all. It was the older one that caused harm. But they had heard about the medicine man before, that he had some kind of medicine that would do that. They hadn't seen the medicine, you know, they just heard talk about it.

After that I stayed with my aunt at the same place as before. Black Horse had an older daughter at home with him, and after he was taken to Santa Fe the daughter took the whole bunch of sheep over to the other side of Gallup where there were some of her relatives. She got all the sheep. While I was with my aunt, she married Sam Smith and they took us toward the east where Sam's mother lived. We began to live together with those people.

Black Horse got that name because he had so many black horses before he went to Santa Fe. Twelve years later when he came back he was called by another name.[26] He was my real mother's brother.[27] If this trouble hadn't come up, I might have gone to school.

When we put the two homes together, we each had a little bunch of sheep. We put them together to make one herd, and I was the herder. Then I found out that Sam Smith's mother was married to the medicine man who had the bad medicine. He was living out by Chinle and doing medicine around there a whole lot. That's what a man told us when he came to join us [when he comes out here to us]. We didn't see him very often, he just came over once in a while, riding a donkey.

I had an older sister who was herding for Big Fred[28] east of us.

> Big Fred is a Singer—Lucky tells of an Apache Wind Way he conducted (LS 373, 375, 376), and he has sung Blessing Way for Bill's family (Social Relations 16).
>
> Big Fred married Lucky's mother's sister (Social Relations 16).
>
> Bert is Lucky's cousin, the son of his mother's sister and Big Fred (LS 426). Following the Navaho pattern, [Lucky] speaks of both [Ralph and Bert] as his "brothers" (LS 481–482). Bert was one of the young men who went to war in 1917 (328) (Social Relations 15).

She came over to see me once in a while. Big Fred had a wife who is getting pretty old now though she is still alive (in 1940). He and she had a bunch of sheep. One day when my sister was herding, I had my sheep there and there was another boy herding with me. We put the sheep pretty close together and all three of us were playing there pretty nearly all day long. Big Fred came over and found us where we were playing. While we had been playing, the sheep got all mixed up. Big Fred beat us pretty hard with a horsewhip. This was in the summer, and there were a lot of squashes and corn. Sam Smith's outfit raised a lot of corn.

In the fall, when I was herding with this boy we used to make a rope out of yucca. We would split it in little pieces and make a long rope with it, braiding it. We could rope the sheep all we wanted all day. My folks didn't know this was going on.

Just about the time the snow began to fly, one of Sam Smith's sisters had a girl who got sick. She was just about a year old and she got sick and died. One day when I was herding with the boy, Sam Smith's brother came over to where we were herding. He wanted me to come home with him, so I went. That's when the child died. Its mother wanted me to help take the child away from there. We carried her out away from the home. I didn't know about burying dead people. We took the girl out and found a good cedar tree that had two big branches. We laid some poles across, between the branches, and when we had them well fixed, we laid the child on top. Then we put some more poles to cover it all over.[29] After we did this, when we got home we stayed there doing nothing, no kind of work, even to go out for firewood—doing nothing for four days. Then they made us bathe. After we took a bath, we all moved to another place.

There was a lot of ripe yucca fruit around and a lot of people were gathering it. The people said it was good food and they fixed it some way so it would keep. In those days there was a lot of grass all over the country. Almost everywhere it was about three feet high. The people used to talk about the wild food. There was a lot that grew in the country, and they used to gather some and it was good food. I was fond of it. I don't remember just how they cooked it. We were living down in a draw. We built a hogan up on top of the hill, this side of it. We all moved there and lived there again.

When we were living there, my grandfather got sick. When he was pretty sick they got a medicine man, not Navajo Indian Medicine Way but Ute Medicine Way. This old man used to live back near Ute country and learned the Way down there. We found him and got him over to where the sick man was. He used some medicine for the patient to take, and while we were singing he worked the sick man over with his hands. He stayed for three or four nights. The old man got well.

Right after that, Sam Smith's sister got sick. When I came back with my sheep in the evening, a man was working at something over on the west side of the fire inside the hogan, a singer from near Gallup. I didn't know about it and I kept watching there. He made a round circle that had a horn, eyes, and a mouth. Afterwards they told me that he was drawing the sun in a sandpainting.[30]

After the medicine man finished the sandpainting, the sick woman was called inside and she sat by the sandpainting over here. She pulled off her shirt and the singer started singing. The sick woman sat on top of the sandpainting. When he finished singing, they took the sandpainting outside, over to the north side and dumped it in the shade there.[31] At night the singer sang some more songs.

Next morning he started to make another sandpainting. He started with white this time, drawing the moon. The rest of the day I was out herding and didn't get to see the rest of it. About sundown I came in with my sheep and came inside the hogan. There were a lot of people, and I didn't know who most of them were. That night they started to sing, and they sang all night long.

When everybody went home, one morning I began to think about the sandpaintings. The first one I saw was the blue, was round, and had eyes and horns. I understood that they were going to dump it on the north side. I thought I'd go over there and look at it. I was thinking that if I found the sandpainting in good shape, I might pick it up and hide it someplace. I looked for the sandpainting and found the place where it was dumped, but the blue stuff was all mixed up with the sand. I didn't find anything else, so I let it go.

We lived there all through the winter and I kept herding all the time with the same boy as before. We had a little dog with us. We had a kind of sling that the Indians used to make—a leather with two strings at the ends. The leather is where the rock sits, and you can throw it very far off. One day when we were using it, the other boy slipped his rock and hit me right close to the eye here. You can see the scar right here.

I thought my eye was gone! We used to make a bow and arrow and shoot most anything, all kinds of birds and lizards. Along about this time of year (spring) the goats were having little ones while we were herding. Some would have twins, and we would have to carry the little ones all the way home. One day when we were herding Sam Smith came up. The dog we had was mean, and when Sam walked to us the dog bit him right in the leg. Sam got mad and shot the dog. That made me mad and I hit Sam with some sticks. From then on I remember pretty nearly everything.

Early in the spring we moved from where we were to right south of here about two miles. There is a spring there, and we lived there through the summer. There were a lot of pinyons that year. In the fall we picked pinyons, they were falling off the trees. Mr. Clark used to have a store right above there and people were camping around.

I and some other boys, three of us, came to the camping place. The other two were brothers, and the younger one was pretty small. We came to somebody's camp and there was nobody there. We saw a gun there, leaning against a brush hogan. I picked the gun up and worked it back and forth, pulled the trigger back, and tried to shoot something around there, but it wouldn't shoot. The younger brother was standing right by me, and I pointed the gun right at the center of his head, pulled it back and pulled the trigger. It made a crack, that was all. I tried to get it to shoot, but it didn't shoot for me. I held it up in the air and pulled the trigger again and it *did* shoot off. It made a lot of noise and scared us, and I just threw the gun away and beat it off. I was wondering why it didn't shoot for me when I was pointing it at the little brother. I didn't know the gun was loaded, but afterward I found out it was. The rest of the day we picked pinyons and came back home at night. When we came home we told each other not to tell about the gun. If that gun had shot for me when I pointed it at the boy, maybe today it would be time for me to come home from prison! All that time during the pinyon picking was the only time I had a new pair of shoes, pants, and shirt. When the snow covered the pinyons, the other boy and I were herding.

About that time my other uncle came after me to take care

of some horses for him. These were the horses that belonged to the uncle who killed his wife. There were too many and he couldn't handle them by himself. I went back with him and looked after the horses, but I couldn't ride a horse {was not permitted to} and had to walk all the time. Soon I quit that man. Old Man Wood[32] wanted me to herd lambs for him about lambing time. He took me home and I herded for him.

> During our stay we met Old Man Wood and heard a good deal from him about his early years long before Lucky knew him or worked for him. He had been given strenuous physical training—racing, rolling in the snow, swimming in icy water—when he was a boy so that he would be a brave and strong fighter. Those were troubled years for the Navaho people, and he recalled narrow escapes from the Mexicans and the hardships endured on the trip to Fort Sumner. He had volunteered as a scout with the United States Army, and most of his reminiscences had to do with warfare against the Apaches. His English name had been given him during the scouting days by a white man as one that would be suitable to use for army records (Social Relations 8).

One day Wood and his wife were herding around Kainti, just the other side of where the store is now. There was no store or houses or fence around there at that time. Wood and his wife had lunch and about noon we were going to make some coffee. The herd was beginning to spread out. Wood said, "While we are making the coffee, get on this horse and go around." He told me to make a circle, riding around the herd and making it come in together. I had never ridden a horse before, and I didn't know how to ride a horse. I got on the horse and rode off a little way from there. There was a whip on the saddle horn and they told me to whip the horse to make it go a little faster. When I started whipping the horse as hard as I could twice, the horse started running as fast as it could through the bunch of sheep and ran over some lambs. I didn't know how to stop it. All I did was take hold of the saddlehorn and hold on as tight as I could. When the horse stopped running and just trotted, trotting all over the place, I didn't know how to stop it. Wood started running up and caught the horse with me. He made me get off the horse, and he got on and rode around the sheep.

I kept herding there for a long time and all those people taught me how to ride a horse, so I knew how to ride a horse and how to stop one. Old Man Wood bought me some clothes and sometimes he gave me a little money. I always had a place to stay there. While I was there with the old man he taught me a lot of things. I learned how to take care of the sheep, and he told me how to do things right and what not to do. He told me I should stay with him as long as I could because I had no mother or father. He told me I wouldn't find any better place to stay. Wood's old mother told me the same thing. I stayed with them about two years, and they wanted me to stay longer. They gave me a little money and bought me a pony and a saddle. After those lessons from Wood I got along all right with people.

After I had been there two years and a summer, Wood's daughter (now Ernest's wife), who was about Clara's age (eighteen or so), got sick. I was moving the sheep then and I just heard that she got sick. They didn't know what was the matter with her. She had been doing work at home all the time, every day, just like Clara, and nothing was the matter with her. Then she just fell asleep and didn't know what was going on. A young man was there singing for her. Wood wasn't living where the girl was, but a little way off. Toward daylight the girl got up and was just the way she had been before, seeing things and talking. She has been like that off and on ever since. A lot of singers have tried to cure this girl, but she still acts the same way.

There were more than ten people there. Those men were the pick of the best men around. Some were good singers, some were not singers but were there to talk things over. At that time there used to be a good singer, who lived this side of Stony Point, named Red Beard. He is still doing medicine. He was a big singer who knew a lot of prayers, and some kind of medicine to smoke whenever a person gets sick in the head, out of his mind. All these Ways were tried over the girl, but she stayed the same, getting worse all the time. The way she would act, she would be all right for a little while, maybe half an hour or an hour, then fall down again. She tried to run off, too, and other people tried to help her. They had hand-trembling and did anything the hand-trembler suggested, the same with star-gazing.[33] They tried everything in the Medicine Way, and besides that they tried the War Way.[34] At that time there weren't all these white people living around here, only Navajos, and no doctor nearby except one colored doctor at Zuni. The girl was getting worse, and those men talked and talked about who was the best hand-trembler and they had tried almost everybody.

The men thought about one more man and decided to try him. He lived out south from there to the XR ranch, then about three miles east from the ranch. They decided to send someone to get that man. The girl was awfully sick and they had little hope left. She didn't eat much. One man started off late in the evening and brought back the man they wanted, way after dark. His name was Tall Tree. They explained to him what had been going on, how the girl had been sick for more than a month already; how many medicine people had come but hadn't helped the girl; how many hand-tremblers had been used. They told him they had tried everything they could think of or heard of. He answered that he didn't think he could do any more than the others, but he would try for them anyway. He would do hand-trembling, not star-gazing.

The first thing he did was wash his hands. He was sitting on the south side, and he washed his hands there, then walked over to the west side and sat in front of the patient. She was lying down there. There were a lot of men sitting on the south side and some women sitting on the north side. After he sat down he said he wanted everyone to listen, and didn't want anyone talking while he was performing, he wanted to have it quiet. No one must go out. They sent word over to the kitchen[35] not to let any person come in or dogs or cats or anything. [And they sent the word outside where the kitchen is, not to let anybody come in, don't want no dogs to come in or cat or anything.] Someone was watching outside.

Then first he gave some corn pollen[36] to the patient, got her to take just a little bit of it. He rubbed corn pollen on her feet and knees and each hand, her two shoulders, back side and front side, and put some on her mouth. After that he used another kind of medicine that he pulled from his pocket, about the size of a corn-pollen pouch.[37] He used that medicine, rubbing all four fingers and his thumb too. He pulled his sleeve way up above his elbow and put the medicine up to there. He held his hand out straight then and he prayed a long time.

After he was through praying, he sang four songs,[38] praying to some Person. They say that this Person gave hand-trembling to the Navajo Indians. The man said that this Person lived south of here about three or four hundred miles at a place called Big Mountain. It is on top of that mountain that the Person lived and they called it Tinlei, or Gila Monster. When the man was praying he was talking to Tinlei just as you would talk to a man sitting right near you. He was telling him that he was the one who had given them hand-trembling. Whenever people can't find something they want to know, Tinlei wants to be called and wants his prayer and also his song to be used. That's the reason the man is using his prayer and song. The man said, "I want you to explain everything about this sick woman. We want to know what's the trouble with her. I surely want to get to the truth. And all these people in this hogan want to know. They've been talking about it and trying to find out what to do with their heads {that is, trying to figure it out}, but they can't. They have asked us to help them." And he went on, "You must tell the truth tonight—not tomorrow or the next day, I want to hear it now. I'm getting paid for this and you are getting paid, too."[39] That's about all I remember. He said more, but I don't remember it.

Then he started hand-trembling. He began with one hand, and now and then he would rub his hands together and use the other hand, changing from hand to hand all the time. As he hand-trembled, he marked on the ground with his fingers. The people couldn't understand what the marks meant. He pointed off to the west many times, and also to the southeast, and sometimes {he made a motion} as if he was throwing something down with his hand.

When he got through, he sat back on the south side where his place was. He said, "Well, men, this may be the truth and it may not. The way I got it," he said, "there is no medicine man or sing or prayer that can cure this girl. But who's singing over here to the west. Does anybody know?" They didn't answer for a little while: Then one man said, "Yes, there is somebody singing down there, the man called Big Singer. He's singing down there for a man." Tall Tree said, "It seems to me that one or two of you could go down where that man is singing and bring him over here. The way I got it, I want you to question this man. I think he did something bad to this girl. And another thing, I pointed off to the southeast so many times, something like a mile and a half from here. This man, Big Singer, took something over there and buried it, and that's got to be taken out right away, especially if you get him over here tonight. I want you to ask him what he buried over there, and tell him to change it around and cure the girl instead of killing her. When he admits that he did that, tried to kill the girl, if you find out that much the girl will be safe. If he doesn't want to admit it and make it good for the girl, she will die right away. If he makes it good before you people, he's going to die himself.[40] If he doesn't admit it, he will be safe."

Only one man started {was sent} to go after the singer. The others said they were going to do just the way the hand-trembler told them. The man who was sent didn't want to go. He said it was way after dark, and maybe the singer couldn't come now. Maybe he would say, "I'll come tomorrow or the next day." The people told him to get down there and tell Big Singer that the people wanted him over here tonight because the girl was getting worse every day and night. Tell him that they wanted him to do a little medicine, and he had to do it tonight. They said, "You might get him to come that way, to give the girl a little medicine. Tell him we want him to sing for her a little, not much."

The man went down there and brought Big Singer back toward daylight. He didn't want to come for a long time. He let him ride behind and they rode back double. [He let him ride behind, ride double-back.] When he got there they made room for him in the middle of the people. Three of the best men were asking the questions. They just told him what the hand-trembler had said about him. The three men said that they thought he had been telling the truth. They said, "The way he was doing hand-trembling was the good old way. Before, in the old days, all the People[41] knew how. We believe that anything that comes from way back there is the truth. We don't want to have you mad at us, and we don't want to be mad at you, but we want to cure this girl. Just tell us the truth about it—if you did it, say you did it, if you've got something left to cure the girl with. We think you know because it's your job to know how to cure her."

They talked to him like that, but he got mad about it. He said he didn't do it. He asked, "Who did the hand-trembling?" They pointed to the man who did it, and he said that man was telling them lies. They kept questioning Big Singer until daylight. The three men told him that if he didn't want to talk about this they wouldn't let him go out. They would keep him there until he told his part. The rest of the people said, "We are not going to drop this. You think you are going to get by with it, but you are not. We won't even let you {out of here to} go to the toilet."

After he heard that and more talk, Big Singer said, "I'm guilty of this." First he asked the people what they were going to do with him if he had done it. They told him they were not going to hurt him, all they wanted was to hear the truth. And they wanted him to use good medicine that would cure the girl. That was all they wanted. They were not going to hang him or send him to jail or anything like that. If he did it, they might send him back where he was raised.[42] After that he said yes, he did it. He was trying to kill that woman. I can't remember what this bad man said about why he did this to the girl. After he said that he did it, they didn't ask him anything more.

After he said he did it, they wanted to take him over where he had buried the things. A lot of people didn't want to take him there, and a few went over, leaving the bad man in the hogan with some people to look after him. They took the hand-trembler with them and he did hand-trembling twice more out there. While he was doing it, he pointed the way they should go where the thing was in the ground. They found a little tiny bundle there, just little pieces, in two places. They asked Big Singer about these bundles and he said yes, they were his. There was some of the girl's hair that he said he pulled out and a piece of her buckskin moccasins with the mud and dirt that comes when your feet sweat. Big Singer said he used all those things, and he used a bad prayer about the girl when he had them in front of him, so they took the place of the girl. That's what he told the people. "Right now," he said, "I am going to say a few prayers for this girl," and he sang several songs, maybe four or five, and said, "You will be well now."

He told the people that he would sing over this girl for nine nights and that would correct everything. He asked what they thought about that. They said they thought they would let it go. He said he wouldn't charge anything for singing, but {so?} they let it go and turned the man loose and let him go back to where he'd been singing.

Those people talked it over after he had gone. They all said that if they had let him sing he might have made it worse yet, so they just went by what the hand-trembler had said. He had said that if the man was guilty it would be hard for him, so they just let him go. The girl began to get better every day.

They watched Big Singer pretty closely wherever he went. In about a month he wasn't feeling very well. From then on he got thin. This happened in lambing time, and from then to fall this man got pretty sick. When he got too sick, he went back home near Chinle.[43] In December one of his brothers came down here. Big Singer had some horses down here that the brother took back. He said that Big Singer didn't live very long after he got home over there. He had died. The girl got all right, felt good, did her work, said everything was all right now. She is Ernest's wife, who was at the sing last night.[44]

> Ernest, who appears rather early in the life story as Wood's son-in-law (LS 49), is Agnes' brother. It was Ernest who once got money and goods from a storekeeper for a calf which died the next day (LS 166).
>
> Ernest was one of those who were drunk at the Hand-Trembling Way sing. He and Coho had a gallon of whiskey which Lucky finally got away from them (LS 484–488) (Social Relations 23).

When that woman got better, I herded sheep with her for quite a while. I was still working for Wood then, and it was in the summertime. In the winter I herded all by myself. I kept doing that for three or four years.

YEIBITCHAI

After that I got a three-year-old blue horse from Wood that hadn't been broken for riding. This was in the fall. I heard they were going to have a Yeibitchai (Night Chant) over this side of Stony Point. I had never seen the Yeibitchai dance.[45] One day we corralled my horse with some other horses, and some men were going to help me saddle that horse. I asked them if they would help me and they said yes. I was thinking that when I saddled the horse I would go to the dance. When we put the saddle on him, I got on. He started running with me away from the corral toward the west and kept running as fast as he could for two miles and a half. While he was running he turned and made a circle and came back with me. I pretty nearly fell off when he turned. Then he ran back the same way. We came back where we started. The other horses were there, and when I got to the corral I saw two women there, both riding horses. They told me they were going over to the dance this side of Stony Point.

When I heard them say that, I thought it would be a good thing for me to follow them, have them ride ahead and I could ride behind and this would make my horse go better. They started off ahead and I rode my horse behind the two women, going north toward Stony Point. When we had gone quite far, we came to a big canyon. We rode across the canyon, but when we got out on the other side, my horse was wild. While I was riding behind, my hat blew off. This was the first time I got off that bronco. I had a long rope tied to his neck. As soon as I got off he started running, but I had the long rope in my hand so I could stop him, and I tied him up and picked up my hat.

I couldn't get on that horse again. I tied him up with the end of the rope and tried and tried to get on for a long time. In the end I got on, and when I got on he started running off with me. But the end of the rope was tied to the tree, and he would run off a little way with me, then get jerked back. I had another hard time to untie the rope. I was on the horse now, and the horse was tied up, but I made the horse ride up to where he was tied and I unfastened the rope. I just reached through and untied it while I was on the horse.

The two women had gone on a long time already. They kept going when my hat blew off. I tried to get them to wait for me but they didn't pay any attention to me, they just kept riding. So I started to ride again where the women had gone and I got to the sing about sundown. There was a big crowd of people there when I came. I got off the horse and tied him to a tree.

In just a little while, Wood and his mother came up behind me. They told me they wanted me to see the two people that were called the Yeibitchai. The reason they wanted me to see was that I had never seen anything like that before. Wood said, "You can't see the dance without first seeing the two Yeibitchai," but if I'd seen them, then it was all right to look at the dances.

> Both Chief Wood and his mother urged Lucky to attend this event {Yeibitchai} and to go through the proper procedure with the other boys and girls so that he could safely see such dances (LS 63–77) (Social Relations 6).

Young boys and girls aren't supposed to look at this dance, and if they go right in and look they will go blind right away. The Yeibitchai would make them blind.[46] So two of the Yeibitchai {masks} had been put on one side and they were telling all the boys and girls to go look at them. So they made the young boys and girls wait outside.

This was after dark. They made the young people wait outside for a little while. Then they told us to get ready, to wrap a blanket around ourselves. They would send out one of the Yeibitchai and he would take the children in. They had one man out there to explain these things to the children so that they would know what to do. They listened to the man. He told them that before the Yeibitchai comes out, he'll call and when he hollers everybody should walk inside. The boys go in first and the girls go behind the boys. They mustn't get mixed up. They should cover their heads so they won't look around. When they get inside, they will sit over on the north side of the hogan. After that there was a lot of explaining of all the little things they had to do.

This was the big hogan—maybe twice as big as this one here (some eighteen feet in diameter). There were a lot of people, and the singers were down by the fire. This is what is called the Yeibitchai dance, the biggest sing; it lasts nine nights.[47]

When the boys and girls came in and sat down over there, they told them all to undress. They told them to keep their eyes closed and not look around. While they were doing this, the people were all singing and they had a basket drum going.[48]

They started with the first boy on the west end of the group. There were two Yeibitchai standing there in front of the boys and girls. They told the first boy to stand up. I had my eyes closed, I wasn't looking at what was going on. The Yeibitchai were hollering, that was all I heard. I didn't know what they were doing to that boy. There were two boys ahead of me, so the third time they made *me* get up. There was one man there who talked to the children, telling them what they can do and what they ought not to do. When they made me get up, the Yeibitchai had cornmeal in his hand and touched me right here on the knee. They had a yucca leaf about two feet long, and he hit me with it where he touched me with cornmeal. Then he did the same way up to my chest, made me turn around and did it to my back, turn again and did it to the top of my head, to the palm of my hand and my elbow—no, the top of the head was last. Then I sat down. They told us not to look yet and they kept going with the next one. We just heard what the man was saying.

When they got through with the boys they started on the girls, and when they were all finished they told us if we looked up we would see two men standing over here. They told us to look at these two people. We saw them—they were the ones who had been doing it. They were all dressed up but had no clothes on—dressed with beads and bracelets. One was wearing a big deer buckskin over his shoulder; the other had nothing over him. After we had seen these two people they told us there was something else to see back on the north side, and that was the masks they had been wearing, dressed with feathers. Then one of the Yeibitchai walked over there and picked up the mask and held it over the boy they had started with before. He held it right up against the boy's face so he could look through it, and after looking through the boy would blow toward this Person (Yeibitchai). Then he took the mask off that boy and did the same with the next one. He kept doing that till he finished the boys and then did the same thing with the girls.

When he finished with the girls, he laid the mask back where it had been.[49]

Then they gave us some corn pollen and the first boy sprinkled it on the mask, down between the eyes and up across the eyes. He passed the pollen to the next boy and he did the same, all the boys and the girls. When they all got through, starting with the first boy again they each sprinkled some corn pollen on the two men (Yeibitchai) standing over to the north side of the fire. When that was all finished, the singer walked across to the north side and took two red-hot coals and set them over next to the children. He had a little sack in his hand and he pulled out some of the medicine and laid it down on the coals. He told the boys and girls to smell it. Then he said, "Put some water on the coals and put them out," and he threw the two coals out. He said that was all for the boys and girls, they could put their clothes on. They told the boys and girls it was all right now for them to look at the dance. They could go anywhere they were having a Yeibitchai dance and see it. So we all went out.

There wasn't anything doing for a while and I came back in after a little. Two or three more Yeibitchai were getting ready on the north side of the fire, inside the hogan. (What did you think of all this when you were sitting with your eyes shut?) Over where I was herding the people had scared me about the Yeibitchai. Before I saw it, the people at home scared me by telling me that when I came to see the Yeibitchai they would whip me with the yucca leaf. So when my eyes were closed I was thinking about that. I thought I was going to get a good whipping there. But it didn't hurt me at all. That's all I thought about.

The three who were getting ready told me their names. I don't remember just how they were dressed. They also pulled out a mask, all three of them. They were sent over to a brush hogan about a hundred yards away. The singer said to the patient, "After these three go out, you must go out, just outside the door." They sent the patient out and a man was also sent out with a buffalo skin. He was told to take it out and have the patient stand on it.

When the patient was ready, standing on the buffalo skin,

the three Yeibitchai started coming toward the patient. The patient was holding a basket with cornmeal in it, and the three came together right in front. One Yeibitchai was in front, leading the other two. The last one had a hump—he had put something on his shoulder to make a hump. They walked pretty close to the patient, then started off to the south. As the first one passed by, the patient threw some corn pollen on top of his head. They walked off a little way, then turned and came up to the patient from the south. Then they turned back and came from the west, then from the north. Then they walked back to the brush hogan. The patient walked back inside and sat down where he had been before, on the west side of the fire.

Afterward four more got ready. They all pulled off their clothes then and the singer mixed up in a dish some white clay which they rubbed all over their bodies. After that they put on moccasins. They had sort of a dress they put on (waist to halfway down thighs), and they put on a lot of beads and bracelets. The medicine man told them to go out to the brush hogan and said they could use blankets until they got there. He went over there also. They took their masks with them.

Outside the hogan there was a crowd of people, kind of in a row, with wagons and teams behind them. That was on the south side. There were more, the same way, on the north side, and right in front of both a fire was burning bright. There was space in the middle where they would see the dancers. They made the patient go outside again. Those four came over toward the patient with the singer leading them. As they came along, the patient sang his song, and they came up to him and stood there until the song was finished. The patient and singer stood in front of the four and the singer prayed for the patient for about thirty minutes. After he stopped talking the patient took some cornmeal out of his basket and walked along where the four were standing, throwing some cornmeal on all four of them. The patient had a chair out there which he sat on while the four started dancing. Each one danced about an hour, each holding a big rattle in his hand.

When that singing and dancing was finished they went back to the brush hogan, then came back to the big hogan and went in. People gave them some water on the south side of the fire, and they washed the white clay off their bodies and dressed up in their clothes. The singers washed him off. The part of the sing up to these four was called "First Songs." These were the *real* First Songs; at small sings they have just small First Songs.

That meant that the singer and the Yeibitchai had finished their special part and now it was free for everybody who wanted to, to get ready and dance. There was a brush hogan for the dancers and they could all get ready over there. There was white clay, too. Each dancer should take all his clothes off and dress like the four in the First Songs. There would be six main dancers, male ones, and six more, female. If there weren't enough for the female ones, maybe they would have just two. If there were enough dancers they would have twelve. Each bunch would dance about an hour, then they would put on their clothes and another bunch would come in, all night until daylight.

The way they do it is that, after the four dance in the First Songs, the next dancers would be the people who live right near where the sing is held. If they have enough dancers, they will dance first. After that dancers from different directions will make up teams, and it keeps on like that till daylight. People coming from places like Shiprock or Ft. Defiance kind of dance against each other to see which dancers are better. They have the Morning Dance for that. People from far off know that they can at least dance at the very end. Then everything was over and everybody went home.[50]

I went back to where Wood's mother and my horse were. We started off from there over to the other side of the railroad, where there used to be a store. I didn't know it, but Wood had some cattle there. Barney was a little boy at that time, and he was with some cows when we got there. So was Wood.

> Bill told us that Barney is Old Man Wood's grandson. Lucky mentions that Barney used to drive Wood's cattle (LS 78–79) (Social Relations 11).

The cattle had been bought way over at Black Mountain. Wood was trading for cows that had been brought there, and they were just camping by the store while last night's big dance had been going on. There were about eight or nine head of cows, and Wood and his mother bought three, giving six dollars in money. After that we started driving the cows down this way. We brought the cattle past the place where they had the dance and kept on with them until we got on top of the hill. The sun was down when we got that far and we camped there.

Next morning Barney started off with the cattle. Some people there who raised good squashes gave us two of them. Wood told me I should carry them on my horse. I didn't want to, but he made me do it. We put them in a gunny sack and put it over the saddle so that there was a squash on each side. My horse was still pretty wild, and I was a little scared when I got on him. He began to look back at each side and started running with me. I couldn't hold him. There was a big valley there, and when the horse was running the squashes went up and down, hitting the horse on each side and keeping him running. I couldn't stop him for a long while. Then I went on a little way in this direction and caught up with Barney. We drove the cattle on across the canyon and came back to where Wood lives now.

After we got home I heard about another Yeibitchai up at Mack's home. I began to think I would go to it. They had told me at the first Yeibitchai that I could go to that kind of dance any place I wanted. (Why did you want to see another?) When I saw the first one, the way they dressed up and danced looked pretty good, so I wanted to see this one. I heard the singer from the first one was going to sing at Mack's, too.

I went to Mack's place and saw it again. I didn't go inside the hogan, just saw the outside dance. (Bill, the interpreter, added: "I remember that dance, I was there too. I had bought a new pair of white boots that were too tight. Toward daylight I got pretty sleepy, and took off my boots and laid them beside me. When I woke up I had only one boot; someone stole the other one. I put the one on and went barefoot with the other. People laughed at me. Mack was pretty rich then.") I saw the dance, but I haven't any story about it because I didn't go inside the hogan. I came back home to Wood's place and went back to herding for him.

SHALAKO AT ZUNI

One day when I was herding someone told me that the big Zuni dance was coming pretty soon. The Zuni dance is called

Shalako, and they have it once every year. After I heard about it, I began to think I would like to go to it. It was about ten days before the dance would start. When the time came, Barney and I started off on horseback and got there about sundown. There were a lot of Navajos in Zuni village. Barney had a friend there, a Zuni man. We went to his place and unsaddled our horses and the Zuni fed our horses. There were a lot of places where we could go to eat, food was free for everybody. We went around all through the village.

We came to a house and went into it. This house was a big long square room that looked very pretty. There was a lot of buckskin hanging on the wall, good blankets, it was all fixed up with good things inside. We went into about six houses and they all looked like that one on the inside. I heard from other people that the dances would be in these houses that looked pretty after a while, and there would be dances outside. There's a big arroyo that runs right through the middle of the village, and they said the dancing was on the north side of the river. Barney and I started to walk over to see the dances there, following some people going that way. We got to the place and saw the dancers. They were about as tall as this stovepipe (ten or eleven feet), maybe a little taller, and big around. People said they were called a Navajo word that means Tall Dancer. There were six of them there and also a lot of Zuni people.

All the Zunis began to sing, all standing up while they sang. While they were singing standing up, I could hear something sort of crack.[51] We couldn't see very well because it was pretty dark. They started off with one of the dancers who walked in front of the people who kept on singing as they followed him. They told us that they were going to take this first one over to a good place inside a house. When he had gone, they did the same with another one. They were taking these dancers to the houses we had seen with all the things in them. They took all six of them, one at a time. After that we went all around. We saw one dancer in one house and another in another house, scattered out, one to each house. When they were all in houses, the Zuni Indians were praying in there. The dances hadn't started yet, praying was going on.

They didn't start dancing until the middle of the night. Each pretty house had a dance going on in it. After that we saw some other dancers, some that they called mudheads.[52] These were funny looking. There must have been about ten of them, going around to different places. When they went inside, they would dance there. There were others called the Dancers' Boss who had a big yucca leaf about three feet long in their hands and wore crow feathers around their necks. They did like the others, going around to each pretty house. They would go in and dance for a while, then go to another house and do the same thing. The houses where they had these six big dances had singers, too. They had a big drum and they sang for the dancers while they were dancing. People crowded in everywhere when a dance was going on. They traveled around from one dance place to another, and kept doing that all night long. The mudheads were more fun than any of the other dancers. They did a lot of funny things. While the dances were going on during the night, the people kept eating, too, inside the houses. They quit dancing about daylight.

I left before sunup and came back on a horse in a hurry. I had corralled the sheep at home and they were alone all night. I got home and took the sheep out and herded them. The other people got home late in the evening.

Lucky Moves On

From that time I herded the sheep from a camp, a dog and I. People brought food up to the camp. We herded there all through the winter. There were a lot of pinyons that year and the pinyon nuts were on the ground during the winter. Early in the spring people were picking pinyons south of Kainti on top of that mountain. When lambing time came, some boys went over to the {other?} side of Zuni to herd sheep for a Mexican. I left my herding and went with them and started herding for a Mexican down there.

Before I left, a woman had come there who had run away from her husband. She didn't want to go back to him and wanted to stay at Wood's place. She stayed for quite a while, herding for Wood. The woman asked me to marry her, and when Wood heard about it he said I could. But I was afraid of that woman and that made me run away and herd for the Mexican.

Although Lucky avoided Wood's place after this {the approval of the marriage}, there is no indication that he was on bad terms with Wood himself. He attended a Yeibitchai dance held for Wood and was present at an Apache Wind Way in which Wood was the patient (Social Relations 6).

There were three of us, me and two others. I went on horseback and camped one night on the way. After we got there, one of the boys took the horses back home. The sheep were lambing when we got there and the Mexican put us to herding right away. We didn't stay very long, just till the lambing was over, a little over twenty days. Then we started for home. We got to Zuni the same day, stayed there a little while, then started off again. We camped overnight just this side of Zuni. Next day we got home.

NAVAJO WIND WAY

When we got home we heard that a Sqaw Dance had just ended that morning. It was over to the west of where Wood lived. I didn't go back to Wood's place but to Sam Smith's place. They were talking about having a sing there. They said a man named Steve had gone to get the singer. Steve came back from the singer's place near Stony Point and said he would be coming the day after tomorrow. He wanted us to get ready for the day after tomorrow and told the people to start getting ready. One of the men went to get some plants for medicine; another went to get different colored rocks for sandpainting; some started hauling wood. When they brought all these things back, the medicine man arrived.

I heard that his name was Red Bead Singer. When he came he asked if the people had everything, the different plants, different kinds of rock, and some other things he would use at the sing. They told him they had everything. This sing was the Navajo Wind Way.

About sundown they cut some of the plants up in little pieces. After dark they spread a blanket out on the west side of the fire and brought in some kind of plant. There were four different kinds of plants, and they laid some of these plants on the blanket in five places. The patient was a woman, Sam

Smith's wife. The singer started singing and sang two or three songs. Then he stood up and walked over to the patient and picked up one of the five plants. They were tied with string. He held the plant in his hand and moved it all over the patient's body, then he untied it at her feet and laid it north of the fire, with the string on the west side of it. He picked up another one and did the same thing, but untied it at the knee. He laid this plant on top of the other one, and its string on top of the other string. He kept on doing this until he finished all the plants.

Then he picked up the string and moved with the patient's string. He had a cup of medicine; he picked it up and gave it to the patient to take a drink. After that he picked out two coals and laid them right next to the patient. He put just a little of the smelling medicine on top of the coals and the patient smelled it. He poured some water on the coals to put them out and threw them outside through the roof.[53] They took the plants that had been used outside, away from the hogan. The singer said that was all he was going to do that night, everybody could go to sleep now.

Before we went to bed the singer said we must get up early in the morning. He wanted some of the boys to bring him some small dry cedar sticks. They should bring some in and put some outside the door, making two piles, one on each side of the door. And one man should start grinding stones for the different colors.[54] He wanted another man to go get some dry oak and bring in an armful. That was all the singer said.

Another man started to tell a story, so we didn't go to sleep right away. His name was Tall Man. Down below where we were there are two hills, and when you see them from far off there's two rocks that look like a woman who is going to have a baby, standing there with a big belly. That rock is called Pregnant Rock. Tall Man said, "I came by those two rocks. There used to be peach trees there, and I looked around for them. I found the trees with a lot of peaches on them. I ate a lot of them, and when I'd eaten enough, I started off again." I thought he was just joking. He didn't say much, just that, and then we went to sleep.

When we first got up in the morning, four of us went out to break the sticks and bring them in and pile them so there was one pile on one side of the hogan and another on the other.

This was pretty early, before we ate. One man started grinding on the north side of the fire. Another brought in four small pieces of oak and stuck them into the side of the hogan on top of the door, on the south side, west side, north side. They took all the ashes out, fire and everything. Another man brought some cedar bark and they laid it west of the fire. The singer pulled out of his sack a piece of stick about nine inches long. He cut a little piece out of the side of the stick and laid the stick down beside the bark. He threw away the little piece.[55] They brought a stick like a spinning stick and the singer tied a stick (like the one he cut the piece out of) on top of it. When he put the butt end on the ground, it was the same size as the hole he had cut in the other stick. The singer said they were going to start a fire now.

I was sitting south of the fire, watching this. The stick that had the piece cut out—a man took hold of it and held it solid to the ground. Another held the spinning stick between his hands, with its end in the hole on the other stick. He put a little sand or medicine in the hole and started twisting the stick as fast as he could. When they were ready, the singer started to sing, and I was watching the sticks. One man gave out and nothing had happened. I wondered what they were trying to do, and I thought they were crazy. Another man gave out, too, and after a third man spun the stick a little while, I saw some smoke rising. Now they had started the fire, they put the sticks away and picked up the fire and put it in the fireplace. They broke some sticks in little pieces and built up the fire with them.

They brought in some dirt and poured out just a little on the east side, south side, west side, and north side of the fire, four places altogether.[56] They brought inside the two piles of wood and stacked them inside. Another man spread out the dirt they had brought into a long smooth shape. One man started a sandpainting on the east side. He drew a black snake on top of the dirt, the snake facing to the east and a straight body. Another man did a blue snake on the south side, a crooked one with four bands, facing away from the fire. There was another one, yellow, made on the west, with a straight body, and to the north a crooked white one—two straight ones and two crooked ones. At the same time they had a pail of water in the fire, heating it to boiling. When it started to boil they put lots of medicine in it. They put lots of blankets at the door, making it thick so no air would come in. They brought in a basket and set it over on the west side. They brought in four new sticks like pokers. They were different kinds of sticks. One was a pinyon and I don't remember the others. They laid one down from the east side of the fire, from the south and from the north. Then the singer said for everybody to go out and let the people come in, and about that time the patient came in. I went out with the other people.

I went over to the kitchen. There they told me to haul some water and wood, so I didn't see what went on in the hogan. I went to look for horses to use on the wagon, way off to the south where I had seen them. When I found them, I caught one and I thought I would go down to the place where the man said there were peaches. I found a few peach trees there but all the peaches I saw were about the size of little marbles. I picked two pocketfuls and came back, eating them as I went. They didn't taste very good, so I tried throwing them to the birds. On the way back I got on top of a hill and looking this way, I saw a big rain coming right toward me.

When I saw that, I thought I would try to beat the rain home. I started running my horse as fast as I could and kept him going. The horse stepped into something and I fell down with him. I fell ahead of the horse, and he started to roll and rolled on top of me. I saw stars, that's all I saw. I don't know how long I stayed there before I tried to get up. I couldn't get up. The whole earth kind of tipped over with me. I fell down again. I felt the rain that I had seen digging at my face, when I woke up. My horse got away and walked off. I trailed him and found him a little way off. I got mad at him and beat him all over with a stick.[57] Then I got on and rode back home with him.

Then I felt sick, my head hurt and I almost vomited. I told my folks I couldn't find the other horse. They gave me something to eat but I didn't eat it. They asked me what was the matter and I said I had a headache, that was all. I was sick and just lay down by the kitchen while the sing was going on. One of the days near the end of the sing my uncle came in a wagon.

They told us to haul water with that team. Four of us put some water barrels in the wagon and started off. I was better by then, but my head was hurting a little bit.

When I started off in the wagon, I saw that the two horses had two big sores on their backs. As we were going toward the water, a big rain came along and we got caught in it. There was hail falling, big hail. We stopped the horses with their sore backs. When the hail hit them they started to jump around, twisting their backs, and it made me laugh. When it stopped raining we went to the water, filled the barrels and started home. The roads were very muddy and we didn't get home very quickly.

I heard what they did the first night of the sing. They did the same thing every night. The last day they did a lot of sand-painting, but I didn't know what that was for. The last night they used the basket for a drum, and sang all night till daylight. Then they were finished and everybody went home. I didn't watch the sing very much; most of the time I stayed out in the kitchen. Everybody went home, the singer went home. That was the first time I saw that kind of sing.

"THEY PUT ME ON THE BUCK HERD . . . "

After that they put me on the buck herd. The Indians living close together put their bucks together. It made about fifty head. They told me to ride the burro while I was herding. I always had fun when I was herding with that burro, teasing him and making him pitch. I also had a rope, and I could rope the bucks with it from the burro. Have you noticed two bucks fighting each other? They get apart and then they run at each other. When two of them started doing that, walk back and start running, I would rope one of them from the burro and they would miss each other. So I, the burro, bucks, and billy goats had a lot of fun every day!

I would herd them in the morning, bring them in at noon, herd them again in the afternoon till sundown. Their wool was my pay. In the summer I had a lot of trouble with them. If you put them out early in the morning they eat a lot of new green grass and some weeds. They start to bloat all at once, and some of them get away. I lost a lot of them. At that time {of year} you don't have to herd them all day, just start about noon. They get in the shade in the summer and they won't go off till late in the evening, if the sun is shining.

One day it rained very hard, water was running. Another boy and I went off to drown some prairie dogs. One place there was an arroyo with water running in it. We tried to cross it. We went into the water, and I was walking ahead as we started across. I came to a deep place but I didn't notice it. The water was too strong for me; it pulled both of my legs away and I started to wash away. I washed about fifty yards and pretty nearly drowned. I had a lot of water in my stomach, my ears, and my nose. The water was running down straight but down below there was a little curve, and the bank was almost level with the water. When I got to the curve, the water was just over it, and I just pushed myself on top of the bank. In just about an hour, I think, I got straightened up. My clothes were all wet and I started back home. We were about frozen when we got home. I dried my clothes, got on my burro, and started herding again.

CONSTRUCTION, AND THE FIRST LOCAL STORE

At Kainti there were no houses then, and we were living just this side of where the store is now. A man was building a wooden fence there, and I helped him at noon when the bucks were at home. They would dig a squarish hole one place and set two posts in it, then set another pair of posts about five or six feet away. They would tie a wire around each of the posts about a foot up so they could lay a pole on it. And they would do the same thing higher up on the posts so there were three wires. They kept on building the fence that way. There were four of us building the fence, three others and me. That's the wooden fence you can still see on the west side of the store. It's not the same shape (now), they keep changing it around different ways. I didn't help a whole lot with it, just when I brought the bucks in around noontime. The other three men did most of the fencing and it took them twenty days. The next thing they did was to hoe weeds out of the cornfield, and I helped with that. Then they cut some pine trees, east about five miles. The logs were about six ax-handles long, and they squared them up on two sides.

These logs were to build a house for an Indian woman at Kainti. She's that old blind woman now, called Old Lady Cloud. Her husband's name was Mister Cloud. That house is now the store, and this was going to be the very first house on the place. The name of the place wasn't the English name we use now. After the logs were cut and squared, they started to haul them back to this lady's place, and I was helping. There were three of us hauling logs. They were pretty heavy to load on the wagon. We hauled two at a time. I think it took us about two weeks to get them all hauled down there.

The next thing was to dig out the place for the foundation and put it up. So after that we hauled some rocks and built up the foundation with them. We built it up square with four corners. We started the foundation about a foot down in the ground and another foot above the ground—two feet altogether, built up with rocks. On top of that, we started building up with the big logs we had hauled. It took about a week to get all the walls up.

About the time we commenced on the roof, a white man from Manuelito came there one day. He wanted to put a little store there for the Indians. He talked with those people and the old lady that the house was being built for. The white man said that if they would let him have it, they would have to put a roof on, a lumber roof and roofing ply. The Indians told him it was all right with them, so we sent two wagons out to Manuelito. We hauled some lumber and roofing ply from there and made the roof.

This white man brought over some groceries—flour, coffee, sugar—and some clothing. The Indians began trading there for their wool, cattle, horses, rugs, and the trader used to pay money for everything he bought. His name was Andy Day. There were some Indians who used to haul freight for him with their teams and wagons.

After they had been trading there for one year, the store man said the house was too small. The store was getting bigger all the time and he wanted to make the house bigger. He wanted some men to cut more logs. He picked out the men who had cut the pine logs and sent them over to Willow Spring where there were some pines. They cut out some more logs that were pretty long, like twenty-four feet. They just peeled the bark, didn't square them off like the others. After they got them cut and peeled, they hauled them down close to the store. Then some more men hauled rocks with their wagons and teams and built a square foundation with them. The storekeeper was paying for the work the Indians were doing, but the Indians owned the land. There were quite a few men working together there and it didn't take very long to finish—just about three weeks. After that the store man had a big store. Another white man was working there who used to go without a hat all the time. We never did see him wear his hat, and the people named him Bareheaded.

They built another house next to the new one, just a lumber frame, and the roofing was all tin. In this house he had hay and grain. The old house he first used for a store was made into a kitchen. The next thing they built was a corral where they bought stock from the Indians. Inside that little fence was the only place where there was any farm around there. That's the fence we can still see on the west side of the store. There were no other farmers or white men.

"I HAD NEVER HEARD ABOUT DIPPING SHEEP BEFORE"

After that they began to talk about dipping sheep. A few of the Indians got together and talked it over. They wanted to put it right near the store, so they built corrals and dug a long pit where they could put a vat. After everything was built, the next thing they (government people?) told the Indians was that they wanted the Indians to buy the medicine with their own money. The Indians got together and talked it over and decided each home would have to put up one sheep. So they did that, put the sheep together and sold them to the store for the money to buy the medicine.

One Navajo man who was at the sing last night used to work every day for the storekeeper. We called him Big Ears. They had built one big corral first, and this man made some more fences inside the corral so that people could keep their sheep separate. All this work on the corrals and the dipping place was finished in about one month.

I never heard about dipping sheep before—this was the first time I heard of it. The only way people can say "dipping" in Navajo is to say, "The Indians are going to wash their sheep."

When they said it that way, I thought they might be washing their sheep with laundry soap. I wanted to be there! I wanted to see how it could be done. I wanted to be there all the time, and the time was coming close. One day when I was around there, people said they would start dipping sheep there on Monday.

Monday morning men started working at the sheep dip. They had a big tank full of water and they built a fire underneath it. That was right near where they put in the vat. After the water got hot they turned it into the vat, filling it with water. They poured some medicine into the vat, from the tank—dark red medicine. Then they stirred it up well. Wood's sheep were in the corral. He and his mother had a lot of sheep then—two herds. Their sheep were to be dipped first. Right alongside the vat were some long sticks, curved at the end. A man there was talking to the Indians, saying that all the Indians were supposed to help each other.

The corral was built from the end of the vat out and kind of sloped down into the vat. One man should watch to see the sheep didn't get too crowded. A lot of men would have to push the sheep toward the vat. Along the vat on each side men and women should stand, holding those sticks so they could keep the sheep moving along and not let any run back. At the other end of the vat was another small corral about two or three feet high. They wanted the medicine to drain off there and run back into the vat. Then there was another big corral and they could let the sheep in there when the little one was full. They did that to one herd, then started with another. About the time they started with the second herd, they would take out the one already dipped.

(Interpreter says: "I remember, too, the time they started to talk about dipping sheep. The Indians said that the reason they were going to dip them into this medicine was that the sheep had some sickness—fever, sore throat, headache, cough. They'd never seen it before, so they made a lot of talk about it. There were two white men working there where they were dipping. One took care of the water and the other counted the sheep after they went through the dip.")

After Wood's two bunches were dipped, a lot of people kept bringing their sheep in. At first, when they were going to make them pay for the medicine, they had said that was all they would have to pay. But after the man counted the sheep, for every hundred sheep the owner had to pay $1.50, that's a cent and a half a head. The man counting sheep said that if the sheep owner had some goats or wethers in the herd, he had to count the goats separately, and keep track of ewes, wethers, billy goats, like that. They kept dipping every day but didn't work Sunday. A lot of people were helping, and the ones who had a lot of sheep had to kill one or two for the people to eat.

The people living around here to the south, and all the Indians living over around Dale, and people back this way on the other side of the railroad all dipped their sheep here. It took about four weeks to get them all dipped. I just watched it, it was kind of new to me. After the dipping was finished, the two white men told the Indians they should take care of the corral and everything around the dipping place. They were going to do this every year.

Enemy Way

A few days after that I heard about a Squaw Dance down this side of Stony Point. I'd never seen that dance, and I began to think I'd like to go over there. Two other boys and I talked together about going and we started off on horseback. We got there just about sundown.

The word that we use to name that "Squaw Dance"[58] means something like "a man picks up a big stick and carries it off to some other place." It means a *big* stick, and they certainly gave it the wrong name in the first place, wherever it started. It is just a *little* stick, just about as long as the spinning stick and a little bit bigger around {that is, about two feet long and about half an inch in diameter}. When I first heard that name, I wanted to see it. I thought I would see how big the stick would be, and whether they would carry it on foot or riding a horse. That was the main thing I wanted to see.

When we got there, there were about a hundred people there. In one place a bunch of people were singing, using the Indian powder (?) jar for a drum. They were singing just as loud as they could. I saw the stick there, inside the hogan, but it was only a little stick. It was dressed up with different colored yarn, with big eagle feathers tied at the end. They sang there till after dark. A little way from there was a woodpile and they had fixed the wood so it all stood up. They set it on fire and it started to burn well. The fire gave a lot of light. I heard they were going to dance there, men and girls together. The dancing was going to start.

One of the girls carried out that stick I was talking about.[59] It had two feathers and was brought in from another place. There were a lot of girls out there to dance. All the girls had to do was to walk up to a man and take hold of him and bring him down where it's light near the fire and dance with him down there. They would dance twenty-five or thirty minutes, then turn the man loose. The man had to pay the girl before she turned him loose. They were dancing there about two hours. I myself danced with the girl who was carrying the stick.

After dancing, the girls went off and the men started to sing again the way they did before. There was a big bunch of people standing all around. The ones who rode horses could get off the horse and help sing in there, holding the horse while they sang. They kept singing all night like that. When daylight came, they took the drum inside the hogan and the singers began to go off.

The people who had brought the stick to the hogan had brought it from the mission over east of Gallup. They had a camp on the east side of the hogan that they were using. The people who stayed at that camp at night had their saddles and things all piled there, but they all came over and helped sing all night. In the morning, when they went back to their camp, they got fed, and then they walked over to the hogan where they sang that night. They were singing right outside the door, all facing the door. Some women had come with these people and they all lined up in front of the men who were singing.

While they were singing there, the hogan inside was full of Indians. One came out and started talking to the people outside. There were a lot more people over at the cooking place. The speaker was walking around talking to all the Indians, asking all the people to help him. He said, "Calico cloth, that's what I want!" He said, "We're going to throw some things to the singers. Everyone who wants to help, come inside the hogan." All his friends began to go in. They knew this would happen, so everyone who wanted to help had calico. Then everyone started to throw the cloth to the people who were singing; both men and women did the throwing. Some just walked up to the women singing and spread out the calico and put it around their necks. By the time they got through, these women had so much calico on their necks, they could hardly walk.[60] There were only two or three women at the place of the sing—most of the women had come from the other place.

After they finished that, one of the men that was doing the singing outside had the drum, in his hand. One of the people in the group lighted a cigarette, took it out there, passed it through the mouth of the man who had the drum, took the drum out of his hand and carried it into the hogan. The rest of them went back to the camp, and when they got there they saddled their horses and went home.

I saw another new thing there. They told me that this sing wasn't finished yet. One of the boys who was with me lost his horse that night. We started looking for it and found it right away. One of my friends started for home and the other two wanted to go on to the other place where the sing would go on that night. People there were talking about how they were going to get a lot of people together and move toward those people who had gone home in the morning from their camp. Down at the home of these people there would be the main dance. If we went there, we would stay overnight between the two places. Staying there would be the second night of the sing. People didn't say they were going to *camp* there that night, they said the people would "bed down." When I heard that, I wanted to see how they would "bed down."[61] They told everybody they should get ready right away and start off, there was a long way to go that day. They were on horseback and wagons.

While they were getting ready, another man and I started off ahead. We got to Gallup that evening, and from there we went east. We reached the place we were going to camp that night and there were some people already waiting there. A little after sundown all the people from where we had been got there, all together. After that, people from all directions began arriving. There were hardly any automobiles then, just a few in Gallup. After dark there were a lot of people, a big crowd of three or four hundred. They got together and started singing as they had before, and they had the big woodpile the same as the night before. The girl who carried the stick was out near the fire, and there were a lot of girls there who started to dance. They danced for over two hours, then quit and started to sing a different way, and kept on till daylight. I remembered about the "bedding down" but I didn't see it all night long! The main dance was still farther away, and after sunup they all moved on to that sing.

We went off in a different direction, across the railroad track, and came to where the dance would be. As we got close, about half a mile away we could see the hogans. We saw a man riding his horse toward us. He came up to us people who were moving, and when he got near us he just turned and ran his horse back as fast as he could. We started running our horses as fast as we could, after him. A lot of people started after him, running their horses as fast as they could go. When they had run them a little way, some people started shooting. When we got up to the hogans they had been running around, some around the hogans, and we could hear a lot of shooting. I thought maybe a war was on! I never saw this before, never saw it before, so I thought they might be starting a fight and some of them might get killed. After we got pretty close, everybody stopped and everything was pretty quiet. When we came to the hogan, I looked around for some dead people but I didn't see any![62]

Where they were running their horses and doing all the shooting there was one hogan and also a big brush hogan. I understood that that was the kitchen. They told us to make a camp over by a brush pile. Everybody got off their horses and helped build up another brush hogan so that we could camp there. Everybody started digging holes, and when they were ready they set a tree in each hole. They made the brush hogan in a few minutes, with a lot of people working together.

The family who had the stick we've been talking about were the ones who were going to camp inside the brush hogan with some of their friends. All the rest of us made camp around the outside of it. After we got located, they brought up some food from the kitchen in a wagon—bread, meat, and coffee. They took that food inside the brush hogan, and the people outside could help themselves. The ones who had their own dishes could come in and get a plate of meat and some coffee and take it outside. Everybody got plenty to eat.

Some people who were there that night, maybe half of them, got very drunk on the old whiskey that they used to have—the kind that was in that country before 1916. While all these people were eating that morning, a lot of them scattered out away from the brush hogan. They got sick from the whiskey and were vomiting. On one side they were doing that and on the other side they were eating! After everybody had had enough to eat, they took the dishes back over to the kitchen.

They had brought up one jar from the place where we had the first dance, and the stick that they carried was being brought back to the place it came from. Then I knew that this was the place where the stick started and that it had got back to the same place this morning. The people who had just made the brush hogan took the jar and stick outside. All the people inside bunched up in one place and started singing. That was the signal for the rest of us to get ready and come inside. They said they were ready now, and the people who were singing started to walk over where the main hogan was, where they did all the shooting. Later I heard what the shooting was for—all that went on for the patient. He was sitting inside the hogan. Those people who rode their horses around the hogan did it four times while the shooting was going on.

We came to the hogan and lined up outside just the way the other people had done it at the other place. While they were singing, they first threw a cloth or calico out the chimney hole, and after everybody saw that, they started to throw out more cloth, apples, cookies, Cracker Jacks, candy, tobacco. Some people got hit, you know! When they finished throwing they did the same as before: lighted a cigarette and gave it to the man who was holding the drum.

The singers went back to their camp. All the women who lined up in front had a lot of calico around their necks. When they got back to camp they started eating the apples, candy, Cracker Jacks, and everything else. There was nothing going on at the camp where we were, but over at the hogan some singers were doing some kind of work. You could see they were busy doing something over at that hogan.

(The interpreter said: "I was at that sing, my brother and I. I remember how they all got drunk that second night. They were singing and hollering all over and some were fighting. My brother and I got in a fight with some men that were drinking. After a while they rode off and their hats were knocked off by the trees. My brother got the hats and tied them to the back of his saddle. He went to sleep on his horse, and when he woke up the hats were gone.")

We could just hear the singing over where the patient was. What they were doing was what we call "Blackening a Patient."[63] After it was finished, they took the patient out of the hogan. They had a brush hogan built just east of the hogan, with a big green cover of pinyon and cedar on top and brush just on the south side. There was nothing on the north side— just a whole roof and one wall. When everything was finished inside, they took the patient out and made him sit in the brush hogan in the shade.

When the patient has a wife, the way they do is to blacken the patient inside the hogan, but they both have to be blackened. They do the woman outside under the brush hogan. When they finished blackening both of them, they were through. When it was finished, the patient went to the kitchen and stayed there the rest of the afternoon.

After that, the cooks could haul more food over to the people in the brush hogan that was put up that morning. They gave us plenty, and after we ate they saved what was left over for the last night that we were coming to.

Late in the afternoon, right in front of the new brush hogan we had built, the men started a big circle dance. We had one drum and the other side also had a drum. They signaled from over there that we could bring their drum over to the circle dance. There were just a few girls in the circle dance, the rest were men. The patient could dance with the people there if he was able. The men kept coming in until they had a great big crowd.

When they first started the dance they sang a song and started dancing the way the sun goes. When that song was finished, they sang and danced the other way. While the dancing was going on, the other side started horse races. There were people over there at the races, and it was crowded at the dance.

We heard that someone was thrown off his horse. That's all we heard about it. The horse races and dancing went on till just about sundown.

Way after dark, people from the new brush hogan started walking toward the patient's hogan, singing a song. When they came to certain words in the song, they would stop and yell out. They went in a row toward the hogan, and they did the yelling four times before they got there. They came right close to the door. They had a singer with them. The people inside threw out a basket to them for them to use. As soon as he saw the basket, the singer outside picked it up and laid it on the ground, upside down. The rest of the men stood in a row behind him. The singer started a song and as he sang he threw the basket up four times. After that he turned it upside down and hit it four times with the flat of his hand. He did that for one song, then threw the basket up. Then he stood up. They kept singing till they had sung four songs, which are also called First Songs. After the four songs were sung the singer went back to the brush hogan and everybody sang for not quite an hour.

The basket was for the singer, they paid him that for the first time he started the group from away over toward the patient's hogan. That was the end of his job, and then everybody was singing there for pretty nearly an hour. After singing that long, everybody started back to the brush hogan.

All the patient's friends around where he lived had come together for this sing. When they took the stick down to the other place for the first night's singing, they all lined up in a row on one side and they "sang against" the people they brought the stick to—the two sides were singing against each other. Then on the last night we had now reached, when they got to the brush hogan they did some more singing, everybody, for about an hour. After that they started a big fire, and when it began to burn they danced again.

You {to A.H.L.} remember that I danced with the girl who had the stick on the first night? I danced with her again on the second night, and the third night down there I danced with her a few more times. That made three nights of dancing with the same girl. That got me pretty well acquainted with the girl, and afterward I married her![64]

After they had danced about two and a half hours they quit that and started some singing for everybody. They kept on singing until nearly daylight, and when the first brightness came they called for the patient to come to where they were singing. He came into the sing and they all faced toward the east. They sang four more songs that they call First Songs and that was the end, just before daylight. Everybody began to go home.

We rode back to Gallup on horseback and went on to the place of the first night's sing. We got something to eat there, then came back to Kainti. We found out that way the meaning of "Squaw Dance."

I don't remember how long after that Squaw Dance it was when we started a dance right here in Kainti. The storekeeper started it. Wood and some other men were talking to him and he said he would like to put up supplies for a Yeibitchai dance for someone. Wood said he would like to have one and be the patient. The storekeeper said, "All right, let's do it." He said he would put up a hundred dollars for Wood, mostly in groceries and trade. He said he wanted some men to cut more trees down for hogan logs. He told them to get them anyplace, and he wanted to put on the dance right away.

So the storekeeper hired about twenty Indians to cut hogan logs at $1.50 a man a day. They started cutting, and five wagons were hauling the logs. It didn't take long, and they began building the hogan on the west side of where the store is now. They made the hogan with the logs standing up, quite a good-sized one. It took them fifteen days to get everything finished.

FIRE DANCE

At the same time there was another big dance about to start—that is called the Fire Dance.[65] The storekeeper wanted to have his dance right away, but the others wanted to wait until the other one was over. That was another thing that I didn't know about, and I wanted to go to it with the people. When the time came, one of my uncles told me I could ride a mule that he had over to that dance. I had the mule with some other horses. I corralled them and put a rope on the mule, led him up to the hogan and put a saddle on him. The mule was in pretty good shape, fat. When I put the saddle on him he was gentle, but when I started to lead him off before I got on him, he began to jump and pitch around. I was holding the bridle line. The saddle went over his neck and kept on moving until it was right between his two front legs. I turned him loose, let him go, and the saddle and everything slipped right over his head. He ran off without anything on him. Two other men and I went after the mule and drove him into the corral again. I put on a rope and saddle and got on him. The mule didn't try to do anything like he did before, and we started off to the dance, the three of us. It was pretty near sundown when we started.

When we got to the dance, there were lots of people there. We could see one of the Yeibitchai running around. This Yei-bitchai was holding up a young deer's skin that had some corn-meal in it. There was a hogan there at the dance and the Yeibit-chai began sprinkling the cornmeal north of the hogan. He made a circle about sixty feet across, perfectly round, with no corners. He left a doorway on the east side. The ground had been all shaped up and smoothed off. This was in the woods where there were lots of trees, not far off. They call that place Trees Standing. One man was in charge of this, and people had to do whatever he told them. Everybody wanted to do some of the work.

We were to build a brush hogan around the cornmeal circle, build a high and thick brush fence, a little higher than this roof (eight or nine feet). We started right on the line he had made with cornmeal. Everybody got some brush and brought it over—it was all green branches, pinyon and cedar together. We didn't use any horses to drag the branches; what-ever we cut, a bunch of men would get together and drag it over. We started from the left (south) side of the doorway and laid every branch with the small end pointing the way the sun goes. The first fence we made that way was only about a foot high, and we kept working on it until we got to the north side of the doorway. Then we went to the south side and added more brush, leaning it against the low fence, butts down and tops sticking up. We made it pretty thick and high around to the north side of the doorway. The corral was finished then, after sundown. I was thinking about that fence—the first such one I had seen. It was a good fence and might corral horses or sheep or cows.

Meanwhile the sing was going on in the hogan south of the fence. The singer over there and the patient and medicine bags were all brought out to this brush hogan and put way over on the west side. When the patient and the medicine man got located, then the crowd outside began to move in. They moved in some saddles. First they moved in close to the singer on the south side, then on the north side, too. They brought in some wood and stacked it in front of the people. It had already been cut outside, and they stacked it in a few places on the south side and the north side in front of the people. Some places on each side, they told the people to make some room and build a little fire to make some coffee. This big dance was reaching its last night; it was a nine-night sing. They stopped feeding people outside after they built the corral. They had to eat their own food in there. People who had come from a long way off kept moving inside and it began to be very crowded.

I skipped something: before they moved into this corral, they had started a fire inside the hogan by spinning a stick, at the very beginning. When the medicine man and patient moved in, they brought the fire from the hogan inside the fence to start the fires there. After that, people took a little fire from that to start the small fires here and there where they needed it for cooking. Along about eleven o'clock they lighted a stack of wood in the middle of the corral. When it started burning it made a big fire and gave people lots of light.

After the light got bright, we saw ten people come in the doorway, plastered with white clay all over their bodies. No clothes except the white cloth they wore between their legs. They each had a stick about the size of the spinning stick, with soft feathers tied right at the end. They started running as soon as they came in before the people, sticking their sticks into the fire, calling their sticks "white" all the time. After they had done this several times, the feathers were all burned away. They acted funny as they ran around. They would put the sticks back in the fire, trying to make it white again, but they couldn't see any white. Every time they did that they would shake the stick and see if the feather came back. The first man to see his feather come back says, "I see white; mine came back!," and he runs outside with it. Each one did that, and at the end maybe there were one or two who couldn't get it back. They went over to the hogan, washed off the white clay, and got dressed again. We call these people "whitings." When they were all washed up they came into the corral and watched what happened. There were some others getting ready over in the hogan.

Then we heard hollering over there. When they were ready, they came inside the corral, plastered with white clay in the same way, and walking in a special way. This bunch had kind of a singer at the head, and each one had a bunch of cedar bark about six inches thick and eighteen inches long. They came in pretty fast as if they were jumping toward the fire. They motioned to the fire with the bark, then backed off, went to the south side and did it again, then repeated it on the west and the north sides. After they did this at the four sides, the lead man lighted his cedar bark. When it was burning, the others lighted their bark from his. Only four were lighted at first. When the first one was burning well, he threw it right over the corral on the east side. The next one was lighted at the south side and thrown out there, and the same for the west and the north.

About then the rest lighted their bark, and when it got burning they ran around the fire, shaking the fire onto each other. They were running and jumping and putting fire on each other. It made all the people laugh. When the bark burned down to where they were holding it, they ran out with it. Some were thrown down in front of the people. After they all went out, back to the hogan, the people could pick up the cedar bark they threw down to use for burn medicine. (They take it home and save it to use if anybody gets burned.)

About that time the singers on the west side started singing and using the basket. They didn't use a drumstick, but they had a stick with notches that was rubbed with another stick, and the basket makes the sound louder. (In brief: The singers come in, then more dancers who carry sticks dressed with feathers—one group after another till daylight, each dances about an hour. Each group of singers and dancers comes from different areas. There are four dances after the Morning Songs. They hold up spruce branches and make a big opening in the south side of the fence and at other cardinal points. The crowd leaves through any of these, and the sing is over.)

Then I started back home. I had found what that corral

was for—not for sheep or cattle, but for the dancers and the people watching them. I came to a man with a broken leg, in a wagon, named Dick, and talked to him for a little while. He had been drinking at the sing that night and his horse fell down on him and broke his leg. We came home.

When I got back, they had already sent off for the man to sing there for Wood's dance at the Kainti store. Wood had some kind of trouble with his head—it hurt all the time. He said he had been dancing with old people many times. They say that when you dance in a Yeibitchai dance, wearing a mask, you are not supposed to talk or cough. Wood said he thought he had made some mistakes while he was doing that kind of dancing, so he wanted to have this sing done for him. (What do you mean, "he danced with old people"?) The others were old and he was the only young one in the bunch. The others knew it well, but he was young and made some mistakes.

It was Big Fred who had been sent off to get the medicine man on the other side of St. Michaels. He came back with a big load on his horse—the medicine bag and also the buckskin masks. The medicine man did not come with him, and Big Fred said it would be two days till he arrived. I was home at Sam Smith's place, but I heard that the medicine man came and they went on with their business. I just thought about the other dance like this one that I had seen down at Stony Point.

For the time that I had been herding for Wood, they gave me six little young goats, six of them. One day I went to pick them out from the herd. I drove them over to the store with Ernest's wife and got 75 cents a head, $3.75 altogether. (cheated) {The parenthetical "cheated" appears in the Leighton manuscript with no explanation, but I think most probably the word reflects Bill Sage's judgment.} I went to the sing with that money in my pocket with Ernest and stayed there with him. Ernest said he wanted to go to Mr. Clark's store, about three miles east of here, to sell a calf. He said that the calf's mother had died and they had been feeding it at home as a pet. When we got to the store, Mr. Clark talked Navajo pretty well and Ernest told him he wanted to sell the calf. Mr. Clark asked him where it was and Ernest said at home. Mr. Clark asked what kind of a calf it was and how big, and Ernest said it was a pretty good calf. The storekeeper said he would give him twelve dollars, half trade and half cash. He said he knew that Ernest and Ernest's father had some cows. So he traded six dollars and gave him six dollars in money. We came back to the dance, and the next day the calf he had sold died! We just laughed about it.

We were at the dance, all the way through to the last night, just as I saw it at Stony Point. There were a lot of people there, a big crowd the last night, coming on horseback and wagons but no automobiles. In the morning when everything was finished, everybody went home. That was the first time I saw a storekeeper put up one hundred dollars for a dance for Indians. Indians and whites got together and put on this dance till it was finished. (Why did the white man do it?) I didn't know it at the time, but I found out later that he wanted to make a little money. He put up a cooking stand to feed the people. Also, they were trading at the store all those nine days and nights, and people brought in a lot of cattle and sheep to sell at the store. Do you understand it now?

I didn't have any regular home, I just stayed with my aunt at Sam Smith's, with no father or mother. The women didn't make good dresses at that time. Now they put color in the middle of the dress and at the bottom, but they didn't do that then. I remember it pretty well, about twenty-five years ago. About one more year after that {when, by Lucky's reckoning, he would have been fifteen or sixteen years old}, I married the woman I'm living with now. We were married about twenty-four years ago. I remember pretty well everything that happened from that time on.

CHRISTMAS

That winter I heard about Christmas, and I saw my first one down at Little Pine Springs. I went down there on Christmas day with some people to a Mexican's store. When we got there, there was a big crowd of men and women. It was snowing that day and I went into the store. There was another room there, and I went through the crowd to it. I saw a man I knew pretty well and the Mexican was there with him. The Navajo said, "Come sit by me," and while I sat, he talked to the Mexican. He had a little glass about two inches tall sitting on the table. The Mexican reached down under the table and pulled out a big bottle of whiskey. He filled up the little glass and handed it to me. The Navajo told me to drink it up. I took a little bit of it and tasted it, but it wasn't a very good taste. I asked what it was and he said it was called whiskey. I never had had even a taste before. I took the rest and threw it down my throat, and it burned from my throat to my belly. I went outside where some other people were. On one side they were cooking a lot of meat and making a lot of coffee. At noon they all ate there. The storekeeper told them that was all. So I found out that's what is called Christmas.

The man that we call Arnold today was down in that crowd that day. He had a bottle of whiskey and started to drink from the bottle. They had been buying this from the Mexican. A lot of people had gotten drunk already. While we were drinking that bottle, I got pretty drunk, too drunk, to where I didn't know anything any more. The man I was drinking with and I started to walk off behind the corral. Another man told me afterward that I didn't come back for some time, so he walked after me and saw me behind the corral. Somehow I had gotten on top of the corral fence. I was wearing a black handkerchief around my neck, and somehow it got around one of the poles. I must have jumped down, and there I was hanging with my toes just touching the ground! I had pretty nearly hanged myself when they found me. The man said he pulled out his knife and cut the handkerchief. I don't know how I did that. I don't know where I went next, but I found myself at Arnold's home next morning. Arnold was telling me that I almost hanged myself yesterday. I came back home to Sam Smith's. They asked me where I had been and I said I had stayed with Arnold. I didn't tell about getting drunk and hanging myself!

After that I saw another dance, a small sing for Wood called Apache Wind Way. The singer came from near Gallup. I had seen this sing a few times before.

One day after that, Dick, Robert, John and I, four of us, went down to Little Pine Springs. The other three had already decided to go there and asked me to go with them. When we got there it was the same place where they had had Christmas. I found out that these boys had gone down there to buy some whiskey—two pints and one quart were bought.[66] We came on home and drank just a pint on the way. Next day we went down to Manuelito, where they were holding a meeting for Indians.

THE TRIAL IN SANTE FE

When we got there we still had some whiskey, and while we were there two of the men got pretty drunk. We had two little bottles of whiskey tied to the saddle on the horse, and someone there reported it and they took the whiskey away. We came home that same night. A car came down from Manuelito to Kainti with the sheriff from town. He picked up all four of us who had been down to Little Pine Springs, took us over to Manuelito and from there to Gallup. In Gallup they told us that they wanted us so as to be able to prove where we got the whiskey. We told the court that we got it from a Mexican at Little Pine Springs. Then they let us go out.

Later they called us in again, took us into another room and asked us some more questions, taking us one at a time. The other three told me I should be the last one. They said, "Tell them the truth about what we saw down at the Mexican's place." After that, the officers took us into the room, and there I saw the Mexican who was selling whiskey at Little Pine Springs. There were a lot of other people there besides him. First they asked my name and I told them. Also my age, and I don't remember what I said for that. They asked me if I knew a place in the country named Little Pine Springs, and I said yes. Then they asked if I knew the Mexican sitting in the room. I said yes, I knew the Mexican. They asked how I got to know him. I said that this was only the second time I'd seen him. The officer asked if I knew the Mexican was selling whiskey there to Navajos—when did he sell some. First, they said they wanted me to tell the truth about this. I said, "Last Christmas Day I was there," and I told them that two of us Navajos had bought whiskey from this man. They asked what I paid for a bottle, and I said, "We didn't buy it in a bottle. He had the bottle and just poured it out into a little glass. He handed it to me and I drank it up. That's all I saw Christmas day." They asked me if I'd seen some more whiskey at that place before that? I said no. Or any time after? I said, "Yes, three others and I went to Little Pine Springs, saw the Mexican, and three of the boys bought three bottles of whiskey that cost them about $6.50." They asked me if I put up some money myself, and I said no, I was just watching the other boys. They asked me if I helped them drink it up and I said yes.

Next thing they asked was how did I start drinking whiskey, where did I learn about it? I said, "At that place—Little Pine Springs. That was where I first saw whiskey on Christmas Day. That's where I started to drink." They asked me if there was a store there, and I said yes, there was. They asked me what the building was like, how many rooms, how many doors? I said, "There's one big house with two rooms in it. He has his store on the north side with one door out to the north, and on the south side there are two doors."

They asked me if the other three Navajos were already drunk when the four of us went to that place. I said no, they were not drunk. They asked if they drank any there after they bought it. I told them we didn't stay there long, we went home right away. They asked if I was telling the truth, and I said, "Yes." They pointed to the Mexican and asked, "Is this the same man?" I said, "Yes, it's the right man." They asked me what made me think that this was the same man. I said, "I know that man. I can tell by looking at him. His face is hanging down and he's big and fat." Then they said, "After you left the store, how far away did you begin to drink?" I answered, "One man used his pocket knife to open the bottle." He asked, "Was he drunk?" I said, "He didn't get drunk, he didn't drink much." Next they asked me if I was at the meeting at Manuelito. I said yes, I was. "Were the others there too?" "Yes, we were all there together." "How many bottles did you have there?" I said two.

About that time, one of the officers walked over and opened up a shelf where they had a lot of bottles. The sheriff had brought in those bottles, and they wanted to know if I could tell the right bottle. I stood up and looked them over. I picked out two, and they told me they were the right bottles. Then they started talking with the Mexican man. He said he didn't understand the language and didn't know what had been said. They got up and started talking, hitting the table with their fists. They let me go out to the other room where the other boys were.[67] After that they let us all go. Ernest was at Manuelito and was at the trial, too, so I walked out with him.

The Mexican came out there, too. He shook his fist, that big Mexican, and he said, "You goddam son of a bitch!"

Before they sent us out, the officer came up and said to us boys, "I want you to keep your story just the way you told it here. When you go home, we'll send word or a letter to the Kainti storekeeper, and he will tell you what day I want you to come in again. We want to take you to Sante Fe to tell the court down there the same thing that each one of you said here." After that, we came back home to Kainti.

We worked around there with the Indians near Kainti for three months, then the storekeeper told us it was time for us to go back. They wanted us to ride our horses to Manuelito and take a train from there. When we got to Manuelito, there was a man waiting for us, and the train got there at the same time.

We got on the train and another man who had come with us took the horses back home. When the train stopped at Gallup we got off, about this time of day (5:00 P.M.). We waited around the rest of the day and night, till toward daylight, all that time at the depot. We found some more Navajos waiting there, too, who were all being taken to Santa Fe for the same thing. We had a lot of friends there. Just as daylight began, the train came and we all got on and started off from Gallup to Albuquerque. They told us we could spend twenty minutes there, so everybody got a little to eat there, but they didn't get any whiskey to drink! We went on from there to Santa Fe. We began to look out the windows at the country. We passed by some villages, and I thought that some Zuni people were living all along there.[68]

When we got way up near Santa Fe, I think, the train stopped, we got off, and the train went on its way. But there was another train there, headed toward the north, and a big tall man who took us over to it. That other train took us to Santa Fe. The tall man took us from there {Lamy?} to the main town. It was early in the afternoon when we got there, and the tall man said we could wait in the middle of the town under some shady trees. He went off someplace and was gone about half an hour. When he came back he gave each man a dollar. Some of the men spoke English and one of them told us that the money was for everybody to get something to eat. The tall man said when we had had something to eat, to come back right there.

The people began to talk about who that man was. Some of the boys knew who he was and told us he was the Ft. Defiance Indian Superintendent for the Navajos.

When we had eaten, we came back to where we'd been waiting and waited for a long time. Our trial wouldn't come up for four days because there were a lot of people in front of us. The man said they would take care of us and give us some money for food every day, and give us an order for a place to sleep. While we were all together there, there was an Apache man that some were talking to, and the Navajo boys gave him some money. That was to get some whiskey for the Indians. I was just watching and didn't put in any money.

We slept one night there, and next morning they gave us just one order for eating that would be good for everybody. They did the same for the place where we slept at night, so we didn't do anything but eat and sleep and come back to the same place in the morning. We were just getting fat.

Our time was still two days off, so we went over to the other side of a hill after we ate breakfast. We saw a big river running over there. When we got farther up we saw a lot of woods. We all went—thirty-four or -five people went over there in a bunch. Then we split and ten of us went still farther. They began to talk about making a sweathouse, and so we built one there. While we were building it up with rocks and wood, we started a fire too. We were taking a sweatbath in there for a while. The people who stopped went home, and we came back to town in the afternoon. This was along in the fall.

When we got to the trial, they told us to wait till afternoon. They took us into a room in a big house, and we waited there until they started our trial in the afternoon. They took us upstairs one at a time. They would bring one man back and take another up. I was the tail, the last one.

When they took me up, there was a big table in the middle of the room and there were three or four of those officers there. I didn't know there were a lot of people there, I was facing the other way. When I turned around, there were a whole lot of people—Americans, Mexicans, some baldheaded. I got scared when I saw so many people. They made me sit where the judges were sitting. A man asked me my name and I told him. Where did I live? I said the other side of Gallup, in Indian language.

They had a Navajo interpreter there and they asked me the same things they asked in Gallup. Before I got to the court the other boys had told me that the Mexican had a lawyer there. When the lawyer asked me anything I told him "I don't know," but I told the judge the same things that I said in Gallup.

After I had told my story to the end and after the Mexican's lawyer had tried to ask me some questions, the judge told me that he knew the Mexican was in the room and I should look around and see if I could find him. If I found him, I should point him out. I looked around at all those people and I saw that Mexican way over there. He had his face shaved, was wearing glasses, had new clothes and a haircut. But I knew him by his face.

Next, they told me to walk over to another room. Another man walked with me, and in the room was another sheriff. I saw a lot of bottles in there, some tall, some half-full, some with just a little. They all had names on them. They made me try to find the bottles. It took me a long time to find the two that time. I picked out two and they told me those were the right bottles.

When I came back and sat in the same place, the Mexican's lawyer talked. He asked me my tribe; I said Navajo. He asked me where I lived; I said Kainti. He said, "What place is that?" I told him it was right there. He kept asking and I kept telling him Kainti. I answered just a few questions, but the rest I said I didn't know, all the way through. I think it was one of the judges who turned and made a big, long speech. After he stopped talking, everybody clapped their hands and laughed. I thought they were laughing at me. I went downstairs where the other boys were.

A man came down then and took all of us upstairs. When we got before the judges, they told us we did pretty well on this case. They said, "We'll let you go home. The food, beds, and train trip here are all paid for. We want to give you each sixty dollars—in a check. When you get out of here, you can cash the checks at the bank. You can buy your own food and pay for the train ride home. It will cost you about nine dollars to Gallup." So we took our checks over to the bank and they cashed them. We all got something to eat and went to the depot, and the train was already there. We started to get on, but they sent us back to buy our tickets. One man took us over there, everybody bought his ticket, then got on the train. We went south from Santa Fe, stopped at the little station, and our train went off. They told us to wait till twelve o'clock when another train would come along.

About twelve o'clock the train came and we got in. It made a stop in Albuquerque for about half an hour, and we got to Gallup as daylight was just beginning. On the way the others were sleeping, but I didn't sleep at all. When we got to Gallup we first came into the waiting room. The seats were nice and soft there and I lay down on one of them. The people were all there when I went to sleep. I don't know how long I slept, but when I woke up it was about nine o'clock and I didn't see any of my friends around. I was all by myself. I came through the middle of the town and saw some of my friends there, almost all of them drunk again.

Then the men that came from Kainti got together again. We started out for home, and when we were ready to go they talked about more whiskey. They wanted to buy a gallon to carry home. They all put their money together except me. We walked all the way to Kainti, taking turns carrying the jug one mile at a time. They tried to get me to carry it, but I didn't want to.

When we were leaving Santa Fe, the judge told us he wanted us to come back in six months when the leaves were green. He wanted another trial then. (What did you think of Santa Fe?) I thought that the train would be like riding in a wagon, rough. But when I got on I hardly noticed when it started. I'd been to town a few times already, and I don't remember what I thought of Santa Fe.

After we walked home, the next day we had a sweatbath. That took a long time, pretty nearly all day. An old man, Ernest's father, killed a sheep for us while we took the sweatbath. We ate a lot of meat, now we were back home, after we took the sweatbath.[69]

In the fall there were lots of pinyons all around here. There were more on the south side of Kainti, and there were lots of camps in the woods there. People came from far away to pick pinyons. There was a Yeibitchai dance going on north of here—the man's name was Mister Big Hail.

Lucky's father-in-law was Old Man Paul. We first hear of him in the life story when Lucky went to help the family move after the death of his wife's sister from influenza (LS 312). He had just completed moving their goods when he discovered that his mother-in-law was also dead. When Old Man Paul was informed of this, he sent Lucky to notify his oldest son, Big Hail (LS 314) (Social Relations 43).

Sometimes he used another name. I went to the dance one day before it ended. Lots of people from all over the country, and all the pinyon pickers around here, were there. They were dancing all night long. Next day I was around there, just a little way off, and in the daytime I slept. About sundown or a little after dark we went back to the dance. This was the last night, and the dancing was just the same as I'd seen it before. Men and women were coming in on horseback together, with the horses dressed up pretty nicely and the men and women likewise. A lot of women used a silver bridle on their horses. Everybody saw the dance that night.

On the next-to-last night, they danced all night long. The dancers came from different places a long way off. Each bunch of dancers was given a sheep the next morning. On the last night they did the same thing, but the dancers were dressed differently—they had no clothes on. They wore moccasins and blue stockings woven by Navajos. They wore a little cloth from their waists, held in place by a silver belt. They wore a good bracelet on each arm, lots of beads, and a mask over their heads. Each man was using a big rattle. After dark they started dancing until daylight. As soon as everyone had seen that dance, they all started going home in the morning. When they got home they just slept that day. By that time I had seen four Yeibitchai dances in four places.

Through his frequent attendance at Sings, Lucky has not only learned the songs but has acquired a wide circle of friends and acquaintances. He has often joined with small groups to go off to work as a laborer or to trade or to gather pinyon nuts or

salt. Many of his stories are of long gambling sessions or bois-
terous drinking bouts with his companions. There have un-
doubtedly been a good many affairs with girls, but Lucky pre-
ferred not to discuss this aspect of his life for the pay we were
offering, especially since the year had already entered on the
season when such topics are more or less taboo (Summary of
Social Relations 1).

One day when A. L. asked Lucky, "Did you have any time
for the girls?" Lucky answered, "Oh yes, I was acting like a little
billy goat!" (Social Relations 37).

To Work at Fort Apache

I didn't do much after that, just stayed home, herded
sheep, hauled a little wood all winter that year. I didn't stay all
winter there, but started off to Ft. Apache a little after Christmas. Another man and I went there together. We went from
here to Manuelito and from there to Gallup. After dark we
talked about freight trains and hung around the depot. After
dark one came and stopped there. We got pretty close and
waited for it to start again. Just as it was starting, the other man
hung onto it and so did I. We got up on top and walked along.
We found an empty car and got inside it. We were sitting down
in it, each of us with a blanket. We lay down and went to sleep.
The freight train stopped a few places, I don't know where. We
didn't know when we left Gallup, but it was way after dark.

We got to Holbrook just about daylight. The train didn't
stop but went slowly. While it was slow, the other man and I
got out of the car, went down the step, and he jumped. I saw
him run off. He told me to do the same as he did, and I tried
but the train was going too fast. I tried to put one of my legs to
the ground but couldn't make it. Finally I jumped off but I just
fell, I didn't do it as he did. I started rolling way down the side
of the dirt pile. I kept rolling until I was down under the place,
pretty far from the other man. I started walking to the other
place. My side was hurting, and I was about a mile from where
the other man jumped. When we found each other, we went
to the depot. When we went in, it was pretty warm. We looked
at the place where my side hurt. There were a few places where
my hide had been rubbed off!

There I saw two of my friends, Arnold and his brother,

and another man and his wife. They said they were going to Ft. Apache, and a train was going there pretty soon. They said it would go pretty near that place. They were going to get off where they wouldn't have to walk very far. We all paid for our tickets, got on the train, and went off. When the train stopped we got out and all started walking toward Ft. Apache.

We didn't go by the road but took a shortcut. There was a road, but it went a long way around. We walked about five miles, and got into timber where there were a lot of pines. There was snow on the ground after we came into the timber. We walked till sundown and kept on walking after dark. I gave out first. When we got there, the rest of the people were tired out. It must have been about this time (8:30 P.M.) that we got there. We found some Navajo Indians camping down there who were just about going to bed. We knew some of the people who were camping. They had a hogan, and when we went into it they told us we could make some coffee and cook something for ourselves so we could have something to eat. Two of the men started to cook. I just lay down, took off my shoes, was pretty tired, and went to sleep right away. They woke me up when they were ready to eat and we all ate together. After we ate we felt good and washed the dishes. We told our story to the other people, then went to sleep.

Pretty early, before daylight, the whistle blew. The people got up and so did we. After we ate breakfast the people got ready and went to work. We new people followed the others to see if we could get a job there. We went down to a big sawmill. There was a big building on one side and on the other a big lake. There were a lot of logs floating on the water. When we went inside, they sent me off on one side and they put all four of us on a job. They put us where we would be stacking lumber, and they took the others somewhere else. They paid me $2.50 a day. About noon, when the whistle blew, we went over where we had stayed overnight to get our dinner. Then we went back to work. We worked till quitting time, just a little before sundown. At quitting time they took us to an empty house, a little cabin. There wasn't any stove in it, but we put one in and all four of us moved in. We worked from there.

After we started working they gave us an order to the store so that we could buy on credit. We could buy flour, coffee, sugar, potatoes, lard. We made a lot of naneskadi (Indian bread)! We all felt good because we were working and had a lot of food. I wasn't a very good cook, I always burned the bread, but the others knew how to cook. We started work before daylight, took one hour off at noontime, and quit at five. There were a lot of Navajos working there and Apaches, too. The Navajos told me that nobody stayed on that job very long.

I stayed with it for three weeks. Another man and I were working together, stacking lumber. He could speak English. We got our pay in fifteen days, the end of the month. The man who worked with me had a big stack of lumber fall on his leg and it broke in two on one side. They took him to the hospital. I got scared of that, and I quit that job and went to another place to work.

An Apache Indian and I worked together for quite a while, then they put us on another job. They had a small railroad there, and my job was to haul some dry lumber from a stack out to another place, pushing the car every day. It went to the planer, where the lumber was planed. Then we loaded it into a freight car. We worked around in different places. The man I worked with took me over to where the Apaches were living, and on Sundays I got to know some Apache people.

These Apaches fixed corn some way, soaked it in water, and said they were making some kind of whiskey. It didn't look like whiskey. They drank a whole lot of it, and they told me to drink some. I did, and I didn't like it. It tasted rotten and sour. The Apaches drank it like water, mostly on Sundays. (It was a mild beer. Cf. Opler, *An Apache Life-Way,* p. 369–70.)[70]

They kept me moving all the time at the mill. I worked two months and ten days before I started back home. I got on the train there and came back to Holbrook; I got off that train and waited for another one. After dark, about nine o'clock, another one came and I got off at Manuelito about midnight. As soon as I got off I started walking this way, and daylight came when I was about halfway. I kept walking until I got home at Sam Smith's place.

I stayed around there a while, then went to Zuni where I heard there was another dance going on. When we got there, there was an open place in the middle of the village, and eight men, plastered with white clay and wearing masks over their heads, were lined up in a row. There were a lot of men around there carrying babies on their backs. They were in a long row, and when they got to where the eight men were standing, they walked by them. The ones with the babies were carrying them with a big quilt. They were not too small babies—maybe four years old. Under the quilt was fixed something else pretty soft and thick. It was all tied over the top of their (the children's) heads, and they carried the children that way. The eight men had yucca leaves in bunches about three inches thick, the longest pieces they could find. The first man passed his baby along that row and the eight men hit with their yucca leaves right back of the head where the cover is tied, as hard as they could, each child eight times. A little way off there were steps up to a rooftop and the child was carried up there, and that was the last we saw of him. They did it to every one of those kids as they went by. After they got through, the eight men went off, and they were going to have a dance in the same place.

You remember that in the Navajo way children are not supposed to look at a Yeibitchai dance until they have seen the Yei? This was the same thing—those kids were not supposed to look at a dance until they got hit in that way.[71] The Zunis danced two days after that in the daytime, and after the dance was over we came back and worked around home.

(Before going on, Lucky asked for a drink of cough medicine, saying that he always liked to put a drink in the story.)

A LONG TRADING TRIP

We stayed around home about one year. Then one day Old Man Wood and I started talking about going someplace. Wood talked about going to Black Mountain to trade for sheep and cows. Old Man Wood wanted me to go along. We started off one day. Wood took a lot of beads, a silver belt, rings, silver buttons that he wanted to trade for sheep. We took some food along with us, a lot of naneskadi, and some dried meat. We were going near Chinle. We started off on the trail to Manuelito and got there late in the evening, then we went on north from there. We went to a hogan, about sundown, where Wood knew the man. There were some men and women there. One of the men's daughters was sick and a medicine man was there. They were singing a War Way song.

After dark they took the jar out for a drum, and they were singing just outside the door. They sang till after midnight, then brought the jar back in and went to sleep. Next day Wood and another man were talking together. Later Wood told me that he had said there was a man over toward Manuelito who also wanted to go to Black Mountain, and to take along a lot of things to trade for sheep. So he went back to get the beads and belts while Wood and I waited there that day.

We waited all day long, and about sundown the man came back. The patient was pretty sick and couldn't get up. People had to help her. During the day they did some other things inside the hogan, but I wasn't paying any attention. After dark they took the jar out again and sang outside. They sang until after midnight, then brought in the jar and everyone slept.

In the morning after breakfast we got ready, brought up our horses and saddled them, and went on. Then I found out something else Wood had done that I didn't know about. Wood and the man who wanted to go with us and still another man had talked together at the start, and one was sent to Gallup to get some whiskey. That one had got back from Gallup toward daylight, Wood said. He told me he had sent that man for whiskey to use on the trip. He had two big bottles, two quarts, and the other man had one quart.

We started off and got to Aspen Spring below St. Michaels. Before we got there, we stopped at another hogan to see another man that Wood knew. We got something to eat there, then went by St. Michaels and westerly, up on top of a mountain. We went on quite a long way from that mountain, and as we went off on the other side we saw two men coming along on horseback. When we met, they were dressed like policemen. They looked kind of drunk. Wood knew the men and shook hands with them. They were policemen from Ft. Defiance, both Navajos. They asked Wood what he was doing there, where he was going. Wood said we were going to Black Mountain to trade for some sheep. The policeman said, "That's a long way for you people to go still." Wood asked about which was the shortest way to go and they told us all about it. The one that Wood knew pretty well said he thought Wood had been drinking and asked how much drink he had left. Wood said he didn't have any. The two men had been coming from a long way off, the other side of Chinle, and they were pretty tired. Wood asked, "If I told you I had some whiskey, would you drink it?" They answered, "Yes, I guess we would." Wood pulled out his bottle and gave it to them. Each one took a little drink and gave the bottle back to Wood. Wood said, "Take a good drink," but they said, "No, we don't want to drink much."

Before they started off again the two men said, "Inside the reservation we are watching pretty closely for this kind of stuff, but you people are coming from a long way outside the reservation.[72] Besides, if a man knows how to drink and takes care of himself, we have no business to bother him. We are awfully sleepy and tired, so we'll just thank you for this and go on. But be careful not to give anybody a drink around here or where you are going. There's a white man running a store ahead of you. We just left there a little while ago after we'd been there half an hour. There are some Navajo Indians at that store. If you go there, don't stay too long. Get what you want there and then go on."

We stopped at the store when we got there. Some people were asking where we came from. Wood said we came from Zuni country. One man asked if we were Zuni. Wood said no, we were Navajos. Then he said, "I myself am married to a Zuni woman. Zuni squaws are that big around (holding his arms way out) and my wife's like that." We didn't stay long and went on west. (Did they believe Wood?) They were mostly young boys and I think they believed him.

Not very far from there we came to a little canyon. We found a spring there and watered our horses. On the other side we unsaddled our horses and found a lot of grass. We decided to make a little lunch there while the horses were eating. They weren't hobbled, just had ropes on them. This was just before sundown and it was pretty hot there. It was in July. We didn't make coffee or anything, just spread out our blankets and lay down on them and went to sleep right away. Nobody woke up.

I waked up first, just about daylight, and the other two men were still sleeping. I went off tracking the horses and followed their tracks back the way we had come. I came back by the store and up to where the two policemen had a drink and on this way till I caught them. I rode one back and took them over to where the men were. It was about eleven o'clock when I brought them to where we slept. The men were up and looking for me and had made some coffee. They had eaten but I hadn't, so I started eating. They knew the horses would have gone back home, and they never thought I would catch them because none of them was hobbled. It must have been about ten miles to where I caught the horses.

We got ready and started off again. We came to a big hill and saw a trail going down the way we were going. We followed the trail until we saw some hogans. We'd gone a long way from where we slept.

We unsaddled our horses about noon and fixed something to eat. As we were traveling, I smelled whiskey once in a while. When we were ready to eat, Wood tried to get one of the bottles out, and he found it had opened itself and he had lost half his whiskey. We took a drink there before we ate, then started to eat. The day was pretty hot so we stayed there in the shade. Late in the evening we started off again. We came to a hill called Red Patch, and when we got up on it we saw the big black hill over there that they call Black Mountain, where we were going. Wood was the only one who had been there before. It was the first time for me. We thought that hill was close. We kept going all afternoon and came to a big lake called Blue Lake. We went quite a way farther and camped. We had been passing a lot of cattle through that valley.

We hobbled our horses that night. There were a lot of grasses where we slept there, too. While we were camping there Wood started singing some kind of songs I didn't know. We slept till morning, then moved off to the West. (Was the song due to whiskey?) No, it was for the good trades he would make.

We came to a place where a Navajo was living who had a big bunch of blue goats. His name was Buck Tanner. Wood had known these people before and they were pretty good friends, all the same clan as Wood {they consider themselves to be close relatives}. They had started to cook something for the people they had seen coming, and Wood was talking to them. After Wood told his side, the other man started telling how they got along there, how they had horses, sheep, and cattle. The man who lived there wanted to know if we people had any whiskey.

He kept asking for whiskey, but Wood didn't have any more. He drank it all at the last camp. He said all he had was the empty bottle and showed it to the man. He took hold of the bottle and took a smell of it, that's all he did. "Well," he said, "I wish you had some whiskey left in it."

After we ate the man asked us what we had to trade. The two men opened up their sacks and showed the people what they had. Wood had a silver bridle that the man wanted. His son wanted a bridle, too. They said they'd give four cows and one saddle horse. The trade was made, but we wanted to go on from there and leave the cows but ride the new horse and leave one of ours there. Buck Tanner got the horse for us, a buckskin horse. (What does that mean?) Wood traded a buckskin for it.[73]

By that time we had been away from home for four nights. We were going way off on the other side and leave the stock here. We would make some trades further on and come back this way, but we didn't know when we would get back. We started off and found a place where there was a store. We didn't stay long at the store. We got up on another hill west of the store and found an open place on top of the hill. We stayed overnight again in this place. There was a lot of grass around and our horses didn't go very far.

Next morning when we saddled our horses we could see some more hogans on the north side. We got on the horses and went to the hogans. At the first hogan there was no man, just a woman and some children. The place we were going to was called Stones Lying, and we asked the woman about the road to that place. She came outside and showed us which way to go. We started off again and came to another place where Navajo Indians were living. They had a hogan made with the logs standing up, the shape of a sweatbath. When we went inside we saw an old man, gray-headed, and a big woman. Where we had spent the night we didn't get our breakfast, but here they gave us something to eat.

Wood said we had come from Zuni and wanted to go to the place called Stones Lying. We were trading for sheep. The man told him how to go to that place and showed him what road to take. There was no plain road there, only a trail. He said, "You'll come to a big hill there, and I think on that hill you'll find some sheep tracks. Follow the sheep tracks all the way on and keep following them from the top of the hill till you come to another hogan. Those people can tell you more about the road from there. That's a family that used to live here, but they moved back over there and moved their sheep, too."

We started off and kept going. We came to the hill, got on its top, and followed the sheep tracks until we came to the place. There we saw a man cutting his hay. He had only one arm, the other one was gone from the shoulder. He said he was the one that had moved from the other place. He said it was pretty hard to get to the place where we were going, there was no good way. There were a lot of hills to go through. But he said he came back from there yesterday and maybe we could follow his track back. That would be the easiest way to get there.

We started off west and found the track. We kept following it and came to a little canyon. We passed that and came to another hogan. We stopped and went inside and saw a big man with his head tied up, his wife, another man and woman, and a few children. This man asked where we came from and Wood said from Zuni. Then he asked what we had. We told him we had a lot of different kinds of silver and beads. Wood and I didn't know the man. He said he wanted to see the beads, would like to have some. He picked up one string of beads that had a lot of turquoise in it, good turquoise. He said he wanted that one string and gave {would give?} a good saddle horse for it. He sent the other man out to bring in the horse. When the horse came, we saw its roan color, not very big, just a small horse, and it had a sore back, too. We didn't want to take that horse, and said we would go on. This was the place called Stones Lying where we saw that horse.

We wanted to go still farther, so we started off. We went down into a canyon and kept going down until Wood said we were off on the wrong road. We went up to the top, and it was pretty cloudy when we got there. There was a lot of grass around and we stayed there overnight. That was the sixth night since we left home. The horses stayed around, so before daylight we saddled them up again and started off to the west. Not very far along we came to a sheep camp just about daylight.

A man and three women were at that camp. We talked together and told them where we'd come from and where we were going and that we were trading for sheep. The man said, "We haven't got any meat for you to eat, but if you're not too lazy you can go and butcher a big wether." Two of us went out and roped a wether, helping the herder, and butchered that sheep. After we ate, they gave us part of the meat and we started off again to the west. We came to a place where people were living called Shady Lake. The two women there said the man had gone off a little while ago to look for horses. They started to buy some beads, but didn't. We just showed our beads, but the women didn't want beads very much.

Going on west, pretty soon we found more Indians. They told us there was a store a little way below. When we got to the store we stopped to buy some food. This was a Navajo Indian who had the store. We went on to where another Indian lived and stayed another night there. We showed all the things we had brought, but we didn't trade. At that home Wood was asking about another man that he used to know long ago who had been a pretty good friend. The man owed him some cows. They knew the man Wood meant and said he was living off this way, so next morning we started off this way, coming back.

We came to another hogan and saw another man and woman there. The man had only one eye. Wood asked about his friend there, and the man said he was living back this way. We decided to split, with Wood and me going to see Wood's friend and our companion going in another direction. He had some friends over there somewhere that he wanted to see. After he saw his friends he would go back to Buck Tanner's place. Wood and I started over to the place where Wood's friend lived and found it. When we got there, there was only one woman at home. We unsaddled our horses and turned them loose and waited. The man wasn't home but had just gone to some other place. About sundown he came home. He and Wood sat together there, and Wood told his story from the beginning when he started from Kainti. He told everything that happened on the way. That made seven nights from the time we left Kainti.

The man said, "The cows I owe you are running somewhere over in the woods. We'll start in the morning to look for them." We showed them what we had. He picked up a string of turquoise beads and said he would give a saddle horse for it. It was a pretty good sorrel horse.

When he had his horses up, he told us we had better go out and look for the cows and we could ride some of his horses. He saddled up two of them and started off to the north from there. When we came to an open place, a big valley, the man showed us the brand he had on the cows and said we would split from there. He said when we saw a cow with that brand we should just chase it out to the valley. He said we would meet in the middle of the valley and decide what to do next. He went off one way, I another way, and Wood still another. I didn't find any and came out to where we were supposed to meet. The other man came down there but Wood didn't come. We waited there a long time. He said Wood must have gone home. So we went toward home, the man one way and I another. We said we would meet at home. Wood was already home when we got there. The other man had found the right cows and corralled them there that night.

The cows that we corralled that night got out. We went after them and found them a long way off. We corralled them again, and Wood and I got ready to go back to Buck Tanner's. We were driving two cows and leading the horse, coming back this way. We kept riding till sundown, didn't stop till after dark. The night was moonlit. The cows looked pretty tired, so we stopped and unsaddled the horses and hobbled them, and the cows just lay down. We kept looking at them during the night. They lay there for a long time. I let Wood watch the cows while I slept, then he slept while I watched. The cows didn't get up till daylight. The horses didn't go very far, so we got them, saddled them, and went after the cows. In a few minutes cows can go a long way off! We started coming home again with the cows.

Quite a way from there we saw some Indians living. We stopped where the hogans were, and when Wood told the people why we were there they wanted to buy some beads and silver, trading sheep. They told us two girls had taken the sheep out and sent me out to find the girls and have them bring the sheep in. I found where they were herding, with a mean white dog. That dog kept after me for a long while. I threw a rope at it, not meaning to rope it, but I did. He was mean and I couldn't get past him. I told the girls they could take the rope off the dog, but they didn't want to. They said if they took it off, the rope would be theirs. They took it off the dog and brought the sheep to the hogan. The people killed one sheep right away, for meat to eat. We were trading there till sundown. Next day we were there all day and all night again. By that time they had traded us fifty head of sheep. We tried to start off in the morning but could hardly manage it. There were fifty head of sheep to drive, two or three cows, and some horses. It was pretty hard to do. One man said he would help us on the way, but we didn't know how far he would go with us.

We came on toward home and kept driving all day till sundown, when we camped. We found a corral and put the sheep in it, and hobbled one of the cows. Next morning the cows were there and so were the sheep. We started them off. While we were unhobbling the cow, Wood started off with the sheep. As soon as the other man took the hobble off, the cow ran behind a tree, and I was holding the rope that tied its hind feet. When it got up, it came after me on my horse. It hooked the horse somewhere in the leg. The horse started pitching with me a little, and the cow started running off the other way. We tried to make it run the right way, but it got too mean and fought and wanted to go the other way. We picked up a long stick and made it come the right way when it saw that stick. We caught up with Wood way off toward home. We got back to Buck Tanner's place.

The people said that the man who had come up with us got back there day before yesterday and waited all day. Next day he took the cow and horse that we had left there and said he'd keep driving them along. We had something to eat there, then started driving again toward Ganado, till sundown. It started to rain that night while we were camping there. Everything was too wet to start a fire. We started one with yucca, the slim yucca {that} has dry leaves that hang down under the others.

We stayed there overnight, then kept driving this way till noon when we stopped for a while. In the afternoon we started again toward Ganado. We got that far with the man who was helping us, then he went home, but another man took over the cows. We came by Ganado and on this way, right on a road, following the road all the time. We could keep traveling at night. Everything was loose and there were no corrals for the cows or sheep at night. The cows would start off the other way, but I would catch them pretty quickly. We kept on coming. We passed the place where we met the policemen, but going the other way. We came into St. Michaels, came across that valley onto the Ft. Defiance road, and took that road a little way. We were coming along there about sundown, and we turned off the road. We went up on the hill there when it was after dark and came on driving the sheep. We found a fence and put the cows inside. Off a little way from there was a hogan. That was where the sick woman was on our first night out. We stayed there that night.

Next morning I started with the cows and sheep. They told me another Squaw Dance was going on a little way east of there. We had started moving with the cows and sheep a little way, but Wood made us go back and stay three more days while he went to the sing. Wood left and went to the sing, and next day he sent for the cows. We drove them over. We just left the sheep and horses where they were. When the sing was over, Wood didn't come back but sent another man in his place. As soon as he came, we started moving again toward home.

We got to Manuelito with the sheep. Wood owed about thirty head of sheep to the store there. Wood sent word by the man who came to help us for me to leave thirty head there at the store. We left thirty and brought along just twenty. We came about halfway from Manuelito to Kainti and stayed there overnight. Pretty early in the morning a man came by. It was the man from where Buck Tanner lived, who helped with the cows. He said he got them down and didn't have any trouble.

I was coming over to Mr. Clark's store that's east of here three miles. People told me there was going to be a little cere- mony there and some races, and I was going there. We started moving our sheep along toward Kainti and brought them to Wood's house. He was already home the night before we got there.

That's the only time I went out in that country and I haven't been back since. I went to Flagstaff once, and to Santa

Fe, and down to Ft. Apache, to the other side of Black Mountain, out south to Salt Lake, and to Shiprock. That's all I've seen of this country.

HERDING ADVENTURES, AND MISCHIEF

After that trip I started herding for Wood. Out herding one day I saw a young wild dove. It was a little one, not able to fly very much. I chased one and it flew off with me behind it. I had a dog with me. I was just about to catch that little dove when it flew in between two logs that lay together. I didn't know the dog was coming behind when I got to those two logs. He came under me, between my legs. When he ran under me, I sat down on him and he ran off with me just like a horse. I rode a little way, maybe twenty yards, then he fell down with me. I fell on a big round rock right on my hip. It sure hurt. I crawled around for quite a while before I got up again. I walked off, but the place was hurting badly. I walked a little at a time and sat down. I don't know where the sheep went, but I just went home. Another man went after the sheep and I stayed home. That place was swollen when I got home. Somebody went out to get some Indian plant medicine and soaked it and I drank some and they rubbed some on my back. It got well in a few days, but I was still not doing anything. They told me not to work or herd until I got well. (Who treated you?) Wood's mother, Bending Tree Woman. The place where Wood lived is called Bending Tree and we knew her by that name because she used to live there all the time.

This old lady's stepson and I were taking two herds of sheep out south, down to a place called Sandy Hill. We camped just the other side of that hill, about a mile on the south side. We had two separate camps, but not very far apart. Barney was herding some days with me out south there. When we were herding in a canyon one day, we saw a big bull up on a hill. We walked up there and began to say we were going to kill the bull with a .22 rifle. Right in the middle of the hill was a curved rock, and he ran against that rock and couldn't go down its sides. We started shooting at the bull. We shot him right in the head, but the bull didn't seem to care that we shot him. We shot him all over the neck and head, I don't know how many times. Every time we shot him, he just closed his eyes and kept on going. Then we started throwing rocks and hit him right on the head with a rock. We decided we would just let the bull go!

We went on with the sheep, brought them in at sundown and didn't say anything about it when we were coming home. Next day we herded out in the same direction to see if we could see the bull again. We took a big rifle this time and we went down where we had been shooting the bull. He wasn't there. We got out of the canyon and saw that the tracks went off the other way. That night when we were bringing in the sheep we talked about it. We said we had been shooting the bull in the head. There were two places where Mexicans were living on the other side of where we were, and a white man in another place. They all owned cattle, and the people thought these men must own that bull.

The old lady told us we mustn't mess with that bull anymore. "It's going to be bad if you kill that bull. When they see that you did it, you will both be sent to Santa Fe, or else I will have to pay a fine, your fine. You will cost a lot of money." After she said that, she talked some more, to me especially. She said, "These people might track this bull if it was dead. I hope that bull got all right so they will have nothing against us."[74] She talked about a lot of things we shouldn't do. She said, "Be careful of everything, horses, cattle, all the livestock. You mustn't hurt it like that. The man who owns it won't like it. It's the same way with me," she said. "If somebody shoots my stock the way you did, I wouldn't like it either. So you remember you mustn't do that again! You've been herding for us a long time, since you were a little fellow, I knew you when your mother died, you were just a little one then. Three years after you were born your mother died. Since then nobody looked after you.[75] Also your father died, hanged himself, and you are a poor boy. You still haven't anybody to help you."

I asked the old lady, "Why did my father hang himself?"[76] She said, "After your mother died, he got another woman and started living with her, for some years. Then she got sick and died. They were talking about somebody being a witch down there. He thought the witch did something to his wife that killed her. After the woman died, he went over to this bad man's place, found him herding one day and shot him with a rifle! When he went back near where his wife died, he hung himself. It was right on top of that hill over there."

> Sandy {Lucky's father's pseudonym} committed suicide after killing a man suspected of witchcraft (LS 234–235). Bill pointed out to us the hill where Sandy had hanged himself after killing the man he blamed for the death of his second wife. He said this happened "thirty years ago," that is, about 1910. A white woman who had long resided in the region thought Sandy had killed himself in 1920, but the earlier date is probably more nearly right. A. L. asked if Sandy's death had occurred before Lucky went to Santa Fe, and Lucky said that it had, though he was just a young fellow when he went to Santa Fe. A. L. then asked if Lucky knew about it that time when he hung himself at Little Pine Springs. Lucky replied that it had happened before that and he thought he knew about it (Social Relations 1).
>
> Benito's daughter got worse and died. Her husband then shot Sombrero with a .30-.30 as he was out herding sheep. Two days later he hanged himself on that hill south of Vine's. This man was Lucky's father. (Apr. 14, 1940)

The old lady went on, "If you listen to my talk, you'll be a good worker and a good herder, the farther you go with it. You'll be a good man and you'll do good work and you might get married after a while."[77] (When did you first hear that your father hanged himself?) Before the old lady said that, I'd heard it a few times. But at the time she gave this talk, she told me just like that. That was Jim's and Charles's father. They said he used to be a witch. This old lady had given me talks lots of times before, and so had Wood.

We wintered over there and then came back here with the sheep for lambing. I was herding for a man called {by} one of the clan names. The old lady used to tell me about the clans, too.[78] After we were through lambing we sheared, cut {castrated} the lambs, and earmarked them. They gave me a mare and a colt and bought me a lot of good clothes. One of my uncles took the saddle that I had, and they bought me another saddle.

Down below Kainti a man named Big Head had a farming place. We were working there and I was still working with those people. Tom Sage was helping there, and also Chester Sage. He was with the man we call Arnold. We heard there was going to be a sing to the north. It was a nine-night sing called Feather Way. Arnold, another man, and I started off to it. When we got there they were just starting to build up the hogan. People were working on two places, the hogan and the kitchen. They told us to help, so we did. Arnold said he was breaking a horse on the way there.

We helped only one day and started back about sundown. When Arnold got on his horse it started to buck, and he didn't go very far with it till it threw him off. The people there helped him catch the horse. We got back the same day, down the other side of Kainti at Sam Smith's home. We stayed there overnight. Before we left the sing place, they told us to come back the next day. We went back where they were building the hogan and helped all day. We built two hogans that day, and when we finished they told us to go home. They said the singer was coming day after tomorrow, so we should come back in two days. The singer called Big Hail would sing over the man's mother.

We stayed home two days, then went back. About sundown we saw the singer there. He had come that same day. (What was wrong with the woman?) Something was wrong with her head. Her head was hurting pretty bad, and the pain put her mind off for an hour or half an hour at a time. Wide Man had done hand-trembling over the old lady and told them they should get a singer who sang Feather Way.[79]

Just after we ate that night they started to make that dress shirt that Gregorio was telling about.[80] It didn't take them long to make it. Two men did it, and they picked out two others who told me I was going to be one of the dancers. I didn't want to do it, didn't know how, but it was two of my friends who were picked out, Arnold and John. After they made the dress shirt they laid it at the back on the west side. The two men who made it have to walk one in front, the other behind, all the time. The one in front is called Enemy Slayer (Nayenezgan) and the other one is called Water Child (Tohbahjischini). The front one was painted black and the back one red. They were told to stand outside on the north side of the door and call the patient inside. After the patient came in, they should come in too. Before they went out, both of these men were given a club.

(Abbreviated description:) One club was black, the other blue. They came in south of the fire and put the dress shirt on the patient. Went around the fire sunwise and returned to patient. Waved clubs at patient from each cardinal point. Gave clubs to singer and received arrowheads with which they cut (the shirt?) on the front side, first the east side, then south, west, north, and above the head, then cut all the knots. Hurried with this. Took the cuttings out on a blanket and dumped them north of the hogan. On their return, the first one made four marks on the ground, two straight and two crooked, and made the same sound he uttered when waving the club at the patient. The second one repeated this. Then those two take off their decorations and wash off their paint.

(Verbatim:) Then they sat on the north side and the singer told them what they had to do for four nights: they should stay on the north side here, not go off to work or chop wood, until four nights are over, then they will start something different after that. After that we ate and went to sleep.

(Abbreviated again:) Next day there was the fire and emetic, and Lucky didn't go in. They cut some reeds in inch lengths and painted one for each of many wild animals, some for fish and other water animals. Lucky demonstrated how the man sang. The patient held the reeds while the singer prayed. That was all, same thing each day for four days. Then they bathed the patient, and the two men could do what they liked— take a sweatbath or do some work. On the fifth day they made a sandpainting. It had deer and many other animals in it, also birds and puppies. It filled most of the hogan, and the fire was just a few coals near the door. The singer said that anyone who thought he had the same sickness as the patient should come and get some of the medicine.[81]

(Verbatim:) They would each pay a quarter or up to fifty cents. I only remember that Big Hail's son, the one who couldn't talk and was called Dumb Boy, did this. There were others but I don't remember who. When they were through with the sandpainting, they took out the top and piled the rest on the west side. They did that for four days. I didn't go in because I didn't have any money, nor did I have a mother or father to pay for me.[82]

On the last day they had some ground corn, from kernels that were not plump but wrinkled. That kind is roasted in a pit and kept there in the winter. They mixed it up with water in a big basket. With this meal they made little deer, antelopes, and all sorts of wild animals—all the ones that were on the sandpainting except the puppy. As soon as they were finished, they ate all the animals without any more cooking. This goes with Night Way. Each one who eats prays for himself. The singer said there might be somebody, one or two people, who might have the sickness of Night Way. He said these animals would cure the sickness without singing. It was just about this time (3:30 P.M.) that we finished. There were lots of people there then.

Don was a little boy then, with long hair tied up behind. After the sing was finished they told him to watch the horses. He got on a workhorse that was a stallion, a studhorse, without a bridle, only a rope, and without any saddle, bareback. He only had the rope around the horse's nose. When he started off, the stallion started to run after a mare. Don was so small he couldn't stop the stallion. It caught up with the mare and jumped on top of her, and Don sat on top of the stallion. His hair was tied and bobbed up and down and all the people came out and laughed. A man there said, "Hit him in the face with your rope!"

After that, the singer said there was one more thing we had to get before night—yucca leaves. Somebody went out and brought in four yucca leaves. Late in the evening they made a drum out of this yucca.

(Abbreviated:) Two dancers were picked out, Hashjilti[83] and Tohnenili. A little jar of meat was boiled, and women made a cake in the ground for Hashjilti. When the singer started singing, Hashjilti started dancing north of the fire and Tohnenili on the south. Big Fred was Hashjilti, and the other one was Bow Legs. They are both alive still. Bow Legs is from Hub, far off. They danced only a little at a time. They would rest for a long time, then start again with the drum beating. In the morning before the end of the dance, Hashjilti fed the boiled meat to the patient. Each time they danced they were dressed differently. The cake was taken out of the ground at the end of the sing, and two big pieces were divided between the dancers. The people got the rest. Then the singer packed up.

(Verbatim:) The crowd of people began going off in different directions toward their houses. I and a girl (my wife, but we weren't married yet) started off with another woman. When we had come about half a mile from the hogan of the sing, we saw somebody coming on horseback right near where we were riding, just a little way off. He came to a little tree and got off his horse and went behind the tree to do something. It didn't take him long and he got on his horse and went back. I told the women to go on, I was going to see what he did behind that tree. Right inside the tree was a jug of whiskey—you know those one-gallon jugs with a black top? I picked it up and got on my horse and tried to catch up with the women, but before I got there I changed my mind and went back to where they had the sing.

When I found that big bottle on the way home I started to drink out of it. I tied my horse and hid the bottle in another place and went back to the sing. The Kainti storekeeper was there with some groceries he had been selling, the one called Bareheaded. He was trading, and Roan Horse's oldest son was helping him. I got drunk there right away, in a little while I didn't know anything. I fell down, they told me afterward. This was still pretty early. When I "found myself" I was at the Kainti store. It was pretty near noon, and I got well by that time. But I remembered I left my horse near the sing, and I went back. A white man and a Navajo told me they just tied me up and threw me in the wagon. They told me to go home. I walked pretty fast across the canyon and went back where I'd tied my horse, picked up the jug, and took it over where they had finished the singing. There were a lot of people there who had gotten drunk and were just rolling around there or lying where they fell. A few people who weren't drunk started drinking my jug, and they got it all. I didn't get very much more.

I started back across the canyon and came to where the

girl was living. This was the first time I'd been at her place, and I stayed there overnight. Next day I walked north from there to where Agnes, Bill's mother-in-law, was living. Bill's wife was a little girl then, and another woman, her mother's sister, was living with them. The man who married Bill's mother-in-law had some horses up on the mountains that he wanted to round up. I wanted to help him. We started off and rounded them up in three days. They were very wild. There were only thirty horses, but it took us three days to get them out of the mountains and corral them. By then the corn was about a foot high.

TROUBLE, AND AGNES

The Gallup Ceremonial was coming close. Agnes said she wanted to take some sheep to the store to sell, with her husband, herself, and me. (Which husband?) The one who killed himself—Gregorio's wife's father. They let me ride a white horse that they were using for herding. It was white all over, but right around the eyes it was all red and it had no hair, just felt rough. We cut out ten head of sheep and started toward the railroad. Just a little way along the side where I was riding there was a little ditch about three feet deep and about two feet across. The white horse started to jump with me, but either he was too weak or he didn't jump hard enough to get across. He fell down on the other bank. On one side I had gotten my foot through the stirrup. The horse got up and jumped onto the bank and I got hold of a bush. He tried to get away, but I was holding the bush and he couldn't pull me loose, but the leather of my shoes, right across the toes, broke. I was holding the brush, he was trying to get away, and when the leather broke he got away. I started after the sheep again with just half my shoe!

I herded the sheep over to a store below Gallup at a place called Little Arroyo. An old man, Agnes's father, Long Hair, came to the store and sold the sheep there. Sheep were high then; a sheep with a lamb used to cost eight or nine dollars, and we were paid money for them.[84] These people bought a wagon and bought me some shoes. They bought some other things and then came back home, getting there that evening. Long Hair went home from there, and another man who went ahead of us got home first. There was another man in the wagon coming home and I asked him, "Where do you come from, grandfather?" He said, "From way down by the home of Mr. Martino." I said I didn't know that man, and then he said he had come over to see his granddaughter Agnes. Somebody down there had told him she was living here, so he came to see her.

He said, "This morning when I had breakfast people told me to walk down to the station, the train would stop there and I could catch a ride to Manuelito. When I got down there I was passed by a train, it didn't stop. I called that train Firekicker. Another train came on Many Feet." You know he meant a freight train. I don't know what he meant about the first one. "A train came along and stopped there; Big Black stopped there, going to Manuelito. I went inside and was just about sitting down when a man told me to come outside. I thought the train hadn't moved yet, but I had already got there! They put me off. At first I didn't want to get off but they made me. I got mad and walked off. There were some houses on the north side of the railroad, and I went there and saw some Navajo Indians. I found out that was Manuelito, I was there already! I forgot about being mad and felt happy again.

"I walked from there out of the canyon and to this place. On top of the hill I saw a man driving. I met him and asked where my granddaughter lived. I saw somebody coming, two horses ahead and Big Wood rolling behind the horses (he meant our team and wagon). They stopped there and it was my granddaughter. I told her I was going to her place, so she put me in this thing and took me along. Four hoops were running under us (he meant the wagon wheels)."

I slept there, stayed just a few days. The other man and I were tending the horses. The old man left after three days. I stayed there seven days and then started back here. I was afoot and walked back to Roan Horse's home. They were having a sing there with a singer called Runner. The patient was one of Long Hair's daughters.[85] I was there with the people until the sing was over. (What kind of sing?) Star Way. (What was wrong with the patient?) She had a big sore, running, on the side of her body. They sang a whole lot for that woman, but she died. She didn't go to the hospital.

Lucky Becomes Married

Then I came back over where my girl was. I started to work at her home, hauling water and herding sheep there.[86] This was about 1917. Ernest had just come back from school. He told me the best way to remember was by these years, and he said it was 1917 right then. So I kept that in mind. I stayed there all summer and through the winter. Those people were pretty rich then, with sheep and cattle. The last thing I did there was to herd lambs at lambing time.

> As a young man Lucky became interested in ceremonies and attended them whenever he could. He met his wife at Squaw Dances and finally went to live with her, though the marriage was at first opposed by her relatives. In spite of the fact that the wife has often felt neglected and has disapproved of Lucky's wild ways, she has not divorced him. They have had eleven children, of whom eight are living.[87] (Summary of Social Relations).

While the lambing was going on, one of Long Hair's sons was very sick and lots of medicine men had been there, some leaving and others coming. He was just a boy. He must have been about thirteen years old when he died. (Were you at Ted Sage's wedding?) (See Bill's description of this in his autobiography.)* No, this was in the summer after that wedding that the boy died. I just heard about the wedding, I didn't go to it.

The singing was going on and we were lambing. We went back and forth between the lambs and the sing. I was working for both places. Sometimes I stayed one place three days, then came back. These singers and medicine people sang for that boy, but he never got better. At the end they moved him out to another place. Another singer called Many Streams sang for him, and while he was singing the boy died. (What was wrong?) I don't really know, but I got the understanding from Ted Sage that he hurt himself badly in his side. Ted and he were building

---

* {This comment refers to Bill Sage's own life history, also collected by the Leightons. The editor of this volume is currently preparing it for publication.}

a fence with wooden poles. One day he was carrying pretty big poles nearly all day long. That evening he got sick. Down inside where his kidneys were it was hurting pretty bad.

Drunk and Disorderly

After that boy died, his family moved down below Kainti, then I came back where my girl was. Next morning I went to the Kainti store and saw a Navajo fellow named Don there. He told me there was going to be a sing that night at Wood's. Don and I went over to this sing, and when we got there we saw the singer who came from Ft. Defiance and was called Pueblo Killer. This was just the first night, tomorrow they would sing all night, they told me. We started right off and when we got to the store we met two Mexicans there. They said they had a camp in a little canyon this side of Kainti and had some whiskey there for sale. If we needed any, we could go there. Don said, "Let's buy some." The Mexican went off ahead and we came behind. We went on top of the canyon and found the place. It didn't look like a camp. I saw just one trunk there by itself. We waited there a while and bought two pint bottles.

After we bought them, we heard a noise as if somebody was coming. The Mexican said, "Let's run off for a little while and hide." So we did that. We stayed out there for a while, then came back to the place. We left, and two more men came and started to buy their stuff. Don said, "Hurry up, get on your horse, let's go." We did and we got away. Don was standing by the horse when I came back, and the other people were standing by the trunk. When we were buying our two bottles, the Mexican had the trunk full of bottles.

We started off a little way, maybe half a mile. Don said he had already stolen some whiskey. At the time when the two Mexicans went off, he opened the trunk and put four bottles in his four pants pockets, two behind and two in front. We got off the horses and counted the bottles. We had nine that we took and two we bought, that's eleven bottles. We went over to my house and were drunk there for two days. After that, they told us the sing was already finished.

We went down to the Kainti store, still drunk. I got in a fight with Big Fred. We didn't go very far with it, Don stopped us. We went back to where the girl lived. They were talking a lot when we came to the hogan. All the people there had gotten scared of us and run off. They stayed away all night long and we stayed in the hogan, two drunk men. All the family there, children and all, stayed out. We saw them coming in next morning. When we all got together, we killed a big wether sheep and had a lot of meat there.

Next morning Don's horse went off with the saddle. That night and the next day we tracked him toward the west, but we couldn't find him. While we were looking for the horse we were throwing up a lot. While we were looking for the horse, my wife's family went off herding and took the sheep back home where they lived. Don went home and I stayed home. I slept all that day, afternoon, night, and all the next day and night—the second night. That was on account of drinking so long.

After that I went down to the store and saw some people who were talking about the sing that Wood had. They said that on the last night of the sing a lot of people got drunk. One of my uncles lost his bracelet, somebody took it, and another lost his turquoise beads. Ted Sage was telling me this. After the sing was finished, some of the hand-tremblers tried to find the beads but never did. They used some kind of plant medicine, chewed up the root of the plant. Just one man did the chewing, and I don't know how they used it after that. I understand that this medicine can get you drunk, just like whiskey, and the chewer acted just like that. (This was probably jimson weed, *datura meteloides*. See W. W. Hill, "Navajo Use of Jimson Weed," pp. 19–20.) {See Hill 1938.} I heard about the whiskey, too. After the Mexicans started drinking with the people, they said anybody could go to the trunk and help himself to a bottle. They cleaned it all out. There were four Mexicans, and they saw them go back to Manuelito the next day.

After that they held a meeting to try to find the missing beads and bracelet. I was there and Wood was the one who led the meeting. He said that where the drinking went on they heard that two men had seen the thefts. They had a fight when they missed the jewelry, and they thought that someone said somebody had seen it. It looked as if the ones who saw it had taken them. When they held the meeting the two suspects were there and they questioned them, but they said they didn't see it. They were Roan Horse's son and another boy.

At the meeting, they told the two boys that they got the understanding from somebody that they had seen who got the beads and bracelet. The boys said that there was a bunch fighting, and while they were fighting the man who lost his bracelet had his arm pulled right into the middle of the crowd. One said, "That's about all I can tell you," and the other said the same thing. Other people said they didn't see anything. They wanted to get some evidence, but that was all they saw. Roan Horse's son said he left the fight after that. Roan Horse and Robert were fighting pretty hard.

After they told that much of the story, the people said that everybody was fighting together. They were quite drunk and they talked and just got to fighting. Robert was beaten up pretty badly on his hands and kicked all over. At that time, this kind of thing was happening a lot—every time they started to drink they would start to fight. (What did you and Big Fred fight about?) We were just playing, pulling each other around. We were both drinking and I was drinking most. While we were doing that we got mad at each other and started to fight.

> Lucky is known to be unreliable and is quarrelsome when he is drunk. However, he is witty and amusing and is therefore quite popular (Summary of Social Relations 2).

They told Wood to settle the case, but he said he didn't know how he could do it. He didn't know whether he would call it a case. Many different people were in the fight and each one got home. It seemed to Wood it was better for them to settle it among themselves the best way they could. They let it go at that. But the man who owned the bracelet and the one who owned the beads asked all the people there to look around wherever they went, in trading posts too. If anyone saw the bracelet, he would pay him ten dollars, if he got it back. The bracelet had turquoise all around, lots of turquoise. He said he had paid twenty dollars for it. The man who owned the beads said the same thing and said he'd pay twenty dollars if they found his beads.

About one month after that my uncle found his own bracelet at Manuelito, in pound at the store. It had been put in pound by those four Mexicans. The Mexicans said that when they were selling the whiskey at the sing, people got drunk and somebody put up the bracelet to one of the Mexicans for whiskey. Len was running that store then. My uncle paid ten dollars to get it out of pound.

As for the beads, nobody found them for a long while. I heard that Wood's old lady mother got them. They just kept the beads there, no one knew how many years, then sold them to somebody to the north. I heard that she found them where the fight had been, but a lot of people didn't believe that. A lot of people had looked there after the fight and nothing was found. They thought the old lady might have just untied the beads from the old man when he got real drunk. If she found them, why didn't she give them back to the old man? Not very long after that the old man died, so the old lady had a good chance to keep them. (Do you think Wood knew this at the time of the meeting?) I don't know. A lot of people said he knew and that it might have been Wood's idea. Those were really old turquoise beads and people pay a lot of money for that kind. (Did you see the beads at the old lady's, or was it just gossip?) I just heard about it. Wood and two others went to Santo Domingo one time and traded blankets for beads. They brought home the beads they got by trading, and they used to trade them for sheep out toward Black Mountain. That's all I know about it, and now I'm going on with my story.

MONEY GONE ASTRAY

At that time, Wood used to collect money from Navajos for the agent at Ft. Defiance for the use of the land, five or ten dollars from people. Those living around Kainti used to have a lot of sheep at that time. They would rent out one township here like that. The Indians would bring the money to Wood's place so he could take it all to Ft. Defiance. It used to amount to two or three hundred dollars. I don't remember how many years they did this. Around Mack's and around Dale there were other townships the same way, and also another place to the north, starting this side of the railroad. The agent at Ft. Defiance was Mr. Peters.

One time people got together at Wood's place. The money was wanted for state land and school land, but the government land was free for Indians to use for grazing. Peters and a lot of people got together to talk this matter over with people who knew about it. They said each home must pay five dollars. But some people said no, that was too much for poor people. Some of them had no sheep or cattle. They suggested that the rich people could pay more and the poor people less, but the rich people said let's have it the same for all. Wood's mother had lots of sheep then. She said, "Let's set it at three dollars for each home." The crowd said, "Let's do that—try it and see how it turns out." They did it and collected two hundred dollars, which Wood took to Ft. Defiance.

Another year when Peters got the money he said it wasn't enough. He said that the people who had cattle and sheep should be the main ones to pay for the land, and they should pay about twenty dollars each. Those people didn't like it, but they kept it that way. I don't know how many times they did it that way. Wood, Big Hail, Gambler, and Roan Horse, the four of them, used to take the money to Ft. Defiance. It got lost once or twice. It was collected down here all right and was taken to Ft. Defiance, but something happened to it on the way. It was reported to Peters, who tried to find the money but couldn't discover where it went. Afterward the money was spent by those four men. It was the same in the other two places, except at one place only two men took the money on horseback. After that the people said this was no good, they might as well let it go. They told the agent to work out some other way. I think the government furnished money for the land for Indians only twice.

After that they started an oil well, and when it was producing they sold the oil. The well belonged to the Indians, so they took some of the oil money and paid the government back. After that, they got the money from the oil. Of course, the government was taking care of the oil well and paying for the Indians' land with that money.

COOPERATION, WORK, AND PLAY

I want to go back to the time of the meeting. It was held there for one whole day and people went home in the evening. I was working around home, herding sheep and working on one thing or another. In summer, where people raised corn they used to get together and help hoe. They would start hoeing at one place and move on to the next when it was finished. They kept doing that till every place where there was a cornfield had been hoed. We hoed a place at Kainti, then one called Canyon, and another called Rabbit Corral. This was a place where they rounded up rabbits. Ned's place was next at Narrow Trail. There is a rock bluff on top of the mountain, and right at the top are two big rocks lying together with the trail going between them. I did that with the other people, going around for about ten days. People used to kill young goats that had got fat in the summers for us to eat. We used to run footraces after quitting time, sometimes we had horse races, and sometimes what we call two-stick races. In that race, each side has a long stick which is hooked under a string and thrown off ahead, then they run after it.

One time storekeeper Len was going to bet on one side of a two-stick race. He bet five dollars against the other team. There were six on each side, and one team was pretty good. There was the store, and west of it a pole. The race was to run around the pole, and come back to where they started. There was a small fence between the start and the pole, and they wanted the race to go around the fence. The white man wanted to bet five dollars and the Indians talked it over. Both sides said, "Let's work it some way so we can get the five dollars from the white man. If we beat him, we'll divide up the money." They thought there was enough money to go around, but they tried hard to get the white man to raise it to ten dollars. He wouldn't do it. "Well, when we beat him," they said, "we'll have cigarettes or tobacco, and besides we'll have some fun."

They divided into six for each side. They put Steve on the other side the white man wanted. They told him they knew that his side would get ahead right away, so he must throw the two-stick way inside the fence. Steve said all right, and they started the race. His team was going ahead. Steve threw the stick way inside the fence, and the other team went by and went way ahead, went around the pole and came back, and Steve's team never caught up. The storekeeper was sore, he was mad about it. Robert told the storekeeper it was his fault for having Steve on that team, he should have had a good man there instead of Steve. Steve had one short and one long arm, and in the race he threw the stick way to one side. After that the storekeeper said he wanted to have a footrace for one of the men who ran pretty well, but no one wanted to run against him.

Another game was called the cigarette race. They used to line up people on horseback. They would lay down a cigarette at quite a distance, and they would run their horses to the cigarettes, each one light one and come back with it. While we were there in a bunch for hoeing, that's what they played. They used to race, too, putting their saddles down instead of cigarettes, run down there, saddle up and come back. We had horse races, footraces, and used to bury a sack and pull it out from on top of a horse, then fight for the sack. They don't do all these things anymore. They quit it altogether when the automobile came— stopped the horse races and all the other races. There weren't any automobiles when they were having races. (Why did they stop?) At that time there was a store at Kainti and others at Clark's, at Dale, and another one, too, and people had a lot of stock. The white storekeepers started the racing first and the Indians took it up. At that time they only used horses, just a very few cars or automobiles. Some white people were moving into the country at the same time, so the Indians kind of gave it up. The white people stopped encouraging it, I don't know why. Either the storekeepers got tired of it or the farmers began to fence up. But I don't know just why it stopped.

One day I started over to Manuelito, using George's mother's new saddle. Back then George's mother was well fixed with some sheep and cattle.[88] At Manuelito they were going to have some of the races I've been talking about. They were to be at the store. Three of us went over. When we got there, they first buried the sack. Ted Sage pulled it out and went off with it, and they started to fight over it. Severo was the one who brought it back. They got five dollars to pull it out and ten dollars to bring it back. They used to run the horses pretty hard when they reached down for the sack. The white man had a big long whip and whipped the horses as they went by. They did what they called tug-of-war once. The women lined up in two bunches and had a big long rope that they pulled, {and} the bunch that crossed the line got beaten. The people from Kainti did that against those from Manuelito, and Kainti won. They fed us after that. There were a lot of people, but the food went around. They did those things in the afternoon, and at night they put on a dance with Indian girls. All the crowd came on horseback. After the dance was finished, a young boy began singing a Squaw Dance song, and two groups of singers, one from Kainti and one from Manuelito, sang until daylight. The Kainti people were the best and they got a dollar each.

LUCKY BEGINS HIS DECEPTIONS

Short Leg was living just this side of Manuelito, and I went there and slept the next day. There was the hogan where I slept and another hogan, and at another place there was a tent. It was about noon when I got up and went over to the tent. I saw three women, one called Sally, another Bertha, and the last one Henry's daughter. When I got up in the hogan I saw that a man called Guy's Son had some whiskey, and we drank some and I was feeling good. So when I saw those three women, I went in.

On my way to the tent there were two boys walking right toward it. When I got inside I asked the girls about them. One of them said they hadn't seen any boys. I said, "No? They were headed here." The one called Sally said, "Give us a drink and then we'll tell you where the boys are." "Well," I said, "I haven't any whiskey." She said, "You've been drinking whiskey." "Well, come on, search me," I said. The woman who spoke first got up and took hold of my arm, then they all took hold. There was a pole up above us, the tent pole. I reached up to the pole, which had a bucket hanging on it right above our heads. They wanted to throw me down, but I was holding onto the pole. The pole and bucket were shaking. I didn't know what was in the bucket, but it was all spilling out, pouring onto my head. It was milk, and everybody got wet with it. Then I let go of the pole and they threw me down.

I had two good bracelets on each arm, and they took those off. I was wearing my wife's beads with turquoise, and they took them away. The two boys came in about then. I asked one of them to help me get rid of one of the girls. He was a laugher who laughed about a lot of things and we called him Smiley. Finally he got hold of the woman called Sally and dragged her outside. The other boy dragged another one outside. My horse was tied outside. I heard Smiley laughing, but I didn't know what was going on. I was asking for my beads and bracelets, but the beads were already put in a trunk and locked up. She gave only the bracelets back. She told me to ask the other two girls about the beads.

When I got outside I saw the two girls walking over toward the Manuelito store. They wanted to get hold of the horse, too, but they hadn't, so the two boys outside said. I got on my horse and went to the store, bought some hay and put my horse in the corral, and came back to the store. I didn't know that the two girls had gone out where the horse was, and one, Bertha, had ridden my horse away. A man told me that. I asked a man in the store to lend me a horse so I could ride after the girl and get my horse back. I went over, but she didn't want to give it back.

In telling the story about the three girls, Sally, Bertha, and Henry's daughter, Lucky emphasized his losses without giving much explanation for them (LS 271–274, 280). In order to get money enough to retrieve his saddle and beads from Bertha, he stole some cattle belonging to his wife and her sister (LS 276–277). During a rest period while this part of the story was being recorded, A. L. asked Lucky what they talked about all that time while he was at the girl's house. Lucky said that one night at a dance he had been with the girl all night. So he was bargaining with her mother to get the saddle and beads back. A. L. remarked that fifty dollars was a lot for one night, which made both Lucky and Bill laugh. Lucky replied that there had been other nights besides. He said he had not been with the other two girls (Social Relations 36–37).

Then Bill Sage laughed and said, "Me and Lucky was talking about that the other morning, not in front of his folks but when we were alone. Lucky spoke about that girl at the Squaw Dance who took his saddle, said he had been with her seven times the night before.[89] (May 6, 1940:28–38)

This man, Guy's Son, was living near Manuelito. He and I rode one horse back to where he lived. I asked him if could borrow a horse and go back where the girl was. I rode to where she had kept the horse, and they told me she had gone off with the horse the other way. I rode over there looking for her but couldn't find her.

I decided to go home, and I cut straight across and got down to where my wife was that night. They asked me about the horse, and I told them that it got away from me down there with the saddle, bridle, and everything. I asked if he had come back home, but they hadn't seen it. I turned the other horse loose. I didn't tell them about last night and the next morning. In the morning I was studying over what I was going to do next, after I ate my breakfast.

My wife's mother and her family all had cattle. They were running around all over that area, and I heard from somebody that the storekeeper was buying cows over at the Dale store. I figured it out that I was going to sell some cattle. I started walking over to my old home, Sam Smith's place, and when I got there I found a horse and corralled him. I put a rope on one, saddled him, and started off, but a little way off it started to buck with me, bucking back toward the corral. He almost threw me three times. I lost my stirrup and bridle lines, and as soon as the horse stopped I jumped off and turned him loose. I got another one, saddled him up, and started toward Kainti, up onto the hill with the big field down here, and over by the spring near here. I rode in where there were some cattle— two yearling calves and four grown cows, six altogether—and started driving them toward Dale.

I brought them over close to the store, just over a hill before we reached the store. I went over and asked the store- keeper if he was buying cattle. He said yes, he was, and asked if I wanted to sell some cows. I said yes, I had brought some over. He said, "You go bring the cattle and corral them right here." When I got back where the cows were, they had just bedded down and were lying there chewing their food. I put them in the corral. There were two yearling steers in the bunch, which I sold for 60 dollars for both. The storekeeper said to sell him a cow and calf, but I said no, they didn't belong to me. He said he wanted to buy them anyway, so finally I gave in and sold them. First he wanted to give me 40 dollars for the cow and calf, he raised it to 45 dollars but I kept saying no, and finally he made it 50 dollars. So I got 110 dollars for the three cows and a calf.

He didn't have enough cash to pay me. I got it mostly in

cash and he wrote me a check. I bought a blanket for 13 dollars, a bracelet with some turquoise in it for 9 dollars and some clothes. I started back with the other cow and calf, drove them back where I'd gotten them, and rode on to Kainti. In a hogan a little way from the store some people were playing cards. I played with them for the rest of the day and the whole night. I lost fourteen dollars that night.

Next day, my wife's sister came to the Kainti store while I was there and told me they needed me at home. I said I'd come back right away. She started back and I came along after her and caught up just before she reached home, so we got back home together. I heard that my horse had come back alone without saddle and bridle. I showed them the blanket and bracelet, saying I'd bought the blanket at the Kainti store and that the bracelet belonged to a man who was playing cards—he had pawned it to me. I told the folks I was going to trade the horse back for the saddle.

I started off, going the other way, and about halfway to Manuelito I met another man who was going there, too. There had been a big rain that day, so when we came to the arroyo, the big main wash, we couldn't cross it. We came back this way, then went north toward Stony Point where there is a big bridge. We crossed the bridge, and I went to Manuelito while he went another way.

When I got pretty near to the store, the girl who had my saddle came walking toward me, just this side of the store. I asked where she was going and I stopped, but she just went on. I went into the store and asked a man I saw if those people were living in the same place, was it the girl's home? The man said yes, they were living in the same place. I waited a little while, then went over to the girl's home and got there after sundown. I stayed there that night. I had all my money with me. Next day they gave me back the saddle and the beads, and I had to pay them fifty dollars. I stayed another two nights and two days, then came back here.

> Lucky got this other girl who ran off with his saddle. He had had her for a long time before that, but his wife and her family did not find out about it until a good while after the episode of the saddle and beads. (Apr. 29, 1940:43–44)

I told my folks that somebody just took the saddle and bridle off. When I came back the first time they had asked about the beads and I told them I had pawned them at Manuelito. About the saddle, I told them this time that some people had taken it off over there, and I found out who they were and they gave it back to me. I didn't say who it was. The next thing that worried me was the cows—I wondered if they would put me in jail.

ADVENTURES WITH NED'S BOY

Lucky and Ned's boy seem to have had a great deal in common and went about together. At the time when Lucky was worrying about the cattle he had taken and sold, Ned's boy came along and got him to go with him to hunt a lost horse. The trip was full of excitement and the rough play that Lucky liked. They roped a steer and a dog, attended sings, got meat away from herders, stole watermelons, and shot at a steer (LS 282–295) (Social Relations 8).

While I was there, Ned's boy came over one day and asked me to help him hunt his horse, way down below, far away. I said, "All right," right away.

We went to his house, where they made up a lunch for us and we took it along—naneskadi and some meat, coffee, and sugar. We started off toward the west. It was a white horse that we were looking for. We went by the place where they have the day school now and down to a place called Bad Water, then on to another place called Trail-through-Wash. That place got its name when the war was on; they used to get into that arroyo. An old lady with the same name lived just on the other side, and she was at home when we came by. We said we were looking for horses. She said there were a lot of horses that watered in the arroyo, but she didn't know anything about them. One of her sons who lived there might be able to tell us more about it, but he wasn't home. We heard about a sing they were going to have that night a little way to the north.

We went off to the other side, looking for horses all day long. We talked about going to the sing that night. We walked back this way, but we were pretty tired by that time. The other boy was going ahead and I was kind of hanging back. I got pretty sleepy, so I thought I would run for a little way to wake me up. I ran my horse pretty hard, and the other boy did too. My horse stepped in a hole and fell down with me, and I fell off. The other fellow was running his horse behind me. I got off to stop the other horse, and it stopped so quick that the other fellow fell off his horse too. We laughed for a little while, then went on to where they were having the sing.

We were asking the people at the sing if they had seen a white horse. Nobody had. We stayed overnight there. We had left our lunch way down where we had been hunting horses, so we started off that way from where we had corralled some horses. We had corralled them so we could ride two of them to look for the horse. They didn't belong to us. We changed horses at the corral and went down the other side.

A lot of cattle were grazing around there. We rode up to where there were just two steers, chased them, and tried to rope them. We got one roped and I let the rope go on them. The country was pretty sandy and my horse didn't run very fast. Ned's son chased the cows away all by himself. I just followed his trail and tracked him down. I heard a holler there when I caught up with him, and got another rope on a cow. It had two ropes on it, and he was still chasing it. We had a gun about so long, a six-shooter. He said the cow got mad at him and he shot it right between the eyes. This was a baldheaded steer. It didn't take him long to take his rope off after the steer fell down. We made a big circle and came back to where our horses were.

From there, we went back to the sing and asked the people there if they had seen the white horse. They hadn't seen it. This was summertime, and we didn't stay long after they had supper. They started singing with the basket drum. We didn't stay at the sing all night but went outside to sleep. In the morning we got our horses saddled up and went off to look for horses again. People were just starting off home. We looked for the horse pretty nearly all day, down below farther than we had been. At one place we got off the horses and went to sleep, pretty tired. The lunch was all used up. After we slept we got up and went on again, pretty hungry now. We rode west until sundown, camped there that night. Next morning when we got up, the horses hadn't gone very far. There was a lot of grass around.

When we started on again we saw some smoke in the distance. We went that way to see if we could find something to eat. When we got pretty close, we saw a man sitting by a fire. We got behind a tree and moved closer, but the man who had been sitting by the fire had run away and a little boy was still there. It was a sheep camp. They were cooking some bread which was in the frying pan and starting to burn. We turned it over and set the pan away from the fire. We talked to the boy, but he never answered us. We went over the hill a little way, got off our horses, and waited for the man to come back to where he was cooking his bread. We heard sheep and thought it was another sheep camp, so we went off that way. When we got to the sheep we saw a herder, and there was the little boy again. It was the same boy! We asked the man why he ran away, and he said it was because he didn't think we were Navajos. He said we could go to the camp and get something to eat there, but there was no water at camp.

After he said that we went off over another hill and stopped there. We talked about whether we should wait there a while until the herder took the sheep off, then go to the camp. There was a little patch of cornfield there, and we saw where they had poured out all the water. We couldn't find any water around. We looked for some bread or flour but didn't find any. We saw some meat and put a piece on the coals, roasted it, and ate it. Then our throats were dry and we were thirsty for water. We roasted some of the corn on the coals and ate that, too. We went on then and came to a lake. We watered our horses and drank some water ourselves, then went on in the other direction a long way.

We came to a fence around a big pasture owned by a white man, and started from there to come back this way, going a long way until sundown. After dark we stopped and camped. I got a headache there that night, but went to sleep and didn't wake up till morning. I woke up first before sunup, heard more sheep in another direction. I woke the other fellow up, we found and saddled our horses right away, and started off toward where I heard the sheep. We thought we might find another sheep camp that way. About two miles away we saw sheep going off, and we heard a big bell to the south of where we were. We thought the camp was there, so we went over.

When we got to the camp it was a Zuni camp. Under a tree they had made up some kind of a bed and a man was still lying on it. There was another man with the sheep. We thought the one in camp was the cook. It was just about sunup then. We walked up to the Zuni man, lying down there without clothes, and talked to him. We said, "Friend, we're pretty hungry. We'd like to get something to eat here." We kept talking to him about wanting something to eat, and after a while he got up, put his clothes on, and built up the fire. A whole meat {entire sheep} was hanging on one side, and he picked up an ax, chopped it in two, cut off a piece, and started it roasting. After a while he took the meat off the fire, put it away, walked back to his bed, and lay down.

We were pretty hungry, and we got on our horses and started to go off, and the Zuni walked over to the fire, put some water in the coffee pot, and started roasting the meat again. We thought he was going to cook something for us, so we got off our horses again. But he put his meat away and lay down on the bed again. We told him again we wanted something to eat and would pay him a quarter. Then we said we would pay fifty cents each. He was not paying any attention to what we said. We got on our horses again.

My friend told me to ride up and pick up the meat. It was a hindquarter, hanging by the leg on a stick. When I got it, I'd want to get away with it. I got pretty close to it, got hold of it, pulled it, and broke the stick. We started off from there pretty fast. The Zuni got up and started running after us. I was carrying the meat and he came running, running right behind. He pretty nearly got hold of the horse's tail. He kept running after us for a mile, I think, then we got ahead of him and he gave out. Then the Zuni only made one holler and walked back home.

We went on a long way from there and came back to that lake, where we found two boys. We thought they were Zunis and talked to them as if they were, but they answered in Navajo. We asked where they lived, and they pointed the direction and said their father was home down there. We went over to where they were living and saw that the man was home. We got off our horses, told him we were pretty hungry, we would like to get something to eat from him. He said they had no water—two boys had gone after some, but they hadn't come back. We told him we had seen them. He said they wouldn't be back for a long while. "Well," we said, "we'd like some salt from you. We found a Zuni camp and they gave us some meat." He gave us some salt and we started off. We rode a long way, unsaddled our horses, and started a fire. We roasted the ribs and ate the meat, and both got a headache.

Then we started back this way. We saw another herd of sheep milling around but didn't see anybody, so kept on going. We came back to the place called Bad Water. A little to the south of that, somebody was raising a lot of watermelons. We tied up our horses and got into the watermelons where we broke open a lot, just looking for good ones. After that we started on, leaving lots of broken watermelons behind.

Coming on this way we found a place where some boys were roping horses in a corral. The boys asked us where we were coming from, and we told them we'd been looking for a horse for four days and didn't find it. They told us that a sing was going on just a little way off. We went on toward the sing. We saw that it was the same singer we had seen on our trip. They told us the sing had just started that morning when we got there in the afternoon. A little after we arrived they brought in a lot of food, and after we drank our coffee our headaches were gone. Our heads had been aching for coffee!

About an hour after we ate there we started on our way again and came by another home. A black dog from there went after us, barking. I tried to stop him but I couldn't. The other boy roped him and started running his horse. The dog made a noise for a long while, and we didn't stop until he was about dead. Then Ned's boy got off his horse, took the rope off the dog and left him there, and we came along.

We got to Ned's place then. Ned was home, and we told him we hadn't found the horse. I started home from there, past the Kainti store and to where I was living. After I got home I told them the whole story of our hunt for the horse and what we did. I forgot to tell you one thing: after we killed that cow, the next day we went back to look at it. Our cow was gone!

We just saw the blood there and the cow's tracks where it walked off!

AN INJURED MAN, AND A SING

Over here is a place where we had a cornfield and raised a lot of corn, good corn and oats. After I got back we were hoeing the weeds out of that corn. We moved over to that place. One day my uncle got some horses and corralled them. He borrowed a horse from another fellow. He heard there was a Squaw Dance going on across the railroad, and he was going to it. He was married to my wife's mother then. After he corralled them, he roped one horse, saddled it, and rode off. Somehow it started bucking with him going downhill, and he was thrown off. They said one of his shoulders was broken. The horse ran off with the saddle, and the man was put on a blanket and carried up the hill and into the hogan. That day I had ridden over to Kainti and didn't see this, but they told me about it.

Somebody came down to the store and told me about it, and I came home. I had a pretty bad bellyache coming back. I saw that horse running with a saddle somewhere between Kainti and my place. I was riding a horse but bareback, without a saddle. I started chasing the horse until sundown. After dark I let it go. When I got home I heard how the horse threw my uncle and he broke his shoulder. Next day we looked for the horse and found him, but the saddle and blanket were all lost someplace. We tracked him and found the blanket and everything.

There was a man named Chee who sang Hoof Way,[90] and we asked him to sing for my uncle. He came over and started singing for him and giving him a lot of medicine. He sang for five days. The shoulder had swollen pretty badly, but the swelling all went down. After five days he got better, his shoulder got well. Where it was broken, a big knot still showed. The singer went home and my uncle started walking around. He got better and better until he got well.

One day after that we had a big heavy rain. Big water was running in the arroyo. There had been some cattle in the canyon, and six of them were washed away. Water overflowed the arroyo. Some men went to look at the cows and found they belonged to my family.

ANOTHER CEREMONY

Next, we heard about a Squaw Dance at Hub. They were going to bring the dance over to just this side of Lupton, where they would have it the first night. I and two others made an appointment to go together, and we met here where a man had some saddle horses. We each borrowed a saddle horse. Then we all went down where the dance was, getting there about sundown. The people from the other dance place got there just about when we did. Inside the hogan, after dark, they fixed up a drum, putting buckskin over the top, stretching it pretty tight, and tying it around. They made a little curved stick for the drum. There were a lot of people there that night. They never (rarely) have such a big crowd on the first night, but all the girls who lived around there came that night and some from other places. The three of us who went together danced that night. In the morning at daylight we quit for a while. After eating they started singing again in front of the hogan and then threw out apples, candy, and cookies. The people who lived around there did the throwing.

After that, some of the people who knew each other gave horses or blankets or some money—ten dollars, fifteen dollars—the people who lived around there. They decided where they were going to camp, and the people who came from the other dance site left one man there to give directions. We came back to where we borrowed the horses, went to sleep, and started to the dance in the afternoon.

First we got to the trading post in Lupton and saw a lot of people there, all going to the dance that night. We went on and got to the camp, and there were still more people there. Some people had hauled over some bread, soda pop, candy, and smokes for sale. There were two or three places where they were trading. That night a woman, Curley's daughter, had a baby there. We all moved camp in the morning to the dance. (Did you see the baby born?) Up till midnight we were hearing about that. They took the woman away from the crowd, a little way off to one side, and some people took care of her. She had the baby there about one o'clock at night. The baby and everything was all right, and they put them in a wagon and took them home.

During the day it had been raining off someplace, raining

pretty hard. There were a few automobiles at the dance, which was on the north side of the big arroyo. The main dance would be on the south side, but when we got to the arroyo we found a lot of water running. Only the ones riding a pretty good-sized horse could get across. One car tried to cross, but the Navajo driver didn't go very far into the water till it got stuck there and he walked out. The engine didn't run very long when it got into the water. At the Hub store they had a tractor, and they told the owner they needed help to pull the car out. A man came with the tractor to where the car was stuck. The car was quite a way from the side, but he took the tractor in and it got stuck. The engine kept going for quite a while, then stopped, and they just left it there. Somebody went in with a horse and took the driver out. The people had started moving pretty early and had been waiting there all that time. Toward noon the water went down, and after that they all crossed.

The main dance was just a little way south of the arroyo. After they crossed, pretty nearly all the people started running their horses. Where they had the hogan, they were going around it four times, and a lot of people were shooting, just holding the gun up and shooting into the air. Then they went off in one direction and made their brush hogan there. A lot of food was sent over from the kitchen. As they finished eating, the people went over to the other hogan and lined up and started singing. The same thing happened—throwing out cookies, candy—they threw a lot out. The people who gave horses at the other place got something back at this one. Then they quit singing and went back to the brush hogan.

A lot of them went to sleep, but over at the hogan people were singing while the medicine man blackened the patient. After that they started horse races. One man from each side had a race horse, a sorrel, the other a dun horse. People were betting against each other—saddle blankets, ponies, bracelets, money. The race horses started down the track, even. When they got near the line the dun horse came ahead. Everybody hollered. That was our side. We had been afraid and didn't bet much. A lot of people won a lot of good things—good saddles, horses. After that they had some more horse races, but not betting much, just a little. This was toward fall. Late in the evening they quit altogether.

That night a lot of Mexicans who worked on the railroad came to the dance. There must have been about forty Mexicans, maybe more. That was Saturday night, when they got their pay. They played cards with the Navajos instead of watching the sing. We were in there, playing all night and the next day until noon. That day was Sunday. Some of the Navajos won a lot of money. The Mexicans were still there when we left.

I got back home at sundown. I'd seen the dance, and the Mexicans playing cards. As for the car in the arroyo, the next morning we looked and all we saw was the top, little bits of it. All the rest was in the mud. I don't know whether they dug it out or left it there, or what they did with it. I stayed home, cutting oats. (What did you do at the dance?) All I did was sing with the people until the last day, when I was playing cards. (Where did you learn to play cards?) I didn't know about play-ing cards that time. I lost fourteen dollars down there. I just played then by having someone tell me. Another time I was playing with Barney and he showed me a little about it. Last time was at that dance, but I didn't really know how. I knew a little but not much.

The night I came back from the dance my wife told me that three men were looking for me. They told her I sold some cattle over at Dale. They missed the cows for some time, then asked all the storekeepers. One of the men went to Dale, and the storekeeper told him they were sold there by me. He showed them the bill of sale where I'd made my thumbmark. The man who first went there didn't get the whole story so he went back with an interpreter and found it all out. When they came back from learning about it they came to my home, two men and a woman.

THE PAST BEGINS TO CATCH UP

Next day I started to cut hay, but I quit that and went over to Sam Smith's place. Two days later I was riding a horse and when I got home and got my horse tied up, I saw three people approaching the hogan. I knew those people, they had some white saddle horses and they were riding white horses. I thought they were the ones who were looking for me, so I rode away. I went up a road way past Kainti and up on top of a hill, where I stopped and looked back. They were coming, trailing me. I started off to the south, and don't know how many miles I rode. I made a long circle toward home and came back after dark. My wife told me they had gone by, and they came back there that evening. They said they trailed me off toward Zuni, thinking I was going to Zuni, so they just started back home. They told my wife to have me wait there when I got back, they would come over. They would tell me what the storekeeper said. The storekeeper had told them that they must hunt me up and bring me down to the store, and we would have a talk between those three people, the storekeeper, and me. That was all the storekeeper wanted to do.

The three people didn't want to do that, they said. They wanted to straighten it out some way. There were a whole lot of people who were all ready to send me to the penitentiary, that's what all the people around were saying. But one of the men of the three people said he wouldn't like to do that. They wanted me to tell what I did with the money. My wife asked me what I did with the money. I told her I spent most of it. I had hidden about sixty dollars some place and I couldn't find the place. When the three started off for home, they said they were coming back in five days and I must be home then.

DEATHS FROM THE FLU

Right then there was some kind of sickness around, either fever or flu (probably the 1918–19 influenza epidemic). My wife's grand (?) mother and her husband were living about a mile and a half west from our place. My wife's older sister was ready to have a baby the day I came home, and the next day I heard this sick woman's baby was born dead. A little while after that the woman got very sick, and that night she died too. They sent for me the next morning and I went over on horseback.

When I got there, there was the old man, Old Paul, and his wife, my wife's mother.

> We are not told the name of Lucky's mother-in-law, but he sometimes refers to her as Big Hail's mother or George's mother.[91]
>
> She was the patient at the Feather Way sing Lucky describes (LS 239). At that time she was suffering from severe head pains (LS 240). Lucky once borrowed her saddle and mentions

at that point that she "was in good fix, had some sheep and cattle" (LS 270) (Social Relations 42).

Besides those two old people, there were some others who were just living there together in one home. They had moved outside the hogan and were staying on the south side. On my way I came by the door, which was all open, and saw the dead woman over north of the fire. I went to where the people were, and they told me that they wanted me to move all their things to another place right away. They said I might have to make three trips to do it. After that, they would need a load of wood. They wanted me to go home and get the wagon, and to hurry. I went back, harnessed up the horses, hooked them to the wagon, and took it down there.

I only made three trips, and the last time everybody but one—the old man's wife—got on the wagon. She said she wanted to wait there, she had something to attend to for a little while. When she got through, she said, she would walk over to their new place. We had hauled everything else down, and the wood was next. It had been a long time since I'd brought the wood, but the woman hadn't showed up. I took the wagon back home, unharnessed the team, and turned the horses loose. I decided to go back on horseback. I told my folks I'd hauled everything but the woman hadn't showed up by the time I left. I wanted to go back and see if she got there.

When I arrived, the woman still hadn't come. They were missing her very much and they told me to go back and look for her. When I went back I didn't see anybody outside the hogan. When I came to the door, I saw the dead woman over there and the other woman waiting, lying down on the south side of the fire. I thought she had just gone to sleep, so I went in and tried to wake her up. I shook her, but she didn't move. It didn't feel as if she was alive, she felt all loose. I looked at her face and saw blood coming out of her mouth. She was dead already. I went outside and got on my horse. My home was just a short distance away, so I went there. I told the people there about it, and one of my uncles didn't believe it. He went back with me and saw the woman, then we went on to where I had moved the others. When we told them about it, the old man sent me across the canyon to where his old lady's oldest son lived. When I got there, he wasn't home, he had gone to Ft. Defiance in a wagon. They told me he wouldn't be back till tomorrow night. I came back and reported this.

The man who went to Ft. Defiance, called Big Hail, came back with another man called Yellow Man. They came over to where the old man was staying. They stayed overnight. I was there again that night. Big Hail went to Kainti next morning and brought back two white men. When they got there, the two white men buried the dead women inside the hogan. It took them until about noon to do this. They both went back to Kainti when they got through. All the other Navajos who had come there went home, but they made an appointment to come back together again in five days.[92] I didn't go to that meeting, but I heard that Wood, Chief Wood, was there.

The old lady who died and her daughter used to have some sheep. The people at the meeting talked to this man and settled it some way, dividing up the sheep and cattle among the family of the two women. The woman who died first had two boys, Don[93] and Ray, and they got most of the sheep and cows. Those closely related to that woman got some, too. The old lady's stock was divided up in the same way. Big Hail took some old-timer red beads and old turquoise beads, too. He still has them. After the property was divided, Wood told those people to come to take care of their livestock. The date the three people had set for me had already passed, and they made a new date.

(What killed the old lady?) Those people had flu, at least the younger woman had it, the one who died after the baby was born. They said the old lady had it too, when they moved out that night. The others all had some, so nobody was taking care of the old lady. They didn't know that she was too sick to be left there. The way she was doing things around there, they thought she might have just a little flu. And she said she wanted to do a few more things before she went to the camp. That was the last they heard her say. After she was found dead, no one went to investigate except the two white people who buried her, and they didn't find out what her worst trouble was. The way she was lying when I looked at her there, I think she had been working. They had had a blanket up inside, and she had rolled it up and put it outside. It looked as if she had been doing that and just fell down. That was the way it looked to me when I went in there.

NAVAJO JUSTICE

When my date with the three people came, not very many people came to the meeting. There were my two uncles, Big Hail, his oldest son Roan Horse, Yellow Man, Wood, Stanley and his wife, I and my wife—that was about all. Wood did the questioning.[94] First he said that he had heard I'd sold some cattle at the Dale store, three cows that belonged to Stanley's wife and one that belonged to my wife. Stanley's wife is my wife's sister. He asked, did I do that? I said yes, I did. How much money did I get for them? I got 60 dollars for the two yearling steers, 50 dollars for a cow and calf, altogether 110 dollars. What did I do with the money? I spent it all for one thing or another. How much money is left? None. I don't have a penny left. What made me do that? I didn't know. They asked my wife if she knew, but she didn't. They asked who else knew about it, who was with me at the time? I said nobody, I was all by myself.

Stanley said, "I've got something to say. Three of these cows belonged to my wife. What I think is that we should just send this man to jail. He sold them and got money for them and spent the money. He didn't let us know a thing about it. After he's been to jail, I don't think he'll do it anymore."

Then Wood spoke up. He said he was going to handle this case. "After I heard this other man talk," he said, "I want to do it the Indian way, that's what I think." Talking to Stanley, he said, "I want to ask you a question: how long ago did you marry this girl?" "Just last fall, a short time ago." "And who owned these stolen cattle?" Stanley's wife said she owned them. Wood asked Stanley, "Did your wife turn this case over to you so you could handle it yourself?" Stanley said no. "Well," Wood said, "If I were you I'd keep still and let the other people talk for a while. Let the people who are related to each other talk first." All the time during this meeting Stanley was talking against me, and I think that's why Wood said that to him. (Why did Wood ask how long Stanley had been married?) Well, he was just a new man, hadn't got to know the people yet. Stanley had told them that he was the one who had to talk about this for his wife.

Big Hail spoke again. He said to Stanley, "We want to ask all the questions we can. I wish you would hold your talk back for a while. I, my father, and the old lady are the three who raised these cattle and are still responsible for them. That has been for many years and you just came three months ago. I don't think it's right for us to talk about this. When one of my nieces died after she had a dead baby and the other lady, my mother, died, you people got scared. The old man sent word to all you people, and also to me, but I was on a trip to Ft. Defiance. The old man says that you people didn't show up at this place, but this man (Lucky) did all the work there. He also saw the woman who died in the hogan.[95] All the rest of you people were afraid to look inside after the first woman died, but he went in there and found the old lady had died and notified us about it. He also came over to my place and told my folks about it.

"I heard that just as soon as I got back. It just scared me to death. I unhooked one of my horses, pulled off his harness, threw on a saddle {on the horse}, and came right over. I wanted to hear what it was all about, and here I got to understand it's the way I said. So I don't like to get anybody mad about this while we're handling the case—we want to settle the case, track the whole thing up first. We want to fix it a way that will satisfy all of us."[96] He said that, for himself, he hadn't done much thinking after those two women had died at the same time.

Wood spoke again. He said he thought that the talk made by Big Hail, whom he called his "grandson," was good. He said I had worked for him a long time, herding sheep, taking care of cattle, helping at home. I did good work for him. He said he used to tell me lots of times that I shouldn't do what was wrong, as in this case. I used to mind him pretty well. I didn't do anything wrong except when I got together with somebody and started drinking with them. He had told me not to do that, too. I was poor, didn't have anything, had no home for myself, no mother or father, had it hard to get along with people at the places where I had been. "And if you people want to, you might think that Lucky should pay back something for the cattle he sold. But I don't see how he could do that, it would be hard.

On the other hand, if you send him to jail you won't get anything. So it's going to be hard on both sides. But you people have lots of cattle, sheep, horses, and one thing you might do is put him on the job of herding. Let him work it out. That's the way I think about it."

Two of my uncles, Black Horse and another one, were there. (How long had Black Horse been back from Santa Fe?) He came back three years before this time when they met and talked. Wood asked them to say what they thought about it. The other one started. He told the people they mustn't be too hard on us. They were related to me and that's why he said it. He said, "I had one idea. I thought I might give you two good saddle horses. I have one outside here now, and the other one is down at home. We'll give you that and would like to drop the whole case and let it go at that since it's his first time. If he does it again, you can handle the case whatever way you want. I don't think it's very good to be selling somebody else's cows. We all know nobody will ever like that, but still we feel sorry for this man just the same." He said he liked Big Hail's talk, and he said, "We don't want anybody to get mad here. I think we will do this and let the man come clean. Then we'll watch him afterward." He asked the people what they thought of this.

All the other people wanted to do that, but they asked the two girls what they said to it. Stanley's wife said all right, she would take the two horses. She didn't have any saddle horse, so she might as well take the two horses. The other girl said all right. Wood asked the people if they were all satisfied, and they said they were. Big Hail said he thought everybody was satisfied, and he told everybody to forget about it. They didn't want the case brought up again after this.

Then Big Hail started talking to me. He told me I had done something wrong, which I shouldn't do. They should have settled the case the other way, but they got pretty easy on me. He said that if I hadn't showed up at the place where the two women died, they might have sent me to jail. After I did all that for them, he said, he thought he might tell the people that they should go easy on me. So they did, but if I did it again they wouldn't help me. They would have to go right straight to Gallup and get the sheriff, who would take care of me. But he hoped I wouldn't do it again. He said, "I don't like to see anybody in trouble. Also I don't like to talk about somebody my own people have married." That's what he said. If I did it again, next time he wouldn't be there. He said he couldn't be my helper all the time.

He said, "From now on we want you to take care of the sheep, cattle, horses, do the work at home and help take care of the old man who's lost his wife now. Make hogans for him, haul water and wood for him. Take care of him in a good way." Then he asked me if I would do that again. I said no, I wouldn't. He asked if I was sure I meant that and I said yes, I meant it. Would I do all that work? "Yes," I said, "I'll help." He told me he didn't mean that I should work every day for them but I should just help them along, that's all.

This was the time when the big war was on, fighting the Germans. A lot of people had that kind of sickness everywhere. Some of the boys from here went to the war—Bert and another fellow. That was 1918. Then I stayed there and worked there and herded. (Did you ever see any dead people before those two?) No, those were the first two I saw. (How did it make you feel?) I didn't feel very good. I got scared about it. It made my feet and all over my body kind of shake. I had that for quite a while, then it went away. (What else?) I thought they had died and weren't alive any more, that was all I thought about it. Afterward a lot of people were telling me that if those two women hadn't died right at that time, I would surely have been in the penitentiary for that. I thought about it the same way. If I had gone, it might be that I would be coming back from there today!

Work on the Railroad and Gathering Pinyon Nuts

At that time there were more people working below Gallup on the railroad. I went there and got a job for three dollars a day. They let me camp in a freight car. There were some there and we camped in them. I worked there for one month and got my pay every week. It got pretty cold that month. There was another man I got together with when I started working. Ernest was working with me, too. One day Ernest and I were walking on the railroad tracks and a train was coming. it was a fast train coming, a long way off. Ernest ran off and told me to get away. I just kept walking. The train pretty nearly ran over me. I jumped off and it just about got me. The wind blew me off. If I'd been hit, I wouldn't be coming back today!

I came down home where my wife was and went on herding. That winter we hadn't had any snow, and we heard there were some pinyons on the other side of Ft. Defiance. Sam Smith wanted to go there. Sam Smith, his wife, two others, and I decided at Sam's place to go over there. After we had decided, I went back home where my wife lived. We planned to start tomorrow, and since I was living on the way, Sam Smith and the others were going to come along with the wagon and pick me up. Next day I took my bedding and some groceries and meat to the road. They came along and I got into the wagon. We got started in the afternoon and got to this side of Two Ridges, where we camped for the night. Next morning we went on, past a store called Little Arroyo, on to a place called Blue Lake and then to High Water, where we camped again. In the morning it was pretty cloudy. We went on and through a gap this side of Window Rock, and there it started snowing.

We passed by those tall rocks on the other side and went on by the old Ft. Defiance road. By the time we got to the big black rock this side of Ft. Defiance, the snow was about a foot deep. We went on to Ft. Defiance and went inside the store. A pretty good fire was burning in the store and we got ourselves warmed up. We were about frozen when we got there. It had been snowing there all day, and the sun was down when we got there. We had no place to sleep, the snow was pretty deep, but we found a place where we slept and next morning started west from Ft. Defiance. We went through those big gaps and on over to the other side. We went quite a way beyond there, went to the top of a hill and made another camp there. The snow was pretty deep.

We found a big tree and scraped the snow away from under it. We made a big round circle without snow and camped there. Next morning Sam Smith and I went out to look around, to see how deep the snow was all around. We got quite far from camp and saw a man walking along. We talked to him and he asked where we lived. We said we were camping to the north. What were we looking for? We said for pinyons. He said we couldn't find pinyons with the snow so deep. We asked him where he lived, and he said a little way above. There were some pinyons over there, but they were all covered with snow. We asked him if we could bring our camp over where he was living. We asked about the land, whether anyone was taking care of that place. He said no, and we said that if someone was doing that, they might run us off. He said he thought the land was all open for Navajos. We decided we would bring our camp over.

We went back to camp, and after we ate we moved the camp to where the man was living. The sun was shining nicely and the snow was melting away as fast as it could. We camped there two days and the snow had gone from under the trees. We could see some pinyons and we started picking them.

I didn't start to pick, but instead went off to Ft. Defiance with another boy. We left pretty early and got there about noon. This boy said there was a man who wanted some work done at Ft. Defiance, where he was building a rock house for a missionary. He was going to try to get work there. I wanted to see about that so I went along with him. When we got there and asked about it, the man said he would put us to work that afternoon. We said we couldn't start till the next morning, so we went about halfway back to the camp, to where this boy was living. He told me they were having a sing, not at his home but nearby. We went to the sing and into the hogan, but nothing was going on, so we went back to the boy's home. We stayed there that night, and next morning we went to where the work was and started to work.

Some were building up the wall and some mixing mud. They told me to carry mud. The other boy worked on the wall. Some were working underneath, digging, some shaping rocks. We only worked there two weeks, then they put some men off and kept just a few working. They put me off and paid me twenty-four dollars with a check that I took to the store to cash.

After that, I went back where the people were picking pinyons. I picked too, by myself for ten days. In ten days I had picked enough, fifty or sixty pounds. Another man from home came to where we were, and he and Sam Smith wanted to take the pinyons to Ft. Defiance. I wanted to go along, and told them I was going home. Sam and the other man were just going to Ft. Defiance, then back to picking again. I asked one of them if they would take my pinions to Ft. Defiance so I could sell them there. Sam Smith carried my pinyons on horseback for me.

I was afoot. I could run a long way then, and I started running ahead of the two men. I got to Ft. Defiance before they did.

First they had decided to go just to Ft. Defiance, but then all three of us wanted to go back home to Kainti. They would just come home and go back right away to the picking place. When we got through trading at Ft. Defiance, they told me to go on ahead, so I did. I had gone about two miles this side of Ft. Defiance, and was near a dipping place, when an automobile came up behind me. There was a little hill I was going up, and when I got to the top the car came right behind me and stopped. Three men got out—not Navajo, not Mexican, not white, but some kind of Indian, maybe Santo Domingo. We couldn't understand each other and just made signs. I told them I wanted a ride. Two had been sitting in front and one behind, and they told me to sit behind with the odd one. We came through by Window Rock, through the gap, up the main hill, over the hill, and on this side. The road took a shortcut there, and we went on another six or seven miles. I got off there and started walking right straight south. The nearest place I knew was the one called Little Arroyo, and I got there about this time of day (3:15 P.M.).

I was pretty hungry, so I bought some food there and ate it. There was a man I knew who lived this side of the railroad, who came to the store with a wagon. I asked for a ride and he said yes. I got in the wagon and came to his home. When I got there, I found that Agnes was living there with a man.*

> Agnes and Lucky are members of the same clan and call each other brother and sister (LS 413, 414). Lucky often stopped at Agnes' place for the night or went there to help with some work, such as rounding up horses or driving the sheep (LS 250, 251, 338, 409, 467) (Social Relations 20).

---

*{With this simple statement Lucky introduces his clan sister Agnes, his partner in various unsavory, and some illegal, actions. The first paragraphs of this insert are in the typical field-note style of straightforward factual reporting. I also have included several paragraphs in order to demonstrate Lucky's dramatic narrative style as well as to illustrate the amount of smoothing the text has received (see Introduction, p. xv).}

Another affair that Lucky did not carry to completion for Agnes was reported to Bill, her son-in-law, in the course of his own life story. According to Bill, Lucky was given two pints of whiskey by Agnes and told to hunt up Bill at a sing. One of the bottles was supposed to have "snake poison" in it, and Lucky was to follow an elaborate procedure of pretending to drink with Bill in order to induce Bill to swallow the poisoned whiskey. She gave Lucky a blanket and promised to pay him money after the job was finished. Lucky said he would do as Agnes wished. But instead, he buried the bottles. Once Bill knew about all this, he dug up the bottles and had a meeting called. Lucky repeated the story; Agnes denied everything and said Lucky was lying. It was decided to have the contents of the bottles tested at Albuquerque. The bottles were sent away but no report was received. Agnes had bragged to Lucky that she had killed two men with that drink (Social Relations 21).

Lucky's friendship with Bill is apparently quite genuine and has been of some duration. It will be recalled that Lucky did not bring Bill the doped whiskey Agnes had prepared, for instance. Lucky did not tell Bill about the whiskey for about a year and a half, however. Then Bill asked him, "Why don't you tell me about it? Why don't you come by here and bring me the bottles?" According to Bill, Lucky replied, "You was going to try me with that" (Social Relations 28).

When Bill was asked whether he thought his mother-in-law was a witch, he replied that he didn't believe so. He said her father, Big Head, was a good man, and he didn't know where else she could have learned it (Social Relations 22).

Lucky says, "I used to steal for that old lady. . . . I did lota stealing with old lady. I go together with her one of the time, another time I go with another boy. Old lady sent us out where Navaho living, tell us to get a sheep or two and tie the four legs together, then tie them together and put them on the horse and bring them down here. "We do this," she says. When they bring them down her home, next morning he puts his knife in the fire, get it red hot, and then cut the sheep ear off with it, red hot knife. No blood come. He says that cut will look just like old, he says, and then put him with the herd. "That is what we been doing for her. She had two gentle horses we using that. She used to get me to sell whiskey to the Indians and I make money for her. That is what all we been doing. And then we did lota other things." But he didn't tell me just what all he did. "Where her father live down here, Big Head, she sent us over there taking her father's sheep, and some of Wood's sheep, and some of Roan Horse, Ernest's wife." (Summary of Subsistence Data 18)

{Bill Sage:} Lucky says, "I did a lot of stealing with that old lady. I go together with her one of the time, another time I go with that boy. . . . Old lady sent us out where Navaho living; tell us to get a sheep or two, and tie four legs together and put them on the horse and bring them down here. We do this."

"She used to get me to sell whiskey to the Indians, and I make money for her. That is what all we been doing, and then we did a lot of other things.

"Where her father live down here, that Big Head,[97] she sent us over there taking her father's sheep, and some of Wood's sheep, and some of Red Man, and Irvin's wife. Old Lady got mad with me and one day I was over her place, she hired me with some whiskey and she wants to get rid of it. One day Old Man went to town, brought out two gallons of whiskey. Old Lady says she wants to give me two pints of whiskey. That was for Bill Sage to drink it up, she said. She told me to take it to the dance one of the days that Bill was in the crowd, and told me to give Bill a drink there, a full pint, and to start drinking with him, but not to drink it, just take it to my mouth like tea but not drink any. . . . 'If he drink that up, that is pretty strong, he is going to die on that right away.' She says if I do that she wants to give me a blanket. I get a blanket and something else. 'Then after you kill this man,' Old Lady says, 'I going to give you a lot of good money.' I told Old Lady that I'll do that, but I don't mean it. I take these two bottles with me and buried them over here this side my place under the tree and they still there yet. That has been about a year and a half ago." (Subsistence 5-6)

They asked me where I had come from, and I told them I was on my way back from the other side of Ft. Defiance where I'd been pinyon picking. They gave me something to eat and I spent the night there. I hadn't seen the two men who had started from Ft. Defiance yet. Next morning they gave me something to eat early, and I started walking toward home. After I walked about three miles, I met a man on the road.

I knew this man, a singer, and he said he had just sung over here at Big Hail's place, over his first wife. We talked together for quite a while. I told my story about everywhere I'd been. When we got through talking, I started walking again. When I walked into the canyon over here to the north, a woman riding horseback behind me caught up with me right away. I asked where she was coming from and she said she'd been at the sing last night and was just coming home. She was one of my wife's sisters, not married at that time. We walked along and I told the girl I was played out with walking, could I ride behind her on the horse? She said all right, get up behind. We went up the hill and then away down to where it was pretty close to my home. I got off there and the girl went on. I got back home.

Next day I herded all day till sundown. When I brought the sheep in, they told me Sam Smith got back there and waited a long time. He was just going away again when I brought the sheep in. He started telling the people that I was back there someplace, walking. They told him I had already come back yesterday. That night I began telling my whole story, told them how I got there, how much snow there was on the road, all the camps we made, our safe arrival, how we started picking when the snow melted, my two-week job in Ft. Defiance, how I got home again. We didn't get to sleep until way after midnight.

ACTIVITIES AROUND HOME

I was building a hogan like this one (Bill's), curved on one side, just about half as big as this, I think. The west side and top were just half-done. It wasn't quite finished when I left, and it was still the same. So I started to work on it. I cut a lot of trees, peeled them and hauled them, and started to build the hogan there by myself. Stanley was living there, too, but he just watched me. He didn't help me at all. It took me ten days to build that hogan. When I finished it, we moved inside and lived there.

Then lambing started. We had a lot of sheep and goats, and we lost a few lambs and a few young goats. It took me a long time to get through the lambing. Then we started shearing—just with my wife, nobody else helped.

I tanned a goatskin into buckskin, cut it up and braided it, trying to make a bridle out of it. I had seen some bridles made that way, and I wanted to make one. I would take my sheep out to a good place where there was good grass and they would graze a long while in one place. While they were grazing I would work on the bridle. I'd seen this kind around the places where they were having a dance. People were using it on their horses. I don't know how many days it took me to make the bridle. I didn't make as good a one as I had seen, but it was all right. I put it on a horse and it looked good. I bought a silver button about six inches across, with turquoise in the middle, to go on each side of the bridle.

I took wool out {when I was} herding in the daytime. I would work on it, carding it out. I would get quite a pile done and come home with it (about 2′ × 3′ × 3′). I never learned to spin. I tried it but I didn't know how to do it. Making strings for the warp, twisting it—if a woman started it for me, I could do it. I only knew those parts. They put me to grinding corn between two stones, and I knew that pretty well. I only made one kind of meal. I cooked for myself when I was herding. I would come back with the sheep and then cook, making naneskadi and cooking meat. I made a bow and arrows that I carried with me. I could shoot anything a little way off—was a good shot. I shot rabbits, birds, dogs that I herded with, lizards, snakes, horses. It would make the horse run when I shot him, but the arrow would fall off before he ran very far. (How about a dog?) It could go right through, I could kill them.

One day I was out herding down toward Roan Horse's home. I was walking under a tree and had my bow and arrows with me. I saw something white under the tree, and when I looked up the tree, I saw a big owl with big eyes. I tried as hard as I could to shoot the owl. I thought an arrow would go through it, and I shot it right in the middle of the body. He just made a noise and the arrow jumped back and broke in two. The owl flew away. That was something tough I shot! I thought maybe he had an iron button or something in his body and I hit that.

One day a dog ran a big brown squirrel into a hollow log. When I got there the dog was biting the log, and when I looked into it I saw the squirrel inside. It made some kind of noise. I didn't know a squirrel could bite, and I thought I'd reach in there and pull it out, get hold of it. I reached in with my arm and almost got hold of the squirrel when he bit my finger and squeezed it. When I got my hand out, my finger was split right at the end and blood was running out.

One day when I was herding, I found a horse lying down asleep. I walked up to the horse very gently and got right up to it. I had a blanket with me that I covered his head with. I think that woke the horse up, but he couldn't see. He made a funny noise and tried to get up. He still couldn't see, and I guess that was why he made the funny noise many times. After that he ran water, and after that he passed lots of manure. It made me laugh. I did that just a little way from here. I pulled the blanket off and the horse got right up and ran away.

There was an old ewe who wouldn't stay with the sheep, was always going one place or another, didn't want to go to one place like other sheep. She used to make me mad a lot of times. I made a stick and thought I would kill that sheep by hitting her on the head. The end of the stick was forked. I started running after that sheep, chased her around a big circle four times. The sheep kept just a little way ahead of me, maybe about two steps. When I got tired of running and the sheep was kind of tired, too, I started hitting the sheep on the back of its head while it ran. I just touched the ear with the stick after I threw it. The stick stuck in the ground in front of the sheep and the fork fitted on each side of her throat. That stopped her and I caught her. I hit that sheep many times with the stick, then let it go. The sheep got worse after I punished her.

After shearing was finished and I had earmarked the lambs and little goats and cut them, we put the herds together to make it one. I didn't herd much after that, other people did it.

(What was the matter with your wife when you did the cooking?) She was having a baby and she was pretty slow. I didn't like that so I started to cook myself. It wasn't only for that reason, I wanted to do it myself.

While the other people were herding, I was putting a fence around the corn. There was one big bull that was always coming into my corn and eating it. We bought six spools of barbed wire at the store. Clark used to have a store then. I went over with the wagon and brought the wire back, then I fenced the cornfield. After I put the fence up the bull never got inside the field again. I used three strands of wire. The bull was pretty mean on the crop. He belonged to George's mother. On one side I had a gate, and he got in there when he learned how.

He got inside the oatfield and trampled down a lot of oats. I was thinking I could do something else about that. I put some wire where the gate was and made a circular place in the middle. I found some bailing wire, and got a lot of empty tomato cans. I made holes through every can, then strung them on the wire. After I got all the cans fixed, I put them around the circle so the bull could put his head through. I tied the circle on in different places so it would stay, but not very solidly, kind of loose. I left it that way at sundown. Next morning when I looked, the cans were gone. I thought the bull slipped it onto his neck. After he walked off with it, the tracks started running. He ran all over the field inside the fence, got outside, and ran down into the canyon. Way down below there, I began finding some cans. Further on, I came to a bunch of oak trees and found all the cans. The wire broke and lost all the cans. After that the bull never came to my cornfield anymore. Don and I had tracked him off.

That summer Don, George, and I were hoeing. They had a pretty good-sized file for sharpneing their hoes, and I had been using it. The two boys were sitting away from me, and when I got through sharpening my hoe I called {to} George that I was through with it. I threw the file accidentally, it slipped out of my hand. George was looking down, doing something on the ground. I hollered, "Look out!" George looked up and the file went into his face just below the eye. George pulled it out and just held his head and closed his eye. It just missed his eye. I was young when I did that. George, Don, and my wife and I, my son and baby were all living there while Old Man Paul, George's father, and my uncle were living together west of us.

One day I went over to their place. The girl that I rode behind once came out of the hogan and walked up to me. I was afraid to go inside because my mother-in-law was there.[98] I heard that Old Man Paul was pretty sick and hadn't wanted anything to eat for two days. That's all I found out, so I went back home and told the others what I had heard. They wanted to go back there that night. I don't remember why we didn't go, but we stayed home and slept pretty hard, didn't wake up all night.

When it was just getting daylight, I saw the bright dawn and I heard somebody talking. We were in a shade hogan. The voice said, "Get up, get up, it's daylight." I got up and went out, and it was just about daylight. Right outside was a big pine tree, and the talk came from the top of the tree. I looked up and saw an owl up there, still saying the same thing.[99] It talked just like a Navajo. It flew away and everybody got up and started to make breakfast. Before sunup, Big Hail came on his horse, came inside and said he had come for Don. He told us Old Man Paul died last night. He said, "They sent me word yesterday, about sundown, that they wanted me to come over. I got another man and we went there. The old man was half dead already. A little while after that he died. The man who came with me is over there now. I want him to bury the old man and I want Don to help him." The old man was Don's grandfather. Don went along with him, and we heard later that the old man had been buried by the two of them. We didn't go over. Don didn't come back for four days. He said when they had dug the grave and buried the man, they stayed in one place for four days. Big Hail was there all the time, too.

(What did you think about the owl?) The Indian would think that it was only a little way to the place where the man died. The breath that left the man came over to our place and turned into the owl to make us wake up. That's the way we thought about it. (Does it go into a live owl or make a new one?) The breath turns into a new owl. (Bill commented about this: "My father used to say that where there is a patient, his close relatives who live right near him are supposed to look after him, day and night. When he dies, it has to be known all around. The people around have to be waked up if he dies in the night. The people shouldn't sleep because if they aren't watching they won't know whether he died. If they sleep the way Lucky's family did, the breath of a man or woman that died will turn into an owl and it will go to one of the sleeping homes and do just as he said here. That's what they used to say. This old man was a pretty close relative of Lucky's wife and George and Don.")

After that, they told us what we should have done. I knew

it already. When I went over there and they told me the old man was pretty sick, then came back and told my wife, we should have gone back there that night and watched over him. It was just a little way from here. But instead we went to sleep. That's what brought the owl. (Is it always an owl?) No, sometimes it's a bad coyote, or one kind of blue bird. Some blue birds stay in a bunch in pinyon woods, but not this one. This one always hangs around homes, mostly the ashpile. (Note: Among the birds listed by Wyman as possible shapes for ghosts to assume are the owl, bluebird and pinyon jay. [Nav. Eschatology, p. 19]) {See Wyman, Hill and Ósanai 1942}

(Did you think about that on the night you didn't go over?) First we decided to go there, but we thought he wasn't as sick as they said. My wife said, "Let's wait and we'll go over there early." But we never thought about the talking owl. (Did anyone else hear it?) No, the others were all sleeping. I was the only one who heard it.

MORE WAGE WORK

I started to cut some props for mines around Gallup, seven feet and eight feet long. The people who wanted them would pay twenty-five cents for a seven-foot one and thirty-five cents for an eight-footer. There was a place there where they were needed. I cut a lot of props and was hauling them down, twenty-five props at a time. It took us two days to go down and come back with a team and wagon. One day when I was hauling them with my little dog along, about midmorning I saw a coyote coming behind us. The little dog tried to scare the coyote, but it came right behind the wagon, not paying any attention to the little dog. I got off and threw rocks at it and chased it away. A little way along I came to a home where somebody was living. By then it was sundown, so I camped with those people.

The people who were buying the props paid money right away as soon as they were unloaded. I bought some flour, coffee, and sugar with the money and brought them back to the wagon. I wasn't thinking about that coyote that followed me. When I came home with the wagon and told about the coyote, they said the coyote was after the dog. The coyotes will do that when they see a dog with you.

"ONE OF MY BABIES GOT SICK. . . ."

I had worked around home about twenty days when one of my babies got sick. He had a stomachache. After he had been sick four days I went to Kainti to get a singer. His name was Long Hair, and when I got there he was having a sing at his place with another singer. I told him I wanted him to sing over my baby, but he said he couldn't because he had a medicine man there with him and he wouldn't want to leave while he was there. I told him I'd give him five lambs if he'd go over. One of his daughters, Ted Sage's wife, told him he could go. She told her father he wasn't working or helping, just staying around.[100] So he said, "All right, somebody get me a horse, and I'll go." He gave me his medicine bag and told me to go ahead with the bag.[101] He said he would come just as soon as the horse got there.

He came and started singing right away after he got there. He sang just a little after dark, and he sang all night long. I had to sing. Next day after breakfast he told me to go out and get some plant medicine. He named them for me, all the roots and plants. I went around and collected all those little plants and brought the whole lot home. When I came back with them, he quit and went to sleep for a while.

When the medicine man woke up, he chopped the medicine in little pieces and soaked it. He dropped some on the baby's mouth and bathed him with it, and started singing again. He quit about noon and went to sleep again. In the afternoon he woke up and started singing. He quit for a little while at sundown, then started again, and I was helping the medicine man sing. We sang till daylight, and about that time we fell asleep. When breakfast was ready they woke us up and we all ate. George and Don were there then.

After breakfast the medicine man said we had been singing the Person-got-hurt Way. He thinks the baby didn't get hurt, perhaps it was something else. That was after he had sung two days and nights. He told me I must go get a man or woman who knew how to do hand-trembling.[102] One of Ned's boys came in and asked us to look for his horses and bring them over to their corral. I asked him to go down and get Roan Horse's wife who did hand-trembling. Ned's boy was looking at the sick baby and he asked, "What's the matter that the baby doesn't shut his eyes?" There were flies on its face, but it didn't shut its eyes. The baby's mother was sitting beside it, but she had gone to sleep. After she heard Ned's boy's question, she picked the baby up and it was dead already.

The medicine man picked up his medicine and went home. And the people who lived there, my wife and I, took everything out of the hogan and carried it over a little way to the south side. We moved everything out. She and I dug a hole and buried the baby a little way off from the hogan, and after that we burned the hogan. We lived there five days, then moved to another place, up to where we are now living. I had a boy first and the second one was a girl, this one that died. She was born about this time (April) and died in the fall.

This was just about twenty days after the coyote followed me. Some people said the coyote did that because I was going to lose the baby soon. That's what I thought, too. I didn't talk about it that way, but just figured it out. (Note: See Wyman, Hill and Ósanai in *Navajo Eschatology*)

MORE WOOD HAULING

What Ned's boy had really come for was to get me to go with him to cut some wood between here and Zuni. He said some white people were going to develop an oil well and they wanted a lot of wood hauled there. They said to pile the wood in what I think they called cords. They wanted a lot. I told Ned's boy I'd go there in six days.

When that time came I went over to Ned's, found my man there, and we started over to where the work was. When we got there some Navajos had already gotten together, more than eight men already there. We saw that the white people had the tools we were going to use already there. Some white people came over in a car from Gallup. They explained to the Navajos that they wanted some men to cut up wood so they could buy it by the cord at four dollars a cord. We didn't have to go far to cut the wood, there were lots of trees around there. Any kind of wood was all right—pinyon, cedar, or green cedar. We could use our own food and camp there. There was water just a little way off.

We started cutting after that. We went back to Gallup every night. I got a lot cut already in three days. Of the white men, one was boss and the others were working for him. They had tents and worked there every day. They had a big machine for digging. After another day's cutting, Ned's boy and I made ten cords. The boss came out again. We had the wood piled around in the woods. Everybody working on the wood could cut ten cords. Two of us, working together, had already done that. After ten cords we should quit. We made ten cords first, then the rest did the same. Next they told us to haul the wood over where it was needed.

GAMBLING

Next day we went home to get a wagon. Along the way lived a man named Curley. On one side of that hogan Old Man Vincent sat all by himself. Vincent had married some of the girls in that family, and he was sitting there all by himself because his mother-in-law was over in his house. He only had a little bucket of water, a sack of tobacco, and a box of matches beside him. We told him we were working over there, cutting wood and piling it, and were going for a wagon now. We stayed a long time till sundown, and were about ready to start off when Vincent said, "Why don't you stay here? We'll play cards now. I suppose you have some money if you've been working." Vincent was working, taking care of horses. We told him we didn't have money because we hadn't been paid yet. Ned's boy had fifty cents and I had nothing.

Vincent said, "You'd better pawn me that blanket for a dollar." He took a five-dollar bill out of his pocket but had nothing to change it. I pawned my blanket and we started to play. I got started for twenty-five cents, and Vincent beat me twice. Ned's boy had already lost his money and I had fifty cents left. Since we didn't have any change, we made change out of matches—four sticks for a dollar. I had fifty cents left in sticks, so I divided it with Ned's boy. We tried again and Ned's boy won the game, but I lost again. I got my quarter back from him and won that time. I borrowed two quarters. We kept playing that. Toward midnight Ned's boy won the five dollars. Vincent had another five dollars, and he lost that too. He got out ten dollars, and we won that before noon—twenty dollars altogether. We got pretty hungry and wanted to go, but Vincent said to stay and play some more. We were pretty hungry and went to Ned's home.

We looked for wagon horses around there, found them, and brought them home. Before we started off with the wagon, Ned said we must haul some water. We two didn't want to do that, and we said, "Get someone else to haul the water." We hadn't quite finished one cord, so we would finish that and come back again. On our way we came by Vincent again. He was asleep when we got there. We woke him up and he said, "Let's play some more." He got out ten dollars again, and we beat him that afternoon. He got another ten dollars and we won half of it. We wanted to quit then, and Vincent was going back to work. We told Vincent we'd go down where he was working and play cards there after two days. He couldn't change the ten-dollar bill, and we told him he could take care of the ten dollars till that day.

AND DRINKING

After he left, we started talking about going to Little Pine Springs where the Mexican had some whiskey. When we got there the Mexican was home. Ned's boy went in alone and asked for it. I was waiting for him outside. He got out a little bottle, about a hand-size, that was one dollar. Ned's boy came out and told me about it. I gave him three dollars and told him to buy three for me. He was going to buy three, too—that's six bottles. Then we went together to the store and bought some potatoes, coffee, sugar, asked for flour but they were out of it. We bought some bacon, too. There was another little store not very far away, and we went there next. As we started, we opened one bottle and before we got to the other store we had finished it. It was pretty strong. The second store had flour, so we bought flour, baking powder, and salt. Then we started off to where we were working.

We thought we would take a shortcut. We opened another bottle, drank it up in a few minutes, opened another. We had finished three bottles and we got pretty drunk. We sang as we went along. I remember we opened another bottle, making the fourth, and drank half of it, and after that we didn't remember anything. But we found ourselves next morning down where we were working. We woke up down there. We looked for our horses but couldn't find them or the saddles. I asked the other boys if they knew what we'd done with our horses, but they didn't. We trailed their tracks back. I don't know how far it was to where we found their tracks. They had gotten far away.

The things we had bought at the stores had all fallen, too. We were picking them up as we trailed the horses. The last thing we found was the flour, all spilled. The horse went under a tree, and the flour sack was all torn. One horse was carrying the saddle under his belly—Ned's boy's horse. We lost one saddle blanket, but we tracked it down. We thought that happened when the horse started rolling and the saddle slipped. We had had six little bottles when we started and now only one was left. It made us sick and we were vomiting.

We got back to Ned's house. We told the folks there that we wanted to eat a young goat, and they killed one for us. That's what I like! We ate the little goat up and we felt well again. Ned said that when we got sick on whiskey we should make soup and put lots of chili in it. We did that, too. We gave the one little bottle we had left to Ned and told him to drink it up. The old man did that and fell down right away. After that, Ned's wife told us they didn't want to have us drinking. We had better quit and not drink. She liked to have us doing that work but she didn't like the drinking.

THEN MORE WORK

We took the wagon to where we worked and hauled the wood to the place where the man wanted it. The man we were working for came again and measured out our piles. He said they were good measure and started to write a check for us. He said he'd have to look up his pen, he didn't have it with him. Then he said he'd write it out with a pencil, but maybe they wouldn't take it. We'd cut ten cords and got forty dollars each. We did that in only four days. The other people there got their pay, too—all the men that were cutting wood—and went home. The men that were working on the well continued to work.

When we got back we went to the Kainti store the same day to cash our checks. We gave him both checks, but he wouldn't cash them. Not far away they were making a brush hogan for a Squaw Dance. We went home and got there about sundown. Next morning we got our horses pretty early, before breakfast, thinking we would go over to Tselizhine, where we knew there was a store just on this side. When we got there, the store was closed. The man opened the store for us, and we gave him our checks but he didn't want to take them. We went on to Zuni and came to the store there. It was closed, too, and they told us it was Sunday. We went around to the storekeeper's house. I saw his wife first and she told us he was in the back. We went around and found him and showed him the checks. He saw the checks were all right, but he didn't have any cash. We could trade them out if we wanted to. We said we needed the money. The trader asked why we didn't take them to the Tselizhine store, and we told him we had just been there and the man wouldn't take the checks. He said he would write something on the checks, so he did and gave them back to us. He told us he thought they'd take them now.

We went back to that store again, got into the store, and showed him the checks again. He took them that time and gave us the money—forty dollars each. We traded some of it there for some clothes, hats, ropes. We put on our clothes outside there and started off with good clothes. We had bought something to eat there, so we ate it {and} then started home. About halfway we turned off to the right, to where Vincent was going to wait for us. When we got there we didn't see anybody, the door was closed. There were some houses there that belonged to the Zuni trader. Vincent took care of them and worked there. We tracked him off toward the east.

OFF TO A CEREMONY

After about two or three miles we found a sheep camp with a tent and burros and one man. We asked if he had seen Vincent. He said he hadn't, but he heard there was a sing, out east not very far, at Sage's home. They were singing the Apache Wind Way and Big Fred was singing. We all thought that would be where Vincent was. The sheepherder asked about the Squaw Dance below Kainti, how long before they would have it. We told him they were just working on the brush hogan. We all ate there.

We went on to the sing. We knew the place where the herder had told us the sing was. After we got there, there was nobody around. We looked all around and couldn't find anyone. We stopped at a place right on the road, got off the horses, took off their bridles. The grass was knee-high or higher. We spread a blanket there and started playing cards. After a little while we heard somebody coming down the road. There were some trees there, and we saw someone coming on horseback down the road from the east, toward us. There was a tree right in the way a little distance from us, and the grass was pretty high. We got behind that tree, dropped down, and lay there. The man didn't see us but the horse did. It scared him. He turned right around, and the old gray-haired man fell off the horse. He'd been sitting on a goatskin, and that fell right on top of him. He was riding a black horse with a silver bridle. He lay there for a while, then got up as if he was hurt pretty bad. He said, "Hah, hah, hah," then he started cussing. While he was getting up we ran to the other side of the hill.

We saw two other people coming along on horseback. The man who fell went on. The two said they were going to the sing where Big Fred was singing. They said they knew the way. We went over to the sing with them. When we went inside the hogan, Big Fred was there and Old Man Sage and the old man who fell off the horse. We saw him sitting there with some blood coming out above his right eye. He was telling about how he fell off the horse. He said, "I was coming over here and the horse got scared of something, turned right back, and I fell off. I got hurt above the eye. I don't know what scared him that way." His son, Mr. Mustache, had just gotten there, and after the old man finished talking Mr. Mustache told him, "I know that horse you were riding. He is pretty slow, and lots of times I've seen you whipping him in the head. So when you're riding, whenever you move as if you would whip him, it scares the horse. I think you probably scared the horse that way yourself." Tom said, "These two people were there when you came along." The old man, Benito, said he saw two horses but he didn't see the men. We were there all afternoon till sundown. Benito was telling stories. He was wearing a lot of beads. About sundown they fed the people.

After dark, about eight or nine o'clock, the medicine man said, "Let's get ready and start singing." He was using the cactus, the kind you saw when Bill's brother was having a sing here. We got ready and the patient came in, and a lot of people did too. Big Fred started singing and everybody else sang and helped him. We were singing till daylight. After we got through, Big Fred thanked all the people who helped him sing that night. I knew some of those songs myself and I helped a whole lot there. (Who was the patient?) One of Sage's stepsons, I don't remember his name. He died a long time ago. (What was wrong?) Something in his chest, he was breathing pretty fast.

After everybody went home, Vincent was still there. He owed me fifteen dollars, but he said he didn't have the money there to pay me, he had it over where he worked. He said, "I'll go ahead, and you can come by and I'll give you the money." He went off and we got our horses up and followed Vincent's track. Near the place where he worked there are some hills to walk down. Vincent was walking down the hill without stopping, and we saw the trace of how he made his pee go from side to side as he walked. We went on a way and heard a big bell. When we caught up with the bell, Vincent was carrying it. He said he found it back there somewhere. We came back together where he was working. When we got there, Vincent told me he wanted to play cards with us again. We said we wanted to go home, and he asked if we had change for ten dollars. "Yes, we have some change." We got our money and started home.

We went to Kainti first, and from there over to where they had been making the brush hogan for the Squaw Dance. We learned the Squaw Dance would start in three days. The patient said he wanted some money from us two boys and he needed a whole lot of help. He was telling some other boys, too, that they would help him a whole lot by giving him some money. After he said that, we gave a dollar each, two dollars altogether. Ned's boy went home from there, and I went to where my wife was.

Next day I hauled wood and water, and the day after that my wife and I took the wagon and hauled six sheep down west to a store that used to be at Wide Arroyo. We'd heard the man was buying sheep, paying seven dollars cash for a ewe and lamb. We got there, sold our sheep, and got the money. My wife got her silver belt out of pawn, and we bought flour, sugar, coffee, watermelon, and calico. We started back and got home the same day.

ANOTHER CEREMONY

The day the Squaw Dance started, Stanley and I went over there together. Some people were there already. Inside the brush hogan we saw a big fat man. He was the singer, but I had never seen him before. Such a big man and such a big nose! They told me his name was Peso. After dark they brought a lot of food and fed all the people there. Then the medicine man said they should fix up the jar for a drum. They put buckskin over the jar and tied it up and made a little stick to use on it. When it was all finished, the singer said to put the jar outside. We took it out and found more people outside. The medicine man came out with the rest and sang four songs for the people. He said this was the way he started it, he had been doing it that way for a little while. We were singing all that night long, Peso sang the whole night for the people. When they quit singing at daylight, everybody went to sleep.

{In the morning} after everybody had eaten, the singer sent a man out to get a cedar stick about two feet long. Coho went after it and brought it in. He wrapped it up in a white cloth, I think out where he cut it. They dressed the stick with some grass, three kinds of plants, and turkey feathers. I don't know how much else they used. I was in there a little while, but then I went out and didn't see the rest of it. Some three deer hooves go on the stick, and at the end they put a lot of yarn of different colors—blue, yellow, green. Somebody was saddling the patient's horse. When the stick was dressed, they hollered for the patient's horse. They brought up the horse, and the patient himself took the stick and got on the horse. He ran his horse away from the hogan and all the people followed him.

We went way to the other side of Manuelito, brought the stick down there. They were supposed to give the stick to a man called Slim. They ran their horses right up to his hogan, next to the door. The man carrying the stick got off his horse, went inside, and handed it to Slim. After that we went to another place a little way off and took the saddles off the sweating horses. They had a kitchen on one side and they brought food up to us—lots of bread, coffee, naneskadi, boiled meat, roast meat.[103] People gathered in a bunch after dark and sang there for a little while, Kainti people on one side and the other people on the other side. After we sang for a little while, we built a big fire and started dancing with the girls. We were dancing for two hours, then quit and sang again. We sang till daylight. Kainti won in the singing. Our side wasn't drinking but the other side was, that's why we won.

They brought food and we ate breakfast. Then we got together again and started singing. We walked over to the hogan, singing as we went, till we got to the door. Then they started throwing out tobacco, candy, cookies, apples, Cracker Jacks, soda pop. A man was using a drum and they lighted a cigarette and put it in his mouth, took the drum, and put it on one side. The people outside went back to where they had camped.

Everybody saddled up his horse and started back toward Kainti, going pretty fast. Another man and I were coming together and our horses got played out down by the little store at Wide Arroyo. We went on pretty slowly from there to Kainti. We got back to the Squaw Dance place just a little before noon. I went home from there and went to sleep just after I got there. I was pretty sleepy then, after two nights without sleep. I didn't get up until about this time (5:45 P.M.). When I woke up I got my horses and harnessed them, and my wife and I took the wagon to go where the dance would be that night. We killed a sheep and put it on the wagon. We went to the Kainti store first and bought some food to take to the dance. We gave the meat and food to the patient.

We ate there, then went over to where the dance would be that night. Lots of people passed us on horseback and I passed some wagons. We got there about sundown. The people from the other side (Slim's outfit) came to camp there. When we got there, the people were all eating.

After dark they started singing. I went over and sang there, too, for two hours. We built up a lot of fire and started the dancing. There were a lot of people there and about fifty girls dancing. We must have danced about two hours. Then we stopped that and started singing. While we were dancing, all the women whose daughters were dancing lined up on one side. The girls who danced with the boys got paid every little while, maybe a half-hour's dance, ten or fifteen cents for that much. They would pass their money right over to their mothers. The women were watching to see that none of the boys got away without paying. If the boy didn't want to pay, the girl would take his hat and let him pay to get the hat back. After they quit dancing I was pretty tired, so I hooked up my team and went home. We went to sleep there.

Everybody moved early in the morning to the place where the main dance would be. We didn't go over there until noon, when we went in the same wagon. About noon they were blackening the patient. While that was going on, a lot of people got together and made a brush hogan. I don't know why they do that. They used to do it, but not much anymore. There was nothing to look at or watch, just singing to hear. After that they started to dance in a circle, holding each other's hands. There were little girls inside the circle. They danced like that till sundown. After that we went home, got too tired of it. I didn't see the last night, wasn't there. We came back home and went to sleep.

Next morning, I hooked up the team and took the wagon over to cut my oats and haul them over where I am living now. We used to have one big hogan there. I raised a lot of oats that year and I must have hauled ten big wagonloads. I worked around home after the hauling, and herded sheep.

And Another Ceremony

I heard there was another sing going on at Ned's place and {that} Ned was the patient. It was already under way, a five-night sing. When I got over there it had already passed the first two nights. The singer was Slim and this was Holy Way. (Were all Ned's relatives there?) There were two from Lupton, Jim, Ned's sister from Lupton, Jim's mother—Raymond was there, too, but he was only a little boy. There were a lot of people from around there. I was there till the sing was over three days later. Sandpainting was going on in the daytime. In the evenings they used the basket drum for a little while, with the songs that go with it—that was at night; most of the time I was outside. Three men started to play cards every night. They had their money stacked up a foot high and they played till daylight every night. Robert was playing, too, and he lost his horse in the game.

In the daytime, I was helping in the kitchen, hauling water and wood, and taking food to the people, bringing the dishes back. Next morning the singer lost his horse, which we then tracked all day long, off in the direction where he lived. We came back without it. Way after dark they put the basket down and used it for a drum with the singing. They didn't play cards that night—everybody was singing and helping all night long. We got through singing in the morning. (What was wrong with Ned?) He had learned the songs, that's why he had the sing. He wasn't sick. (Was Slim his teacher?) Yes. A lot of people say that after you learn the songs, the man who taught you has to sing over you before you can start singing for other people. That's what they were doing.[104]

After the singing was over, Ned told us to track up the singer's horse again. There was another man there, who came from the same direction, whose horse was also gone, but he had an extra horse to ride back. He was one of the gamblers. Ned lent the singer a horse and told us boys we should be looking for those horses, and if we found them, take them to Lupton where the man would be waiting. The medicine man left and so did the gambler, and we boys started off too. We went to where we had left the track last and started trailing him from there. We went a mile or two and found another track joining this one, so we followed the two from there. We came to the rim of a hill with a circle of rock all around it. The two horses were at the edge of the rim. I saddled the medicine man's horse and turned my horse loose. Then I slipped a rope on the other horse's neck and went on with them to Lupton. When we got there Peso was there, but the singer had gone on to his home the other side of Lupton.

On the other side, a little way from the store, there were a lot of camps and people who must have been working on some kind of job. We waited there all afternoon, then gave the man's horse back. At sundown we went over where all the people were. A lot of people were gambling, and we were just watching that night. I stayed overnight there. We went on to the medicine man's home the next morning, riding just two horses.

While we were riding, we saw a squirrel sitting on top of a cedar tree right in front of us. He was a long way off, maybe three hundred yards. I had a .22 rifle with me. I said, "Let's bet on that squirrel. I want to shoot him off with a .22 rifle." The other boy asked, "How much do you want to bet?" "One dollar," I said. I got off the horse and shot at the squirrel, and it jumped up and fell down. I almost missed it. I hit him right in the back of the neck. He was lying under the tree with his mouth open when I got there. "You owe me a dollar," I said, "That will be my extra dollar for whiskey!"

We got to the medicine man's home just before noon. He was there and said he got home yesterday, but went on to another place last night to sing over a girl at her first bleeding, and got back again just a little while ago. I saw some cakes there and ate a lot. Ned's horse, that the medicine man rode home, was there. While we were eating, there had been some boys chasing cattle outside before we went into the hogan, and we heard one shot. After that I saddled Ned's horse and started toward home.

A little way off, three girls and three boys were skinning the cow that was shot. It was a big steer. They took the hide off, cut off the head, and opened the front side. They told me to put a rope around the throat and pull it out all the way, the whole insides, guts and all. My friend and I started pulling on the rope, a little at a time. The others were working on the cow's insides, and they got about to the middle of the belly. We got stuck there, something was too tight. We gave it another good pull. Just the lungs and heart broke off and we jerked them out. We fell back down a slope, me in front and the other boy behind. The lungs and heart went through between my legs, over my head, and on to my friend. When we got up we were all bloody! Those people just laughed about it. They took the rest of the insides out, sawed the beef in two, and cut it in four pieces. They were going to haul it to St. Michaels. We went over to a spring, washed our shirts and pants. After that, they fed us there and we started home.

We came by Manuelito, right straight through to Kainti, and from there to Ned's place. Ned asked us if we found the horses. We told him yes, and we'd taken them back to the two men. We gave him the whole story about how we got bloody at the butchering. My wife asked me what made me stay so long, so I told her my story about where I'd been and what I'd done.

Then I helped herding at my own home. After I'd herded a few days there, I went over to Ned's home. I had heard that the boy who had been with me was going over to work on the Zuni Mountains. When I got there, the boy was there. He wanted to go that day, and I decided to go with him. We got up a pinto horse, got our blankets and some food, and got on the horse bareback with our load. We rode off toward the east and went by Tom's home, then Mack's.

I had a .22 and the other boy had a six-shooter. We went on straight east. There is a sawmill up there now, and we heard there was a Squaw Dance going on near that place. We saw the brush hogans that they use. When we got pretty close, we started running our horse up to the brush hogan and went around the hogan, shooting the way they do in the Squaw Dance. We were doing it just for fun. We laughed about it when we went on our way. When we got right under the mountain, we got off the horse and turned it loose, let it go home. A little way from there we found a spring and got a drink of water and started climbing the mountain. There was only a train there at that time, no wagon or automobile road.

When we got right up to the top, we sat down there and looked back this way. We could see a long way from there, but it was so high up we couldn't recognize anything. We ate lunch there and went on. We got down to Murray late in the evening. There was a big sawmill and a lot of lumber around it. A lot of Navajos were camping there, people from the other side of Ft. Wingate and from Gallup. The people said they were still needing some men, and said they got three dollars a day and were paid every Saturday afternoon. We just watched people gambling there that night.

On the Railroad

Next morning we went to the big store there. All those who were working gathered there, and the big boss and the foreman came. We asked them for a job. There was a train going to where they worked—it hauled the men over there every morning and back every evening. The boss told us we could go with the bunch. We got on and went a long way. You know the gap on top of the mountains that you can see from here? The workplace was under the mountain on the south side, below that gap. They were putting a railroad through the mountain on the other side. We got off at a place where they were leveling the ground. A tractor did the leveling. They had built it up with dirt and built a lot of little ditches. We lined up on the place they were leveling.

Behind that place were some men who were doing the leveling, getting it just as smooth as they could. Back of them more men were laying ties, and behind them others were putting rails on the ties. Two workers worked together. We did that till noon, then ate lunch, and after lunch went on with it. After we put two rails together, other men screwed them together, and still others straightened the rails up. Then some more did the tamping with a shovel handle, and back of them came a freight car.

There were about a hundred men working, and they must have done about one mile a day. We quit at four-thirty and got back to Murray at five o'clock. Quitting time was at five. Each of us got a number as we went by to work. The number was on small buttons that were passed out to the people. We wore them on our shoulders. A clerk from Murray came out every day to keep track of the time of the people who worked there. From Murray, he said, he rode "a little colt" to the place where we were working. What he meant is a small machine that runs on the rails, quite fast.

Some white people were sawing logs; a lot of logs and big trees had been cut down there. There were a lot of horses in big teams working on the logs. I don't know what it would be called, but they had a thing to haul the logs that had two big wheels. We kept working there, going down every day and coming back. We worked there a week and got paid on Saturday, eighteen dollars. We came to the office and showed our buttons to the clerk. They had told us not to lose that button because if we lost it we couldn't get paid.

On payday a lot of Navajos came there, bringing meat to sell to the workers, both sheep and goat.[105] Saturday night we started to gamble with the people who worked there all the time. We were just watching, not gambling with them. Mexicans and Navajos were gambling together there.

ANOTHER SHALAKO AT ZUNI

Ned's boy worked only one month and then went home. I went on working pretty nearly two months, then came home with a little money I earned down there. I came back the first of December.

The day after I got home they told me that the Zuni dance would be six days from that day. I stayed there, working around home. (What did you do with the money?) I gave sixty dollars to my wife and kept forty. I stayed around until the six days were up. My wife and I went to the dance. We went one day ahead of time and stopped to see a Zuni friend there. We stayed with him a little while. He would feed our horses and us without charging us anything. After dark I went to the middle of the village. (How did you get to know the Zuni?) The old man who died, Old Paul, had Zuni friends before we did. After the old people died, my wife's mother began to be friends with the Zunis, and then my wife was pretty well known to them. After my wife and I got married, we made friends with Zunis.

After dark one of the Zunis said they were playing cards one place and he wanted to go over. He asked me if I wanted to go along to see the gambling. I did, so I followed him. When we got there, a lot of Navajos were gambling with the Zunis. They had a lot of money. They put up two cards at a time and guessed which one would come first, betting on it. Some people were pretty good at guessing that. Every time one of them was guessing, I helped bet on it. Every time he beat, then I got my money the same as the guesser. I was doing that all night long till daylight. I won twelve dollars. I went back to where my wife was and went to sleep there. I didn't get any breakfast till toward noon. I got up, washed, and ate. Then I watered and fed my horses. After lunch I went to see what was going on around the village. I saw people coming in as fast as they could, from Morton, Dale, Gallup, Manuelito, Hub. The wind was blowing pretty hard.

Toward evening it started snowing, and it snowed the rest of the day and all night. We didn't go around to the dance, just stayed with our friends. A lot of the people saw the dance, but a lot didn't go out. Next morning we bought Zuni bread and some corn from the Zunis and left. It was still snowing, getting deep. Coming along the road, I saw some tracks ahead of me. My horses weren't very big, just two little ponies and a small wagon. I'd passed some wagons already and there was only one ahead of me, but halfway between Zuni and Kainti the front wagon had built a fire and was having some lunch. They were some of my friends who lived near us. They had two little mules. We stopped with them and fed our horses. After we ate, another man, Howard, went by. I came along behind him. Pretty soon I caught up with him and passed him. We came by the place where you went the other night and took the road there to Kainti. When we got to Kainti my hands and feet were awfully cold. The storekeeper built up a good fire, and we warmed ourselves and fed the horses again. We ate supper there. Just as it was getting dark, we moved on. We had the wagon cover on the wagon, and we were all dry inside though the snow was still falling. We got back home way after dark and unharnessed the team.

Next morning there was a lot of snow. The horses were outside, and I fed them. These were the ones I used going to Zuni. After I had breakfast and fed and watered the horses, I harnessed them and put them on the wagon and hauled wood that day, pretty nearly all day. It cleared up that evening. Then I herded sheep for a few days while the snow was on the ground. As the snow melted away, I heard about a wedding at Gambler's place, and I wanted to go to it. Big Hail's son, Dumb Boy, was going to marry one of Gambler's girls. They were going to have it in the canyon west of where Gambler lives now.

A TRADITIONAL WEDDING

I went over there and found people there already. Gambler was there and Big Hail, Dumb Boy, and Harvey; also Short Hair and his wife, Wide Man, and all Gambler's folks. Dumb Boy was sitting way west of the fire, inside the hogan. The kitchen was on the south side. The people were talking about the snow and how they had been to the Zuni dance. I wasn't listening very closely until after dark, about nine o'clock.

Then a man came in, in front of the girl. He carried a little jug with water and a dipper. The girl was carrying mush in a basket. They set it over on the west side near Dumb Boy, and the girl sat on the south side of Dumb Boy. Right away they brought a lot of food inside and put it along the south and north side of the fire. The girl poured some water into the dipper and poured it onto Dumb Boy's hands. After he washed his hands he poured water on the girl's hands, and she washed them. The man who had come in front of the girl took out the corn pollen and made a cross in the mush in the basket, first from east to west, then south to north. Dumb Boy took up some mush on the east side first, then the other three directions, and the girl did the same thing. Then they both ate the mush together, and all the other people started eating. They passed the basket over to the people and everybody got plenty to eat.

After they ate, Big Hail started to talk. He said he couldn't make a very long talk to Dumb Boy and the girl because the boy is deaf and can't hear. But he said, "While he was with me I did a lot of signing to make him understand what he has to do for the people here." He said to the girl, "Now that you are getting married, you must take good care of this boy and do the best you can to make him understand you. I'm sure he will do what you want if he understands. When he was with me he was always a good worker, with sheep and farming, and he likes to work. You must take care of your home while he is doing outside work. You can do your own work at home, and as for us, we can be helping each other. When we start farming, plowing, we can exchange work with our teams; if we work alone we can't do much, can't have much food. The crop we raise and store away in the fall is all used up soon. So we should help each other."

He told Gambler that he should take care of this boy. He could work for Gambler, and Gambler could teach him some things. He already knew lots of things, but there was lots he didn't know yet. He said, "Every boy and girl of this age do like this. Our old people, grandfathers and grandmothers, used to do the same, and so did I. That's the reason we're having this wedding today." But Hail went on, "We always like to have a wedding for our children, that's the way I believe. I like it this way. In the other way, boys and girls get married without a ceremonial basket, mush, or pollen. A lot of people do without it. The way I look at it, I don't think it's very good that way."

The reason I like this way is that I like to hear some good talk to my children before I let them get married. The talk and the ceremonial are what interests me," he said.

Gambler said he thanked Big Hail for what he said, and besides, he expected to have a good helper in Dumb Boy. While he was doing all the work by himself, he said, it was hard for him to do everything. He had just started many things, fencing, cutting trees for hogan poles, clearing more ground, hauling water and wood, and still more. "Of course we can't finish them all in one day," he said, "and first we'll try to learn to understand each other somehow so we can go ahead with our work easily. I hope he and I will get along, and the same way with all the people."

That was all the talk, then we all went to sleep there. Some people who came went home the same night, but all Dumb Boy's folks stayed overnight. Next morning they fed all the people who were there, and after that I walked back home. Some others stayed longer, especially Dumb Boy's father and relatives. When I got home my folks were asking me what I saw there and what the people did. I told them everything just as I have told you. Then I started herding. I didn't herd all the time; part of the time I worked around the home all through that winter.

(Why did they have the wedding?) I think it's just like other people, they always get married so they can have some children. I didn't hear anybody on either side say just why they got married. (What do you think?) It is so they can get together and work for each other and live together—more I don't know. (Why would the girl marry a man who couldn't speak?) I don't know whether he wanted that girl himself, and asked for her, or not. Dumb Boy's father was the one who got the two together, so it's more likely that the old man wanted that girl for his boy. I heard that Dumb Boy's father went to Gambler and asked for that girl.

AGNES THE TERRIBLE

Many days after that I went over to Agnes's home. She was living about a half a mile east. When I got there, she said I could stay there that night. She told me that night that she had moved her home down here from near the railroad. She got mad at her husband up there and moved back down here. She said she had some cattle by the railroad, and she wanted me to go get the cattle and bring them down here. I told her I didn't have any horse to ride. She said there was man named Long Knife who had some horses he wanted to corral. The horses were running around here, and I could ride one of them.

Next morning I started hunting up those horses and found them on the north side. They were five saddle horses that were running together. She had told me that they were on the north side and that there was a corral there, so I must put the horses in that corral. She said she would be down at the corral. I found them and corralled them and she got there after they were in the corral. I tried one but it was too wild, tried the others and they were all pretty wild. She told me I was afraid of the horses and didn't want to ride them. She had her horse that she had gotten from her father, and was all ready to go when she reached the corral. We started off to my home so I could use my own horse, and went on from there about noon.

The man that Agnes was mad at had cattle and she didn't have any.[106] It took us all afternoon to go over there. When we got close we saw some cattle, and those were the ones we were after. But she said we didn't want anybody to see us drive the cattle away. She said she had a Mexican friend over there and we would go there first. She said, "Let's go down there. We can stay there till after dark, then come back for the cattle." So we went over to the Mexican home, and they gave us something to eat for supper. She said she was living there last summer. "I used to be pretty good friends with the Mexicans around here. They'll give me a bottle of whiskey without me paying for it." She went out after dark, looking for whiskey. She was gone for a while, then came back. It was dark then and she said, "Let's go." We came back across the big wash.

After we got across she said she had some whiskey, and she opened the bottle and gave me some, saying, "Drink a little, not much." She said, "When we see the cows again, we want to take the big steer and another one and drive them toward Gallup to the place called Little Arroyo, we will sell them there." We moved on and saw the cows. It was pretty dark and we couldn't see much. First we cut {separated out} two and started driving them away. After a little way the steers didn't want to go in that direction and ran off toward the others. We tried to drive them away, but we couldn't make them go. We tried taking more than two, but they didn't like that either, so we didn't bother anymore. We just unsaddled our horses and stayed there all night, watching for daylight.

We'd been chasing cows for a long time that night, and next morning we tried our best to make the steers go but couldn't do it. I was tired and didn't want to chase cows for another day. I wanted to go home. Agnes and I and all her folks are the same clan, and she called me "little brother."[107] About that time, she said that her husband and his mother were living not very far away, off in that direction. She wanted me to go over there and, if the man was by himself, to tell him she was nearby and he should come right over. She wanted to talk to him about the cattle. I mustn't let anybody else hear me tell him this. I said all right, I'd go over there. She said she would wait there till I got back.

I went in the direction she said, and in about two miles I saw the hogan up on a hill with the hill behind it. I changed my mind about going to that home. After chasing the cows, I didn't want to go over there. I just wanted to go back home without telling that man what she said, so I just went by that hogan and came on home. My wife asked me, "Where is your sister?" Before we started Agnes had said that she owned the cattle, and after we got down there she said they weren't hers. That's why I didn't like it and came home. I told my wife that Anges was down there, and how we got down there and what we did; how I was supposed to tell her husband to come over to where she was, but {that I had} just passed by the hogan and came home. I said I hadn't sent anyone over to her, waiting there.

One day later that woman came back, right near my home. We could see her from the hogan. I don't know what she did after I left or where she stayed that night. After that, whenever I saw her she wouldn't talk to me, she was mad at me. (What was she going to give you for helping?) When we sold the cow she would give me five dollars, she said.

Lucky Works at Home, and then Goes Logging

I stayed right at home another two or three years. I didn't go away for work, just worked at home. After three years, four of us got together and went to get a job at Flagstaff—I, Bert, Chuck, and Ralph. We walked from here to Lupton and took a train to Flagstaff. We paid three dollars and something. When we got there we got off the train and waited inside the depot. A white man came in, pulled out his pocketbook, and gave some money to the agent. I think he was getting small change. He counted it up by putting some in one place, some in another. He counted up one pile and put it in his pocketbook. It looked as if he was in a hurry, and he walked off without paying attention to the other pile. Nobody noticed this for quite a while, so I walked over and picked up the money. It was $3.40, I think, and he never came back for it. We left the depot and went to a place to camp, where we stayed overnight.

A man in the station told me the train would stop right there and start out south in the morning. The work was about twenty miles south. We could catch that train and go there if we wanted jobs. So we came back in the morning and the train arrived. We had food with us and small dishes that each one could eat out of. We rode a long way until we came to a big lake. There were some horses on the edge of the water, and south of the lake we found a camp. We got off and saw a freight car there. They told us a man living in the freight car was in charge of the work. There was another car beyond the man's, and there was a store in it. Some Navajos were camping around there. We could see some women folks in the camp, but nobody in the freight car. We were told that the men were all working.

The boss came back at noon. We told him we were looking for a job and he said he couldn't put us to work today, but he said, "I'll put you to work tomorrow, starting tomorrow morning. I'll write your names down and get your names and numbers." We saw some men working a little way from there. A lot of pines had been cut down. They hauled the logs away, and the branches that were left they chopped up into little pieces and piled {them} up about eight feet high.

In the evening we were called to the office, and the man

wrote our names down and gave us passes, little buttons with numbers on them, and some papers about two inches by two inches. One was worth two or three dollars, and it was a little book with sheets marked twenty-five cents, ten cents, so we could buy groceries with them at the store. Next morning we all went to work with the people. Each man was given a double-bitted ax and a saw. We worked on chopping up the branches and piling them up. The one white foreman spoke a little Navajo. He said before he came to this job he was over at Tselizhine as foreman while they were building the dam.

We worked a week there, and on Sunday we built a sweathouse and took a bath. There were a lot of cottonwood trees by the river. We worked another week, and on Saturday we got a paycheck. We took the checks to the store, and the man cashed them and gave us the money left over after we'd bought our supplies. That night some people started to play cards, gambling. A Navajo came to our camp and said two women had been brought from Flagstaff. They were over the hill, and anyone who wanted a woman could go over there. After they heard that, they kept going over. One man said he was over there, a little while ago. He said there were two tents and a lot of Mexicans, Navajos, and whites. The women charged two dollars from each man. They were Mexicans. We didn't go over. They kept playing cards all night. In the morning after daylight, at sunup, they were saying that the women were still there.

Next morning was Sunday. There was a great big mountain on one side, and Ralph and I started over there. First we went to the top of the hill to see if we could get to the mountain. We looked back toward home to see if we could see any of our mountains from there. We walked down a hill and over toward the mountain and started to climb it. It took pretty nearly all morning to get to the top. It was quite wide on top, and I saw some sheepherders there. I saw a man driving burros. We met him and spoke to him, but we couldn't understand what he said.

We went on again, walking around on the top of the mountain. In a little while we met a man with big long whiskers. Then we saw two men coming toward where we were walking. They had a little dog with them, coming pretty fast. We got behind trees and ran quite a way to hide. The men were looking around, making circles, for quite a while. At last they came pretty close to us but didn't see us. We were afraid the dog might smell us. We went on down the mountain and walked back. (Why did you run from the men?) We were scared they might kill us. There were a lot of rocks, and while the men were close to us, we saw they had guns on the side of their horses and other guns that they wore on their hips. We began to think the two men would do something to us. They were looking all around where we were. We started running and got down off the mountain and walked back to camp.

When we got back we remembered something—the people at camp had said there was a woman right near the big lake who was selling whiskey. She was all alone there. We decided to go over there and started off. We came to a big house where we saw a Navajo boy. He wasn't very near the house, sitting on a rock to one side. He had been carrying water around to the people who were working. That was his only job. He had a little hump on his back. We asked him what he was doing there. He said he was just sitting down. There was a big lake there, maybe three miles across, where a lot of people fished in the summer. While we were talking to the boy a big door opened and a woman stepped out and started to talk to us. We didn't answer her.

The woman came over to us. Ralph understood a little English, and he said that she asked if we wanted any whiskey. She drew her finger across the inside of her hand. Ralph said she had some whiskey at fifty cents for a little bottle. We told her that we each wanted a little bottle. The woman went back and brought out a paper bag with three little bottles in it. We paid fifty cents each, drank it right there, and started back to camp.

Walking along there, we found two tents and stopped there. There were three Mexicans inside, gambling. They wanted us to start playing with them. While we were talking, a woman came in and got hold of Ralph and wanted to take him to the other tent. Ralph was just laughing about it. He said, "This woman wants to take me inside her tent to have me give her two dollars." He said, "If I did that it would cost too much to have a Squaw Dance if I get sick from it. It takes lots of money to have a Squaw Dance, so I don't want to go with her." She came over to me and said, "Come on, you!" and took hold of my wrist. I got scared of her and began to shake and said, No!"

> Near the camp where they were working, Lucky and Ralph found some Mexicans gambling and with them a woman. Just why Lucky was so much afraid to have sexual relations with this woman is not entirely clear. He may have feared disease; or perhaps it was the fact that she was not a Navaho woman which bothered him. At any rate, he was very much disturbed (Social Relations 49).
>
> His reluctance to have sexual relations with the Mexican woman may have been from a fear of disease (LS 424). Ralph had refused to go with her on these grounds (LS 423). When Lucky was asked about his fear, he replied that he was "scared between the legs" (Summary of Survival Data 6).

Then she tried to pull the boy who was with us. He said no, but we two pushed him and told him to go with her. He stayed in there a long while, and when he came out all the others laughed about it. I asked the boy how he liked it and he just laughed about it. Ralph looked at his face and told him it looked as if he had cried in there. The woman came over again and tried to get one of the men. Ralph and I said no, and the last time he told her they wanted to wait a while and eat first, so they would be strong when they came back. When he told her that, she went away. We stayed a while and then went back to camp.

After we got to camp and ate some food, some of the workers were coming back from a sweathouse. There were several sweathouses there. After we ate we went to take a sweatbath. We came out and went in three times. Then we came back to camp and washed our clothes and socks.

Gambling was going on one place there. There were four Navajos, and I knew one of them called Salazar, a Mexican name. Another one was called Dark Man and came from Three Pines, between Gallup and Shiprock. Another man from this side of Lupton was called Dave Rope, and the last one was Seth. Those four gambled all the time and had a lot of money there— a pile of money and a lot of checks. After dark a lot of the men who worked there got drunk and were walking back and forth.

I began to look for Bert. I went a few places and also down where they were gambling. I found Bert there, playing cards. There had been four playing, {but} two had left and Bert and Lefthand joined the game. Bert said he had lost ten dollars, so a little after I got there he left. The one called Dave Rope had the most money, with a big pile of money under him. Each man got ten cards to start with, and each bet once for three dollars or five dollars.

After Bert left I took his place. I was paid twenty-four dollars, but in a few minutes I lost fifteen dollars, and in a little while I lost all the money I had. Lefthand, who was playing, asked me if I wanted to borrow ten dollars from him till next payday. He gave me ten dollars right away. I lost five dollars again and had five dollars left. I had a card there that I played right and I won that game, twenty dollars. The four of us played together all night. I won a game once in a while. I did very well and won all the money. I had a big pile of all the money from the rest of them. Near daylight Lefthand said he had no more money, he'd lost fifty dollars. He was there when I first came and had been there quite a while. I gave him back his ten dollars, and he played it and lost it. After that he used some checks. For the other two, I gave some of their money back, and I loaned Lefthand money until he owed {me} about twenty dollars. About daylight I quit and still had some money. When I got back to camp I gave back to Bert, my brother, what he had lost. I counted seventy dollars left. (Was he your real brother?) Our mothers were full sisters.

We ate breakfast and went to work. At noon we ate lunch. I ate fast and went to sleep. They woke me up for work at one o'clock. We worked there until we had been there one month. The boys played some other kinds of games. Some played ball, and on Sundays the white people played baseball right near the lake. The Navajo men sang Squaw Dance songs at night. Gambling was going on, but I never went there again.

Three of us started home—Chuck, Ralph, and I. We took the train to Flagstaff in the afternoon. We ran around the streets there. There were a lot of houses spread far apart up on a hill north of the railroad. I had about ninety dollars to go home with. I bought a blanket in Flagstaff that cost fourteen dollars, and two bracelets, one for nine dollars and one for seven. We came back to the depot and waited for the train there. We bought tickets {and} got on the train when it came toward sundown. It stopped at Winslow and Holbrook. When it got there it was about nine o'clock, and we got some supper. We got off the train at Lupton.

We started walking south. There is one big mountain and we made a long walk up to the top of the mountain. It was getting pretty bright, almost daylight, and we walked toward home. At a place called Badger Scratch we ate when we came to some water. We came along to that place west of here where you turned around on your walk to come back. There is a place there where you can see both toward Kainti and Manuelito. The men with me walked toward Kainti, and I started this way. Ralph said, "Wait, don't go yet." He wanted to borrow twenty dollars from me. He said he had an account at some store and had only forty dollars with him. He needed another twenty dollars to cover the whole amount. He said, "If you will come to my place tomorrow, I'll give you ten head of good goats, the best ones I have. That will be for the twenty dollars." I said, "All right." I like goats; I want to eat the young ones all the time. I had a little load to carry—not a very good load, an old blanket, old sheepskin, little bundles of coffee and flour.

(Why did you quit the job?) I should have stayed longer, but Ralph told me I should never play any more with these men I won the money from. He said Dave Rope might beat me badly. But I never went back to play any more. One day I was talking to Dave Rope and I saw he had some cigarettes in his pocket. When I asked for some, Dave Rope reached in another pocket and took out a half-full tobacco bag he used for rolling cigarettes. I said no, I wanted an already rolled cigarette. I rolled one and struck a match. It started to burn. I struck two matches, and each time it went out. It was about time to start work at noon, and I ran over to the camp and gave the cigarette to Ralph. I wanted to smoke it myself, but I gave it to him to smoke. Ralph got a headache from it. He said his head went wrong, he didn't know much, and his mind was not working right. Besides that, he felt like vomiting. The next day he vomited. Five day later, at payday, Ralph said there had been something wrong with him after he smoked that cigarette. I had told him right away when I brought him the cigarette that I got it from Dave Rope.

When that payday came, we left because Ralph had gotten sick there. Ralph was going to come by himself, but I decided to go too. I always went around with him while we were working there. The other man who came home with us said he was homesick and he just had to leave.

(What about Dave Rope?) Ralph and I talked about that and we thought that that cigarette must have been made for me, some kind of a smoke that Dave Rope knew about. I don't know one thing about what was in it, but I can tell you about how much trouble Ralph had from it when he came home. I was told to go to his place the day after tomorrow. My wife sent me to Gallup on that day—two days after I got home. I came back the same day and went over to Ralph's place. When I got there he told me he had been sick too much. He said that when he had been down at work the sickness got heavier and heavier all the time, he got more of it every day. One day after he got home he was out of his mind, he said. Things like trees seemed to be going around him. The second night he was home, he was thinking that those trees or logs were all men and women. He was vomiting, vomiting all the time.

The day that I was supposed to come in the morning, he said he felt awfully weak and thought he was going to die. His mother,[108] an old lady, heard about this and came up to see him. She had medicine she soaked in a cup, some kind I don't know, I didn't ask her what it was or its name. After it was soaked she said he should drink it up, and {he} rubbed some on his head and body. He had a sweatbath after that, drank some more of the medicine, and felt good again. Last night he slept well, and he thought he was all right again. I never heard any more about it after that. He died two years ago. He gave me all the goats he promised but one. He told me he'd give me that one next time I came. I brought the goats back home.

From Bill we had the following account of Ralph's death:
Two years ago while Ralph was plowing with some other men, he and Tony were wrestling at the edge of an arroyo. Ralph said he was going to throw Tony down the arroyo and picked

him up by the pants to do it. Tony held on to Ralph's belt so that when Ralph flung, he was dragged after Tony. The arroyo wasn't very deep or steep, about eight feet or maybe twelve. They rolled down and both got up. Ralph took a few steps and fell down, opened his mouth twice and lay still. Tony ran to the other boys who were plowing and told them Ralph was lying down there and didn't move. They ran to him, shook him, but he was loose and didn't get up. He was dead. They went to Wilkins, and he came in a truck with another man and buried Ralph [109] (Social Relations 16).

A TRIP TO GATHER SALT

Two days later, Roan Horse came to my home and told me he was going over to Salt Lake, the other side of Zuni. Roan Horse, Barney, Wood's son-in-law Jay, one of Wood's grand-sons, and I would go. Roan Horse told me I should take his wagon because he wanted to ride his horse. We would take four wagons altogether. We made an appointment to meet in Zuni village. I started from here early in the morning, got to Zuni, and I and the others all started out from Zuni and camped way on top of a hill. Next morning we started off toward Aspera and had dinner there. After dinner we went through a place called Mud Lake, past the lake which was dry then. One place we came to a well, but it was closed with rocks. From there on we were going downhill on the other side. We traveled all day till sundown. Way after dark we camped this side of Salt Lake. There were a lot of windmills there, so we had water.

Next morning we went on to Salt Lake. We went down to a low place in the Salt Lake and began picking out salt. We got there pretty early and had picked as much as we wanted {by} about this time (4:00 P.M.). Roan Horse and I filled about nine sacks. We quit, harnessed up the teams, and started toward home the same day. It started raining as we came back. Stanley was there, too, and when we got up the hill, his horse got sick and was lying down as we went by. It was raining quite heavily. We got back to where we had camped. One man went back to see how Stanley was getting along with his horse. When he came back, he said that two of the horses were dead already. They thought that the hay we had bought at Zuni village was no good. They took two horses back to Stanley and pulled his wagon up to the camp. Next morning, the horses that Roan Horse and Wood's grandson had been riding were hooked to Stanley's wagon, and we continued toward home.

We traveled all that day and passed Aspera. We camped that night on the west side of Aspera and went on the next morning. We ate dinner on top of the hill just the other side of Zuni, and got to Zuni village a little after noon. Roan Horse and I waited there to feed our horses, and the other men went on. Toward evening we started off from Zuni, came about halfway to Kainti and stayed there overnight. We started off again next morning and reached Kainti before noon, and got to Roan Horse's home at noon. I got two sacks of salt, and Roan Horse got seven. We had been gone five days since we started. I walked home from there, got a wagon, and came back for my two sacks.

THE GALLUP CEREMONIAL

That was in summertime, past July, I think. After that, I went to the ceremonial in Gallup and stayed there three days. I saw a lot of races there, and bucking horses. Some of the boys got thrown off the horse. One time they had some buffalos there for riders to try, but they rode horses, cows, and steers because they were afraid of the buffalo. Just one boy rode a buffalo. It didn't buck very hard. There were different kinds of dances by Zunis, Hopis, Lagunas, and a lot of other tribes. They did these in the daytime and also at night. After all the others were finished, they put on a Squaw Dance and everybody there danced till daylight.

A LENGTHY TRADING EXPEDITION

After I had seen these dances for three days and two nights, a man called John told me he wanted to go to trade salt on the other side of Ft. Defiance. He said a Squaw Dance was going on there and we could see that, too. I was afoot, but John was with his wife and had an extra horse which he said I could ride. I didn't want to go there, but I made up my mind to go. We left Gallup in the afternoon and went to where the Ft. Defiance and Shiprock roads meet. (Why didn't you want to go?) After I had been at the dance three days and three nights, I was pretty tired. They said that if they got some sheep in trade, they would give me some goats or sheep.

We took the Shiprock road instead of the one to Ft. Defiance. When we came to a Navajo hogan, John told the people there that he wanted to trade some salt for sheep or goats. He said for a goat or lamb he would give a small sack of salt, and for a big sheep he would give a fifty-pound sackful. We got a little goat there, and we butchered it and ate it. We were pretty hungry for meat after the ceremonial, and we had been drinking a lot there. We built a little fire there and cooked a lot of the meat. The little goat was pretty fat. We asked the people there if they had cut their hay and would sell us some. Some of the men said that one fellow had some and he lived along our way. There was no feed for our horses, so we wanted to go to where the man had hay. We met him on the way and asked him about his hay—what kind of hay was it? He said it was not alfalfa or oat, but some wild hay that he cut in the summertime. He wanted to sell some, but we didn't buy any. The man driving the team said his horses wouldn't eat that kind.

We went on and came to another hogan, where a Navajo called Phil was living. We shook hands, and he called me by a relationship name. He said we should stay with him that night. He said there was no horse feed at all for a long way. He had a little hay that he said we could use, and he had some corn fodder. He told us to put our horses in the corral and feed them there at night.[110] So we did that, gave them some hay and corn fodder. I went to sleep pretty early and didn't wake up till daylight next morning. They took some salt there and told us they would give a goat for it. We told him we would leave the goat there and pick it up when we came by again.

We left and went on to a place where some people were living together, and we stopped at one place. We went in the hogan and found only the women, no men. We told them about our salt and our trading it for sheep and goats. The woman said they didn't know whether they wanted to trade or not, but they told us we could stay overnight. One woman said, "You might trade when the men come back if you work it right." I stayed with the wagon, while the other two went around the hogans. They had a lot of cornfields there. We traded salt for some sheep, and told them we would leave the sheep there until we came by again.

We went on a little way to a man named Lew. He picked out two sacks and said he would pay two lambs for them. We said we would leave them there because we were going on farther. We had dinner there and fed the horses. We left there and came to another hogan, where we saw a woman and two children who said the man had gone away up on the hill. She said to stay and trade tonight when the man would be back. We stayed the rest of the day, and the man came back in a wagon. Two girls came in also with the sheep, maybe a bunch of about eight hundred. They had a two-night sing there, Blessing Way.

After the sing we stayed another night there. Some people said they were going to have a Squaw Dance in two days, right nearby, a little way to the south. Then John wanted to catch a ride to town and come back the same day. He didn't say why he wanted to go. He went to the road and didn't come back that night, but came the next day just before noon. I was taking care of the horses and wagon, watering the horses. John's wife was trading around there. She traded for eight sheep. We camped there, and at night we stayed with the wagon.

The Squaw Dance time came. We could see the big brush hogan from where we were, just a mile away. We went over and got there pretty near sundown. People were coming on horseback, a bunch of people coming from the other side of Tohatchie Mountain. They were bringing the stick over to where we were. There were about fifteen men that came over. After dark they began. The people coming in made a pretty good-sized crowd. I went where they were singing and helped sing. Some people there were drinking. John and his wife had brought the wagon and stayed with it. I didn't know that they had some whiskey to drink. He was selling it to the Navajos right along. A small soda-pop bottle {for} three dollars. He got a few sheep for it, too—one sheep for a little bottle. I got a little drunk, but I was singing all night with the people.

In the morning, I was singing again with the bunch when they lined up in front of the hogan and the people threw out candy. After singing, they threw out a lot of apples, candy, Cracker Jacks, and calico. After that the people all went home. John said he got three sheep that night for whiskey.

We went back to where we'd been staying and were there three more days. We heard about another Squaw Dance coming in three days from then, in the opposite direction. It was to be at a place called Clay Hill, a little round hill, not very big, shaped like a sweatbath. John had one gallon left. We started off in the morning and got to a place about noon where we ate our dinner.

After we ate, John's wife went off somewhere. I don't know how far she went, but she came back and said she had seen something over there and wanted her medicine. She searched in her sack, picked out the medicine, and went back. I didn't talk to her. A long while later she came back. We asked her what she saw, and she said a blue lizard. Its body is just about the size of my hand, and it has a kind of long tail. They can stand up about five inches and can run pretty fast. She said she put some corn pollen on her hand, and also two other things that she didn't name. She held her palm up near where the lizard was and it came over, right up on her hand, ran over the pollen, up her arm, back over her shoulder, and jumped off. She said that's what she does when she goes off for a long way to trade. The way that lizard ran over her shoulder is good, she said. "If you hold out your hand like that and it doesn't come, that is not so good. But this means that we will have good trading." We two men asked, "Why didn't you say that when you came back? We would have gone over there and seen it."

He had a gallon jug, half full still. We went to where the sing was, and I was in the sing again that night. John got about six more sheep. In the morning they did the same as at the other dance—threw out a lot of calico, muskmelons, all kinds of corn, some roasted in a pit. One man there wanted to buy some turquoise beads from John and said he would give ten sheep for them. John said he wanted fifteen for the beads. The man told him to come to his place and talk it over with his wife. The dance was way back toward Gallup, and those people were farther still in that direction.

We went to their place. They lived way up on a mountain, a good place. He lived in a house with a lot of pines around it, it looked pretty. We got there just about noon. He had some alfalfa which we fed the horses; they had plenty to eat there. John got fifteen sheep for the beads, and a bale of hay and half a whole mutton, all that for the beads. Both sides said thank you, and we all wanted to go to the second night of the dance. We looked at the sheep, but left them in the herd and went on to the dance.

(How did you keep count?) We just kept it in our heads. The man we traded with would remember, and we would too.

On the way to the dance we went to another two-night sing where we traded some more. We got three goats and three sheep for one new shawl. John's wife had made some dresses and she traded them for goats—six dresses for six goats. The woman who owned the goats took the dresses, and we left the animals there, all twelve of them. We stayed there quite a while that day, and in the afternoon we went on again. A lot of people went by as we were going along. We got to the Squaw Dance about sundown and found a lot of people there already. We built a fire on the edge of the crowd and cooked something to eat and some coffee. Another wagon with some people in it came to the same place. They got out and built a fire too.

After a little while, those people were talking about how one of the women fell down and couldn't get up again. She didn't know a thing after she fell. Three of us helped the woman up, took hold of her. We didn't know what to do for her. We thought that one of those people who are witches sometimes make a person do that. The people with her said that. They wanted to know who had some medicine that could cure that kind of sickness. One man with long hair tied up came over where we were and asked us if we had any medicine. John and his wife had some and gave just a little bit to the man. They told him how to use it: get a cup of water and drop in some of the medicine, mix it up, and let the woman drink it up. The man took the medicine over, and they did the way they were told. After about an hour the woman got well.

About that time the dance started and went on for two hours. Then singing started again. I went to sleep, I was pretty sleepy. In the morning we went off a little way and stopped. John said he got some more whiskey, another gallon that was brought to him last night, and he had been selling it again. He gave me some. He had given a man who was going to town some money to bring it out to him. Everybody went to the main dance. When we got there, they brought out a lot of food for the people who belonged on this side. After breakfast there was the singing in front of the hogan, throwing out a lot of smokes, candy, apples, cookies, and calico, and it was finished. After that the singer blackened the patient. I was just herding then and didn't go over there.

Just after the blackening, we heard that a man died in the kitchen, a different man from the patient. On the first night, when they were taking the stick, the man who died went with the bunch. When he came back with the others, he sewed moccasins the rest of the day. He had a headache that night, and then a fever. They had a medicine man to sing for him till daylight, who sang for him a long time. In the morning after sunup they knew he was growing worse, and he died just about noon. They stopped the whole dance, quit everything, everybody left and went home.[111] We went away, too, to a Navajo home where John had traded whiskey for five sheep. I picked up those five and started driving them. We came to another Navajo home, where we stayed overnight. Next morning, we got two more goats for salt. We sold two bottles of whiskey and wanted six dollars for them, but the man paid only five dollars. After we had gone a little way, the man who got the two bottles came after us, wanted some more. John said he had no more, but the man didn't believe it. Every time John started his horses, the man would take hold of the line and stop them. Another man came along who was his friend and held him so John could go off.

There was another man who took a bottle at the dance who was supposed to give a yearling sheep for it. We got to his home and he was there. He said he still had the full bottle and wanted to give it back to John because his wife didn't like it. John took it back. He sent me over to where the whiskey was, and I got the bottle and started back. I drank about half of it. John got mad at me about that and asked me why I drank it. I said that if he didn't like it, I might as well go home. I was very tired driving those sheep he had traded from the Indians. I told him I didn't like that, and I might start walking back home. After I said I would leave him, he said I had better stay with them and help them gather those sheep and goats. He let me keep what was left in the bottle. I didn't drink it right away but kept it for a while.

We came back to the next home where there were sheep for us and picked up twelve more. Then we came back this way. At another home, two men were skinning a sheep. The sheep they were skinning was awfully fat. We ate with them and got two more sheep there, traded for a big sackful of salt.

We came to a place up in the mountains where there was a big spring and a lot of green grass, and a big stream from the spring. We went to where it started, up in the hill where water was coming out of the ground in a six-inch stream. Where the water was running out of a hole in the ground, we put in a stick to see how far it went. We got the stick in about two feet and it would go no farther. We watered the sheep and horses there.

We went on to another home for more sheep and goats, the place where they owed us fifteen. We went down the hill with the sheep on a straight trail, but the wagon went around by the road. John's wife and I brought the sheep down to the foot of the mountain, herding them along. John said we would meet at one place at the foot of the mountain. As soon as we got down the hill, John's wife said she wanted to go to where the wagon was and start feeding the horses. She told me to bring the sheep along slowly. When I got there with the sheep, they had dinner ready. As soon as the sheep got there they bedded down right away. We ate, and after that we went over to the store that was very near. We looked around the store while the sheep were still bedded down. We saw some Navajos there. One man asked me if John still had some whiskey. I said I didn't know, they should talk to John. The man said he wanted me to find out. When I asked, John said he hadn't any left, it was all used up. John and his wife went back where the sheep were, but I stayed at the store. The man who wanted to find out came along, and I said there wasn't any.

Then I went back to the sheep, harnessed up the horses and hooked them to the wagon, and started driving the sheep. We were going to the place of a man called Gray Hair. When I got there about sundown with the sheep, John was already there. They had a corral they said we could use, so we corralled the sheep. I went to the wagon to get something to eat, then we went back to fix the corral. It wasn't very good, so we got some more wood and put up some more poles where it wasn't very high. Then we went back to our camp.

We went in to Gray Hair's hogan, where they were telling stories until way after dark, pretty late. On this trip, when we would first get up in the morning, pretty early, before sunup, our horses had not gone very far from where we camped. A lot of times we would see our horses when we first got up. But this time we didn't see any horses around. John told me to track them before breakfast, so I started. The horses had gone out this way onto the road. They went a long way on the road, then turned off on another one. It must have been about ten o'clock and I was still tracking. They went a long way on the second road to a place called Little Trees, a long way from where they started. When I got to them and drove them back, I got hold of one and started to ride it. It's pretty hard to drive a mule a different way from the one it wants to go. I drove it a different way and it started to kick. I got a long stick and made it go with that. We went back pretty fast and got there about noon. While I was tracking them I pretty nearly gave up and went back. My legs were pretty sore from all that walking. I had a long walk.

We stayed there another night, gathered sheep around there and got seven more from Gray Hair. We started home from there. We had gathered all the sheep together, fifty-six head of sheep and goats mixed up together. We traveled all day, stopping for a little while at noon, and got back to another place. We stayed two more nights, trading some more. I was pretty tired then and hated to stay another day. We got a few more goats. After two days, early in the morning when we just got up, John got out one pint of whiskey he had left, that I didn't know about, and gave me some. I drank it up. It made me feel pretty good again, and I started off along the road with the sheep.

Just as we were about to start, another woman came along. She wanted to trade a goat for some salt. She said she lived right on our way and we could come by there. We started off for her place. I drove the sheep the whole day to get there and arrived by sundown. John and his wife got there long after dark, with two more goats in the wagon with them. We corralled the sheep and killed one of the two goats they had brought. We had a lot of meat to eat there.

Next morning they let me ride a horse to drive the sheep

but told me to go slowly with them. But I went pretty fast with them! I came right back up to the top of a steep hill which was pretty close to the Ft. Defiance road. The wagon caught up with me there. John told me I had gone pretty fast with the sheep, it was a long way to where they caught up. We got mad again, all stopped there and started to make coffee. John was walking around and talking about how he didn't like me to drive the sheep fast. I was kind of mad too. They had started me off with no lunch or anything like that. We were still talking that way, and I began to think that after I ate I was just going to walk to the road and catch a ride in a car and leave. But I didn't do that. I started walking with the sheep again after dinner. The others wanted to go ahead and feed their horses in Gallup.

As I came along with the sheep just the other side of Gallup, John met me and we went over to where some Mexicans were living. We stopped at a place where a Mexican had a corral, put our sheep in it, and stayed overnight in the Mexican's home. We walked into town, went to the movies, and stayed there quite a while, then went back to where the sheep were. In the morning after breakfast John and I started the sheep across town, and when we got just past the town he went back. He said they would come right behind and catch up with me somewhere on the road out this way.

Before we started that morning, one of the Mexicans bought a little goat for $1.25. I came along on the road until I got to where Salamon lived. John and his wife were also there and told me they wanted me to go along to where there was a dam on the top of a hill. They were going to stop there and have some lunch. They would go ahead and get the lunch ready. So I went on and got there where they were waiting. After lunch I started off with the sheep again, took a straight trail up this way, came across one canyon, and went along the north side over this way. From there I went on down to where I am living now, this side of where I live. I told John I was going home from there. My home was just north of that place. He said all right and thanked me very much for the help I had given them. Before I left, John told me to come over to their home and he would give me a big sheep, a lamb, and a big wether, all three. I told him I might come over day after tomorrow.

I went home. It was then about sixteen days from the time

we started off from Gallup. The folks wanted to know where I had been all that time, and I told them my story. I told them how much pay I got for going out there with John, {that my pay was} the three sheep. I must tell you that I skipped one trade that I made myself on the trip. I was wearing two good turquoises in my ears and one man wanted to buy them. I sold them for three goats, two little ones and a big one. Three days after I got home, I went to where John lived and brought back five sheep and goats.[112] After that I started cutting my corn.

LUCKY'S SON IS KILLED

My oldest son took the sheep down in the canyon one afternoon on horseback. When he started off with the sheep, I came over this way to where Agnes was living to the east and stopped there to help.[113] The boy was herding sheep in the canyon on horseback. That night the sheep came home alone. The horse he was riding was a mare with a yearling colt that followed its mother all the time when she was herding. After the sheep came in, my wife started hollering for the boy, but nobody answered. She and her mother walked down into the canyon. They found the little colt and its mother, which the boy was riding. The saddle was on the colt, under its belly. They hollered around that canyon for a long while that night, then came back home, and next morning they sent me word, over where I had stayed overnight at Agnes's place. My wife and some others had been looking for the boy pretty nearly all night.

Next morning my wife, George, and Stanley started looking again. They found him in the canyon, lying there dead, just a little way from where they had seen the colt with the saddle. His head was busted in one place and a rib was sticking out. This colt was gentle, not wild, to touch him with your hand. They found a place where the boy had saddled the colt and got on, and the colt started running. They had come up the arroyo, turned around, and a little way below they lost the saddle blanket. They could see that, after that, the horse started to buck and the boy fell off, but the tracks went on a long way. The boy had been dragged from that place. The way he was found, he must have put his foot through the stirrup and that's why he was dragged. Somehow he got his foot out of the stirrup and fell there, where they found him. They thought that while he was dragging, the horse must have kicked him all over. That is what I heard when I came back home.

George and his mother buried the boy down in the canyon where he was killed.[114] I think he was about ten when this happened. He had been riding horses quite well. If he was still alive, he might be as old as Harold now. I went tracking all over the place where he went on the colt, and it looked just the way the people told me. (What was done with the colt?) We didn't do anything, but we traded him off to my father-in-law for a blanket.

Away Again

A few days after that, one of Chuck's sons-in-law came to my home and told me he was going up {to} the Zuni Mountains. A lot of men were working there, and they were getting paid each day. He wanted me to go with him and play cards with those people at night. "But let's go around by the Morton store," he said; "when we get there we can borrow some money so we can play cards with those people." Roan Horse's wife was there and heard what he said. She told me she wanted to send a saddle horse to Roan Horse so he could ride it back home. I said, "All right, I'll go." We got out the saddles, saddled up the horses, and started off for Chuck's place first. We stopped there for a little while, then went on to Morton.

When we got to Morton we went into the store. The trader was loaning some money to Indians that year, and Chuck borrowed fifteen dollars. (Why was he lending money?) To buy lambs. I got ten dollars. The trader said he was going to gather the lambs right away, within a month, and told us we should have our lambs ready so he could come and get them right at the home. We told the storekeeper we would do that.

We started from there and went up by the reservoir and on to the top of the mountain where the men were working. Chuck, but not I, gambled all night with the Mexicans and Navajos. He gambled till the next day and made thirty dollars. He went home right away as soon as he got that much money, but I stayed there. Roan Horse started home the next morning, but I stayed another night. Gambler's wife and the woman who used to be Dumb Boy's wife[115] brought some meat there and sold it to the people that were working. Next day we all came back here together.

I went to Gallup the next day after that. I had heard about a Yeibitchai dance at Manuelito. A man I knew came to town from near Crownpoint. We got together and decided to go to the dance that night. We took the train, which cost thirty-five cents for that distance. We got off at Manuelito and walked over to the dance, up over a hill. That night I danced with some boys there, and I danced with the bunch every night. (How did you learn?) When I first heard about that dance long before, the men who danced were practicing and that's how I learned. (When?) I learned it from way back where I first saw the Yei-bitchai dance about fifteen years before. (Who taught you?) For that dance I didn't have to get one man to teach me the way they teach songs. For dancing you just have to pick it up by watching the dancers, by looking at it. But in this bunch, if I was not doing it right, any of the men could tell me how to do it. I learned in that way, mostly by watching. (What people were with you when you first learned?) I don't remember. It got all mixed up, I've done it so many times.

When that man and I got to the Yeibitchai dance in Manuelito, it was the next-to-last day. Those there had been dancing all night till daylight. The last day I danced in the daytime with people from Hub, but at night I didn't dance. By that time, I was pretty tired from dancing. The last night I just went inside the hogan and slept. The dance was finished in the morning, and we heard some of the people who were going home yelling out to the crowd, "We are going to have a Squaw Dance." People from the south side were bringing the stick to Manuelito that day.

The Squaw Dance was at another place and they brought the stick over in the evening, and there were a lot of people there. A storekeeper from Manuelito was helping with some food, and I was there all night. At the other dance site, the patient was pretty sick, and that was why they were having the dance. It was late in the fall while it was cold. When a person gets too sick and needs a Squaw Dance, they can put it on in wintertime.[116] They don't go a long way for the first day. If the patient is really bad, they can start the sing and take the stick just about two miles. In the morning they did the same as usual, singing in front of the hogan and people throwing out candy and things. They finished for that morning, and they said the second night it would be down near where the singer lived. I just heard them say that. I didn't want to go there. The people who came from the sing all went home.

I went home to where I lived and didn't go over there again. Next day I went over to Kainti, to Ted Sage's home. Ted Sage's wife was sick and they wanted me to go get the medicine man down at Aspen Spring. They sent ten dollars to the medicine man by me and said they would give him five dollars more when he came, fifteen dollars altogether. Next day I started out from Kainti, going by Manuelito and on down to where the man lived. I asked a man where the medicine man lived, and he said he didn't know if he was at home. I went on and found he wasn't home. He had left yesterday and gone west to where there was another Yeibitchai dance going on. Some of his folks told me I could go over to the dance and I would find him there. Another man and I went down to the dance together.

We got there pretty late. There were a lot of people there. Some new boys and girls were seeing the dancers the way I had the first time I saw the Yeibitchai. The singer was from far away. I went in with the crowd and saw the dancers again, my second time. After that they started dancing right in front of the hogan. There was a pasture on the east side of the hogan where I kept my horse that night. They didn't dance very long that night, just for a little while, and then we went to sleep. In the morning pretty early they gave us a lot to eat. I found out the family giving the dance were Bitter Water clan. They started to do a lot of sandpaintings.

While the people were doing that inside the hogan, I went outside and found the man I was looking for. I told him I had come for him, that a man in Kainti had sent me to get him to sing Ghost Way. The singer said he was putting on this sing with the other people and why didn't they get Ned to sing in Kainti or another singer there?

We saw Ned at a sing one night and observed that he seemed only to raise and lower his voice without keeping the words, pitch, or rhythm of the song. Later we were told that he is a very good "medicine man," very old, and that he has been singing that way for over a year now. He does it only when he is helping. He sings properly at sings he does himself. No one knows why he does it. Some people say he does it because he has sung so much in his life that he is tired of it (Social Relations 10).

I told him that those singers knew the songs, but not the big prayer called *hayate*. I gave him the money. "Well," he said, "it's four more days until they finish singing here, I won't go until the sing is over." He wanted me to stay and help. I said, "Give me back some of the money and I'll help you!" but that was just a joke. I decided to stay there.

I went inside and helped with the sandpainting. I did it pretty fast. I knew a lot of the sandpaintings and almost all the figures. I had seen them lots of times at all the dances. I was doing that four days with people, beginning early in the morning and getting through at sundown. About twenty men were working there, ten doing sandpaintings inside and ten more outside, hauling and piling wood, chopping wood, working in the kitchen.

(Abbreviated description:) The next-to-the-last night the people danced all night and were paid with sheep in the morning. The last day they decorated the masks with spruce, then had the masked dance, six dancers at a time. The patient was a woman. After dark the regular dancers came first, then it was open to other groups.

(Verbatim:) After that I went to get my horse in the pasture, but he had gotten out and gone. I trailed him off to where he broke his hobble. So I was afoot and stuck there. I knew well a man, Brave Man, who used to live between here and Manuelito. He lent me a horse and I rode off on it. The medicine man told me he was going to stay there that night and come over the next day. I rode my borrowed horse back to the medicine man's house and got a horse there to go home with. I rode that horse back to Ted Sage's place. I got back in the afternoon, bringing the medicine man's bag. When I got there, they asked me what I had been doing. I said I was helping down there and seeing all of the dance. I told them the medicine man was coming tomorrow. Long Hair, who owned the horse I had ridden down there, told me to ride back and look for the horse, which hadn't come back.

Next day I went back, looking for the horse. I found it about ten miles this way from where they had the dance, and I brought him back. Long Hair thanked me for finding the horse. The medicine man had come. He just sang a few songs and did a little praying that night. Next morning they used the fire just as always.

When I went to Kainti after that, the storekeeper asked me to drive some lambs to Gallup for him. I said I would, and I took the lambs and started to drive them. Dick and I both started off next morning and took the lambs through the big canyon. After we got across, we camped there for the night and went on again in the morning. The second night we stayed this side of Gallup. He paid each of us two dollars a day. The next morning I brought the lambs into town to the other side of the tracks, to the place called a stockyard. That day they were separating the sheep, and they started to work on ours as soon as we got them there. They separated the good big lambs off to one side and the ones with long hair to another. Big ewes were in another corral. They were doing that all day long. When I got back to town, Len and I got into a car and started back to Kainti. I had met two of my "brothers" in town, Bert and another boy, and we all came out in the car. The sing at Ted Sage's was all over when we got back. I stayed there that night.

More Sings, and Mischief

Next morning I heard that John was pretty sick below Kainti. I heard they were having the Apache Wind Way sing for him. I went down and John was still pretty sick. They said his throat was sore down inside. I understood from the other people that John had started to holler and ran outside and tried to run away. People caught him and brought him back inside. He was a patient there for two more days, and then they took him to the Ft. Defiance hospital. Five days after that we all heard that John had died.

I heard about another Fire Dance near Manuelito. John's wife came back from Ft. Defiance by herself, and the next day my brother Ralph returned. He was down there, too. (Is he your full brother?) Same mother, different fathers. I went to the Fire Dance, and Ralph was there that night. I saw the dance. Old Scout was young then.

That winter there were a lot of little sings going on—Apache Wind Way, Blessing Way, Ghost Way. I went around to wherever there was a sing. I went to help sing. A lot of people just go to sleep when they go to a sing, but I didn't do that. I kept helping at sings, and in that way I got to learn all these songs. That is how I became a singer.[117]

In the summertime Ted Sage was having a sing for his wife who was sick all the time. She had been Jack Sage's wife when she first got sick, that time I went to get the singer. A singer from the other side of Gallup called Hunter was singing Motion Hand Way for this woman. He sang Motion Hand Way there for five nights, and the last day Martin Wood and I came to the sing. Walter had a car and we came that way.

Ernest, Walter, and Dick were pretty drunk when they arrived. Ernest and another man named Coho started to walk away from the car. They were carrying a gallon of whiskey. When they got off pretty far, they sat down. Martin Wood and I walked over there, coming pretty close. They walked away again, then sat down for a while, and we sat down at a distance. I said I wanted to go over to them by myself. I said, "If I go by myself, those men might stay so I could get to them." I told Martin he could keep watching. If the men didn't try to get away when I walked up to them, they might start telling a story. If they did that, Martin could go round about and walk up pretty close without letting Ernest or the other man see him. If he could get close, he could grab that gallon and run away with it. Martin said all right, he would do that.

While Martin waited, I walked over where the two people were sitting, and walked right up to them. I sat down there and right away asked for a drink. They knew me and they opened the gallon and gave it to me. I took a drink and gave the gallon back. We started talking, and the gallon was sitting there waiting for Martin to come and get it. I heard a noise nearby but I didn't look around. Ernest said to Coho, "Let's go to my house and get something to eat. After we eat, we'll come back." There was another place where a sing was going on, and they would go on to that one. I said, "I want to go along." Coho had his pony there and he said, "All right, let's go, then."

They put that gallon into a gunny sack, Coho got on his horse, Ernest threw the sack over his shoulder and got on the horse behind the old man, going to ride double. I said I wanted to ride behind, too, three on a horse. Coho said I could walk, but I said no, I wanted to ride. Finally they let me get on behind and we started off, three on a horse. About that time Martin slipped up, got hold of the sack, and pulled it hard. Ernest and I were holding each other and we both fell down. Martin pulled us off with the sack. Martin started off with the gallon, but he lost it when it fell out of the sack. Ernest and Coho started running after Martin because they saw he was holding the sack and running. They didn't see the jug lying there. I picked it up and ran off with it to the south.

It was a little after dark that we were doing this. While I was running pretty fast, I ran into some barbed wire. I was wearing just one shirt and got cut pretty badly, right around my belly, and bled a lot. After I ran into the fence, Martin came over. I asked about Ernest and the old man, but he didn't know where they went. They chased him and he saw them there, but that was the last of them. I told him I had cut my belly with barbed wire. We started off with the gallon.

There were two sings going on near there. We went to one, and when we got there we drank some of the whiskey and then hid it off a little way from the hogan. We came back and saw old man Coho hobbling his horse. I had a pop bottle full of whiskey and gave him a drink. We stayed at the sing a little while, then two other men and I went to where the whiskey was hidden. We divided it up by filling one pint bottle, which one of them took, and also a quart bottle. I took that, but there was still some in the gallon jug, so we hid it again and went back to the sing.

Another man, Robert, who is Ernest's brother, and I started off from the sing. We were getting pretty drunk, so we went away. We were just below Kainti, and we both got very drunk on that quart. I don't know the rest of it. I got up the next morning and Robert was still lying there. I tried to wake him up, but I couldn't. I came back to the Kainti store, but didn't stay there long and went right back to the sing. There I saw Big Fred pretty drunk, talking and making all kinds of funny noises. I saw Martin there and asked him about the whiskey. He said he sold all of it and got a four-year-old pony for it. There was a little left after he bought the pony, so he and Big Fred drank it up. From there, Martin and I went down to the Kainti store.

Lucky Blackens a Patient

We saw my uncle there. He told us we must go to his place. His wife was sick, and he asked me if I would do a blackening for her. This was the first time that I did this.

> Lucky had attended innumerable sings over the years and had often assisted singers. Now his uncle sent for him to do a blackening. Lucky was paid, but his first and second pay for blackening were given to singers from whom he had learned the procedure (LS 489, 491, 494) (Summary of Subsistence Data 6).
>
> Ned was one of the singers Lucky had assisted often enough so that he knew how to do a blackening when he was called upon to perform one (LS 491) (Social Relations 9).
>
> Ned performed a blackening for Bill when the latter was suffering from abdominal pain and vomiting. He was at Bill's place again the next month to do a blackening for an old man there, Old Scout, who was ill with some gastric ailment. We heard of other persons for whom Ned had sung or was going to sing (Social Relations 10).
>
> Coho is one of the singers Lucky had helped with blackening many times (LS 491). When Lucky became a singer, Coho helped make up a medicine bundle for him and taught him Blessing Way, part of Ghost Way, Navaho Wind Way, and part of Coyote Way (LS 497) (Social Relations 17).

I said I would go. Martin was leading the horse he got for whiskey. He wanted to go with me and he wanted to ride his new horse. He put on a saddle, but the horse was pretty wild and got away from him. Steve came along and Martin made him catch the horse. He chased it a long time and couldn't catch it, even with Martin's help. Steve gave it up and came back to the store. While Martin was still chasing the horse, Coho came along on horseback and roped the horse for him, so they got the horse back.

Pretty late, almost sundown, we started out and got to my uncle's place after dark. The people had started to go to bed already, because they didn't think I was coming. (Why did they choose you?) She had a headache, and the woman who did hand-trembling over her said she had the sickness of Ghost Way and that it might help her some to have a blackening. My uncle knew that I knew how to do this. I helped singing all the time for Ned, Coho, and my uncle. Now, my uncle said, I could do it by myself. I might as well do it alone so I would know how to do it by myself. That's what he told me. We burned the weeds for the ashes we needed.

(How much did you pay to learn?) For the blackening, whatever the people pay me the first time I do it, that goes to the man who taught me. But when you start to learn the songs you have to pay for it.

(Tell me more about learning to be a singer.) I just picked it up from the people I knew. After that Coho and Trapper made up a medicine bundle for me. There were some little places where I didn't know a song and I would go over that with these two people and get everything straight, and I had the medicine bundle.[118] But I hadn't done a sing, and so this was my first time. I was just waiting for somebody to ask me. (Did you pay those men?) Yes, I paid them both, the first and the second pay I got. That was for blackening at two places. (What sings did you know at that time?) The blackening part of Ghost Way, that was all. (Have you learned others since then?) I know other songs just in part, not the whole thing. (Do you know any songs all the way through?) I know the Ghost Way all the way through, five nights; Blessing Way all through; Apache Wind Way, two nights. Also just part of nine-night Night Way; part of Mountain Way; just a little of Feather Way, and Coyote Way. That's about all.[119]

(How and when did you learn the ones you know all the way through?) I started learning those songs about six years ago. Coho taught me. He was the only teacher for Blessing Way, part of Ghost Way, and part of Navajo Wind Way and Coyote Way. I learned Night Way from another man and part of Mountain Way from another. Jesse taught me Apache Wind Way, and my uncle taught me Hatnilni Way. That is about all I know, and all these men are still living.

(Why did you learn them?) I was always running around to these sings for many years. Wherever there was a sing I would go there and start learning it, then to another one and so on. I began to know the songs and help the singers. After doing that for many years, I knew a lot of songs pretty well. About six or seven years ago, songs were all that I knew; I didn't have the knowledge, and that was when I started to learn.[120]

I blackened the patient at that place, and that was all I did. Next day, Martin and I got all ready to go when my uncle wanted to take away from Martin the horse he was riding that he had traded liquor for. The horse belonged to my uncle, {but} somebody had traded it away. It was Jesse who did that. We told my uncle that we were going to ride the horse home so we could take our saddle there. He said he would send a man to bring it back. When we got to Kainti, another fellow came after the horse and took it back. From there I went back home.

(How did you feel about your first sing?) I didn't feel much. I liked to do it and didn't feel afraid about doing it. There weren't many people there, just Martin and me, my uncle and his wife. After I got home the next day, I went to the north side of my place and watered the horses. As I started back with them, they went a little ahead of me. I started to run my horse when he got out of the water, which was down in a deep arroyo. We came to a ditch and I got hurt on my bottom. I was riding bareback.

Lucky's Injury Is Serious

At the same time there was a sing going on near here, and I went down to it. The patient was Coho, and the singer was Peso, from Hub. The sing had already passed two nights. The place where I got hurt felt pretty bad after I got there. I was rolling around inside where the people were. When they started singing it began to hurt pretty badly. After the sing was over I started home, and after a while I could hardly walk. I was coming by some hogans and I just lay down there for a while. I got pretty thirsty, so I got up and started over to Roan Horse's home. When I got there, I couldn't walk any more.

I stayed there for a long time, maybe about twenty days,

when the storekeeper, Doug Winter, came over in his car and took me to the Mission Hospital. After I got there, a big swelling there started to hurt. The doctor cut that place and a lot of pus ran out. First I took a bath, and then the doctor had me lie on my belly on the table and {he} cut the place. I don't know what else he did after he cut it, but he worked on that place for quite a while. Right after that the pain stopped. They put me to bed and told me I had been pretty sick. Three days later I was a whole lot better, and the day after that they gave me back my clothes and I came back home. This was the day before the ceremonial. When I left the hospital the doctor told me not to ride a horse for two months, so after I came home I didn't, I walked most of the time.

Lucky has attended sings all his life and had his child sung over when it was ill (LS 357). It is interesting, therefore, that, when his injury from the fall did not clear up after a few weeks, he went to the hospital instead of calling in a singer. He reports that he recovered rapidly after the doctor treated him, and one feels that he approved of the treatment he was given (LS 501– 503) (Survival 7).

THE BIG SNOW

That fall there were a lot of pinyons all over. The pinyon nuts were falling, and people started to pick them. I picked, too, for about two months. One day I hauled a lot of wood to my home, hauling all day. That night it started snowing and {it} snowed till the next morning. In the morning when I went out the snow was above my knees. I had hobbled the horses that night and I couldn't find them. I couldn't go very far in the snow; it was too deep. Next day we looked for the horses and found them trying to come this way. The snow was so deep we didn't go very fast with the horses and couldn't see the road. We just came along about where the road was and got back home. My wife and I were driving them through the snow. The snow was pretty deep where our fire place was, too, but we scraped it out and built a fire.

Next day we started off to the pinyons, going by way of Kainti. We carried some hay on a horse, rolled up in a blue blanket. We got down to where they were picking about sundown. The snow was pretty deep, and this was about nine years ago (the famous Big Snow of November 1931). We couldn't go very far, and stayed at home most of the time. Some people built a sled and we were using that to go to the store with. Sometimes we hauled wood with it. I heard that a lot of Navajos were snowed in around Aspera, and I don't know how they got out of there and came home. I also heard about people's horses starting to die from the snow, and that there were a lot of dead horses between Aspera and Zuni. There were no trails open between homes. It must have been about a month until they made little trails between homes.

The Zunis had a dance. People had been coming past Kainti to get home, and all those people were snowed in. Some of them lived at Kainti, Tohatchie, Ft. Defiance, Window Rock, St. Michaels, Aspen Spring, and they came by here. We had made one road here and they came back on that. A lot of trees were broken by the heavy weight of the snow. I don't know how long the snow stayed so deep. After it melted some people had a hard time and others were all right. A lot of green grass came up all at one time because the ground was pretty wet. There was a lot of grass and feed for horses that summer. I only lost a yearling colt, and my wife didn't lose any sheep. My little horse fell down close to the fence and put its leg through the wire. While he was moving around, one leg got tangled in the wire, and I think the horse lived two days until it died. People got all their crops planted, and most of them raised good crops that summer—oats, corn, squashes, beans.

Right after planting, the government people told the Indians they were going to have a lot of jobs for Indians all over Navajo country, inside the reservation and outside. First they took Indians in a truck to Gallup to take examinations before they gave them jobs. Wilkins was hauling some Indians from here to town. Just after they took their examinations he lent to Indians on credit, so they would start buying and he could get their checks when they got paid.

DEDICATION OF THE KLAGETOH CHAPTER HOUSE

Before we went to work we heard about a big ceremonial at Klagetoh. They were having it because they had built a big Chapter House there and the government wanted to show it to the Indians. After they saw it, they could build one in each district of Navajo country. They wanted to have a lot of dancing at the ceremonial, and would have a lot of food for us to eat. They wanted a lot of people so that they would have a big crowd. The other boys wanted to go there from Kainti. A white man living off to the west had a big truck and wanted to haul a lot of Indians down there for two dollars a round trip.

A lot of boys got together to go to the ceremonial—some down below, some more at my place. He picked us up, and some women went too. We got to Gallup and started down the road but hadn't gone far when we had a flat tire. We fixed it, but before we got to Manuelito we had another flat. There was no good spare tire, so the white man got a ride in a passing car to go get another tire and to get the flat one fixed. In about an hour he came back with two tires, one new and one old. We started off again and had two more flats before we got to Chambers about sundown. They told us it was forty miles yet. We got about halfway there and had another flat. Do you know why? The truck was overloaded. While we were fixing that tire a lot of people went to sleep there.

They found two bales of hay on the road where we stopped. A pickup came along and the man said he had lost two bales. We told him we found it; it was in the truck. He put the two bales in the pickup and said he wanted to give some of the boys a ride to where the ceremonial was. Some boys got in and went on that night; the rest stayed there with the truck. Next morning we started off and got there about ten o'clock. There was a big crowd there, with a Squaw Dance going on to one side of the Chapter House. Behind the Chapter House was a lot of roasted meat for the people, with cooks making bread one place, cooking meat another place, making coffee at still another. There was a Squaw Dance on each side, about a mile and a half away. The boys all scattered out as soon as we got there.

(Usual description follows of the Squaw Dance, horse races, speeches, and food at the Chapter House at noon; exhibition of rugs, beads, and silver. Paper plates and spoons provided. The Ft. Defiance agent spoke to the Indians, and Chapter officers from different districts were there.)

Hunter, the government agent, said that we people could start making blankets like the ones there, on the women's side.

"If you do the best work you can on a blanket, you'll get more for it. You aren't making very good blankets, and so you are just wasting your time, throwing money away. It is the same with your silver. If you make a lot of good jewelry, do it better, you will make more money from that too. Whatever the Chapter officers say, you must listen to them and let them talk to you. They know what they are talking about. We are standing back of them, telling them how to help the Indians so they can go ahead and start learning how to make their own living. That's what the Chapter officers are for. You must have Chapter officers in each district. Whenever we have a big meeting at Ft. Defiance, they can come to it and then come back and tell you all about it, carrying the news to the Indian People. In that way, we can all help you together and we will do the best we can for you people.

"I am Superintendent here at Ft. Defiance. I have both hands full. I can't get around all over the country, so I need your help. You can help me out in some ways, and I will surely appreciate it if you will do that. Let's try to cut down the drinking, gambling and all such things."[121]

EDITOR'S EPILOGUE

Lucky continued to serve as a singer in and around Kainti for at least another decade after he recounted his life history. In the early 1950s, however, he left his practice, his home area, and his family for the fleshpots of Gallup. There he drank, lived with another woman, and died a violent death in April 1958.[1]

For many, many years it was, I think, the ceremonies that saved Lucky's life, almost literally. He relished their opulence: the Cracker Jacks and cloth and cigarettes literally thrown away, the food so plentiful for guests. He relished not so much the religious and historic and philosophical aspects of the rituals as their color: the singer made a face of blue, the stick was dressed with brightest yarn, people wore their best jewelry. And I think Lucky savored the authority of the singer, who told people to leave the hogan or to come in, who sometimes sang and sometimes did not, who chose to perform a ceremony this way or another way. And deep beyond words, I think Lucky was desperate for the welcome sense of belonging that ceremonies engender: people coming together, people engaged in purposive activities, people riding and eating and dancing—

and drinking. It was never the content of the ceremonies that drew him, it was the riches they brought to his life.

But Lucky was fatally flawed. He was very young when his mother died (Mrs. Wood told him, "Three years after you were born your mother died. Since then nobody looked after you"). He was a lonely little boy; most unusual for that time and place, his grandmother and grandfather lived alone, and Lucky seldom was able to play with other children. He acknowledged this social deprivation when he says that, after he lived with the Woods, he could get along with other people pretty well.

When did he begin the behavior that earned him the name Navajos called him? (That here he must bear the name Lucky is unfortunate.) His life history does not tell us when he learned to appear perpetually happy and jolly, to joke, and to expect a welcome because he made people laugh. Bill's children remember him for this, not for his singing or his adventures or for any skills, certainly not as a husband or a father to his children. In the end, being "a jovial sort," as Dorothea Leighton first described him, was not enough. He abandoned the effort and joined a Skid Row community whose delusory color and riches came from the greens and ambers of bottles of cheap wine. There, his death and the manner of it were entirely too predictable.

NOTES

PREFACE

1. In 1953 Rosemary Joy Brough analyzed Lucky's life history for her M.A. thesis in the Department of Sociology at Cornell University (*Lucky, the Opportunist: A Psychobiological Personality Study of a Navaho Singer*).

2. I already had interviewed Ruth Underhill in Denver, and was later to interview Mary Shepardson in Palo Alto and Katherine Spencer in Santa Fe. My focus in these interviews, however, was on same-sex research rather than on Navajo women.

3. The field notes collected by Alexander H. Leighton and Dorothea C. Leighton at St. Lawrence Island, Alaska, in the summer of 1940, after they left New Mexico, have been placed in the Alaska and Polar Regions Department of the University of Alaska in Fairbanks.

4. The ability to speak well is valued in their spiritual and political leaders by the Navajos as well as by other Native American groups. Lucky, I think, spoke well, and he was also an accomplished storyteller, as the reader will discover; these two characteristics accounted for at least some of his popularity.

INTRODUCTION: PEOPLE, PLACE, AND TIME

1. Clifford's term polyphonic (1986:17) is appropriate here. See also Marcus (1986:190), who speaks of "the dialogic context of fieldwork, . . . even to the incorporation of multiple authorial voices."

2. The model for these seminars was developed in the Concrete Sociology course at Harvard, conducted by the physiologist L. J. Henderson, which included

> physicians, lawyers, business executives, governmental administrators, and representatives of the various social sciences [who] presented and discussed a "case" with which they were personally familiar. (Kluckhohn 1956:531n.1)

3. I am grateful to Alexander H. Leighton for this information about their 1938–39 attendance; he remembers that seminar as being only the second in the series (AHL, p.c., Apr. 18, 1990).

4. White's *The Roots of Dependency* (1983) is a persuasive account of the policies by which the self-supporting Navajos, Choctaws, and Pawnees were driven into poverty.

5. Most of the data for the one book-length study of Navajo witchcraft (Kluckhohn 1970[1944]) come from the Ramah area. As Kluckhohn noted, Ramah Navajos were marginal rather than heartland Navajos, and the extent to which such marginality left a space for the malevolent supernatural forces that are part of the traditional Navajo worldview, and for Lucky's concern about such forces, cannot now be known. From within that worldview Lucky reports several credible examples of witchcraft, although only the first, the sickness and cure of Wood's daughter, is specifically identified as such.

6. Lucky's possible incarceration had to do with a drunken brawl he had with Tony, and we are fortunate that Tony pressed the Leightons into service in order to have his version written up for presentation to the judge. I include it here despite its length, preceded by the Leightons' explanatory paragraph, because it documents an instance of Lucky's philandering (Barney's sister, now Tony's wife, he calls *his* wife) as well as his bellicosity when drunk.

> (Mar. 19) At the time of our stay, Lucky had got into trouble with Barney and Barney's brother-in-law, Tony. Barney and his wife had approved a match between Tony and Barney's sister and Tony had gone to live with the girl at Barney's place. Barney and his wife, Tony and his wife, they all get along fine, they was all working together, up till one month and a half. ["All went well for a month and a half."] Then the following incident took place. The account was given by Tony who wanted it prepared for the Crown Point judge.
>
> One day two men came, they was drinking. One was Lucky and the other was Don. Lucky was pretty drunk; Don was not very drunk. They came on horseback but they tied their horse out there and came inside the hogan. When they came in they stood up here near the fire.

Lucky started to talk to Barney's wife. Lucky says they was so hungry, they want to get something to eat. Then he turn right around to Barney and ask Barney what he thinks about it. They told him they give something to eat. And they sat down here.

That moment this boy (Tony) went out, going outside. Stays outside for quite a while. He think about that time these two mens got something to eat. "So I starts to come back inside the hogan. Lucky stepped outside the door and met me there." Says, "Lucky put his arm around my neck and asks me where did I took his wife to?" Didn't say anything about it but Lucky just turn it over to joke. Tony thought it might be just a joke. Says, "We start walking from there on to where the horse is tied up." Don came outside the hogan and come down there to where the horse is too. They got one horse and they said they was going home and they started off. They got one horse; they was riding double.

Tony came back inside the hogan and he sat down inside here. Then he heard a noise, sound like somebody is running a horse up, sound like coming over here toward the door. By that time somebody yell out and said, "Where you are, Tony?" And Tony got hold of the door and opened it, and there he was on the horse, that was the same man again, Lucky. They were riding double yet, like they start off. They was riding back and forth behind the door out there. They got a pail out there and they got that pail all smashed up. Wanting Tony, calling him out. Tony stepped out the door to see what was going on. He went outside for the pail, not for the mens.

"When I stepped outside and I picked up that mashed pail, Lucky dropped over one side and tried to grab me, and I got hold of the bridle and stopped the horse from going around." Says, "Lucky was pretty mad, wanted me to fight." Lucky wanted to know why did he take his wife away from him? Lucky is meaning this girl, Barney's sister. Lucky says he wants to hurt him today some way. "And the same time he got hold of my hair." . . . Lucky is holding his hair with two hands. He told the other boy, riding behind, whip the horse so they can drag this boy (Tony) away. "So he did, he whipped the horse and started off and I was dragging one side the horse." Before they start away for that he get ahold of Lucky too, get ahold of round his body. They go for a little ways, Tony is pulling all that time and Lucky is pulling all that time. They didn't go very far with it. Everything start to falling—the two men and the saddles, everything is fall off the horse. Tony noticed one bottle was broke.

Him and Lucky started to fight there. Didn't take him long to throw Lucky down and he was sitting on top of Lucky. Says, "While I was sitting on top of Lucky, Don come in and try to throw me off. Barney come out and come along at that time. And he throwed Don away and told Lucky to get up, and pushed me over to one side, and told us to stop fighting." There was a quart bottle, half gallon, one gallon, three bottles. He says but these, the biggest bottles, the gallon and the half a gallon, they had very little in it. The quart bottle was full. What he heard, {the} one bottle that was broke was the half-gallon one.

He says he was the one that put the saddle back on the horse. And Barney took the two mens away from the hogan and they lead the horse away from there too. He says that's the last of it that he saw. Says at that time he took the sheep away from home, start to herd out. When he bring the sheep in by sundown, Barney told him that they had all kinds of fight that day. He says he didn't know what they all did that day. He says Barney knows all about that.

A few days after that Barney tell one of the Chapter {officers}. The Chapter man says they must have a meeting over that. This was happen February 8. The meeting was going to be on twelve day of February. They come down at the meeting when the time comes. There is quite a few people there. The three of the officers was there. Says Barney told his story there. And so was Lucky; I make a mistake, it was Don. Lucky didn't say a word there. People talk about that and they decided to drop the case, the whole thing. They says nobody was hurt in that fight (Social Relations 11–13).

The stages by which cordial relations are reestablished are interesting. On April 6,

Barney is mad at Lucky and so wouldn't ask him to sing. Bill says that after the fight at Barney's with Tony, Ben took Lucky and his companion Dan Smith down to the canyon and started them on their way. Then Barney went to Kainti. On the way back he met them again, and they both set on him and fought him. (Bill says fortunately for Barney, Lucky was so drunk he couldn't fight well.) Before the fight they had been at a Sing at Ned's. . . . Barney is evidently still mad at Lucky. Lucky says he got drunk all right, but he doesn't remember anything that he did that night and he holds no grudge for Ben (Social Relations 14).

Neither did Tony hold a grudge for long; for the following occurred on the very next day:

On April 7 Bill told us Tony was here. Bill and Tony and Lucky were planning to take a sweat bath. That night Tony and Lucky came in together. Tony wanted cough, headache and general pain medicine for Barney's wife. We gave him these. Tony asked about his picture and we showed him the kodachrome transparencies. He and Lucky handed them back and forth to each other in a friendly manner. Tony went out for a while but then returned and sat for ten minutes, laughing a good deal at Lucky's account of riding a freight (Social Relations 14).

It is notable that the Anglo legal system dictated that Lucky serve time for the altercation, as did Don, but that in the Navajo way people had talked about the case and dismissed it because "nobody was hurt in that fight."

7. Dorothea Leighton returned to Ramah in 1942 on a different project, and contracted with Evelyn, Lucky's half-brother's wife, to be her interpreter and helper. Evelyn, in turn, had expected to employ one of Lucky's daughters to care for her house and children while she helped Dorothea. The message detailing these arrangements had been sent via Lucky, but when Dorothea and Evelyn drove to Lucky's to pick up the daughter (Dr. Leighton very kindly gave me a copy of her 1942 field notes, from which this quotation is taken),

> We found that she had gone off to El Paso a month ago to pick cotton. Evelyn and Rudolpho were rather annoyed, as they had counted on this girl. [Her father Lucky] is a notably unreliable character, who may never have mentioned the matter to either his daughter or his wife. [Evelyn] said they would pull his ears when they saw him again for doing this thing. Later she said he may have been drunk when they were talking to him, which is more than likely.

LUCKY THE NAVAJO SINGER

1. Singer, medicine man, ceremonialist, chanter, healer—the terms all refer to Navajos who have learned the ceremonies that heal (I have not capitalized the terms from here on since "doctor" or "physician" would not be capitalized). In 1982 (p.c., Mar. 10), Dorothea Leighton's judgment was that

> the medicine men were such intelligent people. How could they ever do their business if they weren't! And certainly they were serving a much more useful purpose than the doctors for 99% of the Indians, because there were at that time something like five hospitals on the reservation . . . {and} no doctor in any of those hospitals ever went outside the door to do anything for an Indian.

2. Navajos generally used to, and in some areas still do, abandon the immediate area where a death has occurred.

3. By far the most common arrangement for a child who has been orphaned is for him to go with the mother's sister or, as here, the mother's mother. (A bit later, it appears that one of Lucky's sisters has gone to live with their mother's sister, who is married to Big Fred.) Kinship terminology reinforces these close clan ties—both mothers and the mothers' sisters are called "mother," and their children are called "brother" and "sister" rather than cousin. They are all members of the same matrilineage, the formal term for a group that reckons descent through the mother.

4. People unfamiliar with the pronunciation of the word Navajo sometimes pronounce the name as if it ended "joe" rather than "ho." For more than a decade in the 1930s and 1940s, including the time the Leightons were in the field, Navajo was therefore spelled with an "h."

5. Delegating burials to Anglos, especially traders, was a common custom of Navajos, who consider handling a corpse to be extremely dangerous. Avoidance goes even farther; in 1942 Dorothea Leighton recorded:

> Evelyn said she thought lots of the Nav{ajo}s wouldn't ride in Mr. V's pickup now because they knew {a man} had been carried in it to his grave (Sept. 14, 1942:59).

Some six weeks later she wrote about another death:

> Barton Davis had finished the coffin and lined it, and all the new clothes and jewelry, etc. were in it. The wife didn't want to touch the bundle of old clothes, but wanted to see the body. Raymond wasn't afraid to look at it himself, but was afraid it might do something to his 2nd wife's pregnancy. . . . They wanted someone else to dress the body, and Evelyn said she would if someone would help her, so I volunteered (Oct. 27, 1942:107).

6. Each of the sons would have gone to live with his wife's relatives, for Navajos are matrilocal. The term is a succinct way to say that, upon marriage, the new couple will be expected to live in the wife's area, rather than the husband's.

7. "Lucky here is referring to his mother's father {who is of course of another clan}. There is no indication in the life story that Lucky had any contacts with his paternal grandparents. The paternal grandfather, Kee, was famous for his knowledge of hunting songs and ritual" (Social Relations 4a).

8. Again, note that such terms as sing, ceremony, hand-trembling, chant and the like are not capitalized.

9. A ceremony, *Kinaaldá,* is celebrated for a girl at her first menstruation. It is a joyful ritual and one with many levels of meaning, from reenacting the ritual that was originally done for Changing Woman, who is preeminent among Navajo sacred personages, to "molding" the young woman for personal and social beauty, to honoring the promise of fertility. See Frisbie 1967 and Begay 1983.

10. "According to the life story, [he] had nothing to do with Lucky's up-bringing. That Lucky did not even recognize his father when he saw him is implied in the account of their meeting at a Sing.

(LS 8) Lucky told us that he was not sure but he thought this was the only time in his life that he had seen his father" (Social Relations 1).

11. Hair washing with shampoo made of yucca root is part of many ceremonies. It is made by chopping yucca root into fine pieces and placing them in water, then briskly whisking the solution into suds.

12. She runs to the east just as the sun is rising, for long life; others run too, but behind her, for to pass her is to risk premature aging.

13. A significant statement, since Kinaaldá incorporates many parts of Blessingway, the ceremony that is basic to all other Navajo ceremonies.

14. Singers often receive extra portions of the food served at the ceremony as part of their professional fee.

15. Understandably, since the singer is awake and working long hours during the ceremony as well as for the entire final night.

16. The cake is made of cornmeal mixed with water until it reaches a near-liquid state; then sugar and raisins are added and the mixture is poured into a pit that has been lined with cornhusks and carefully covered. A fire is built over the covering, and the cake is baked overnight.

17. The "naneskhadi, slapped again, a griddle cake, owes its name to the manner in which the dough is passed in easy fashion from one hand to the other, and then tossed on the stone griddle to bake" (Franciscan Fathers 1968: 207–208).

18. The importance of a child's labor in those years, especially for herding, is emphasized, as here, by their being frequently borrowed.

19. The famous school and mission in northeastern Arizona run by Franciscans. The Navajo scholar Father Berard Haile lived and worked there, and St. Michaels Press has published several books basic to Navajo ethnography.

20. Black Horse is Lucky's mother's brother—an extremely important role in the Navajo kinship system. A mother's brother bears many paternal responsibilities, and mother's brother is particularly important when a child's biological father may not reside in the same camp, as was the case with Lucky's father.

21. A hogan is divided conceptually into quadrants. The south is traditionally the space for men, the west is a place of honor for guests, and the north is for cooking and generally for women. The eastern portion is sacred because it faces the rising sun. There are pictures in Jett and Spencer (1981) of hogan construction as well as of a ramada (p. 186) and sweathouses (pp. 193, 194, and 195).

22. A funeral director interviewed in 1978 told me (Griffen 1980: 14) that Navajos are more realistic than Anglos about the physical details of death—that they frequently want to know them, sometimes in very specific detail; and are capable of dealing with them unsqueamishly.

23. Docile behavior following a homicide and attempted suicide seems quite common; again, more data are needed.

24. For several reasons, my attempts to find the official records of this case (as with Lucky's father's suicide following a homicide) have met with failure. First, Lucky did not know the year in which the crime occurred. Second, personnel of the District Court of McKinley County, New Mexico, informed me that their old records had been sent to the State Records Center and Archives in Santa Fe. That center, in turn, avows that not only do their case files for the McKinley County District Court end in 1912, but a District Court clerk withdrew the docket book from the center and never returned it; in the center's words: "So, without a Docket we cannot locate any proceedings against [Black Horse] or the other individuals. . . . If you can locate case numbers get back to me and we will assist you." Thus far I have not been able to locate those numbers. Then, too, there is the matter of names. Not only is Black Horse a pseudonym here, but for the rest of his life he was known to his Navajo neighbors by the nickname that reflected his sojourn in prison. "Before that he didn't have a name," reported one of the older Sage daughters. He did have a name, of course; he would have had a war name (see n. 26 below) as well as other names, all more or less temporary as they became appropriate because of emerging distinctive physical characteristics, quirks of disposition or personality, or events in his life. Apparently his imprisonment was so major that it overrode other possible labels and became, finally, the only name by which he was known.

25. The daughter would have been born to a previous husband, however, or the relationship would have been incest, abhorred by all except witches. On the other hand, mother–stepdaughter marriage was a common form of polygyny, albeit probably less common than marriage to two sisters.

26. A person may acquire—and lose—several names in the course of a lifetime; however, one's secret name, one's "war name," remains the same. Regarding this, the Franciscan Fathers wrote:

> Some maintain that the war name is in reality a secret name known only to closer relatives and never divulged to outsiders. An occasion for its use is had at the blackening during the war dance, at

which the name of the patient is proclaimed and inserted into the songs celebrating his victory. Others attach no importance whatever to this name (1968: 119).

27. "Real" in front of "mother" or "father" or other kin terms indicates biological relationship, for many people may be called by a kin term, much as an older and esteemed woman used to be called "aunt" by Anglos in some parts of the United States, even though she was not a biological relative.

28. Bill once told Clyde Kluckhohn that Big Fred is his (Bill's) maternal uncle (Social Relations 17).

29. See Shufeldt 1891 on infant tree-burial.

30. Sandpaintings, an integral part of Navajo ceremonies, are stylized representations of various beings and elements. Colored ingredients in powdered form are dribbled in a controlled stream through the fingers of the painters to form the picture on the smoothly swept floor of the hogan. See Franciscan Fathers 1968: 69.

31. The shade referred to is more probably a structure, as in n. 35 below, than an area not exposed to the sun. Brush hogan, shade and ramada are all terms for the rectangular structure roofed with brush or branches, usually without sides, that is used so widely throughout the arid Southwest. For illustrations of several types, see Jett and Spencer 1981: 40–46.

32. "Old Man" is a literal translation, but not an apt one, for what is in Navajo a respectful form of address.

33. Hand-trembling and star-gazing are two of the several ways to find the cause of an illness; such practices can also be used to "locate property which has been lost or stolen; for finding water when a party is in strange territory; for discovering the whereabouts of persons; and for predicting the outcome of a war raid or hunting venture" (Hill 1935: 68). They can also be used to discover witches. I reported to Dorothea that I had had a hand-trembling, and she responded (p.c., June 20, 1984):

> How great to get a handtrembling diagnosis and treatment! I've never seriously doubted its efficacy, but I've never had one nor seen one. Clyde {Kluckhohn} once did a fancy job of hiding something and then getting such a one to find it for him—without difficulty.

34. Presumably Enemy Way, or Anaa'ji.

35. Cooking during the summer is frequently done in the shade provided by a ramada and over an open hearth, especially where, as here, quantities of food must be prepared for visitors.

36. Corn pollen is basic to Navajo ritual and ceremony, and its uses run the gamut from the very personal and informal one of sprinkling a small pinch toward the rising sun for a blessing on the day, to a line of pollen being traced over patients at hand-tremblings and uses in very formal ceremonies. A specialized category of pollen is "live pollen (normally corn pollen that has been shaken over various animals and plants)." "The tiny bags for pollen are made of buckskin and usually also contain small fetishes or other items" (Frisbie 1987: 30, 31).

37. These containers most frequently are about as large as a pack of roll-your-own cigarette papers, perhaps a bit larger.

38. Four is a ritual number for Navajos, just as the number three is for Europeans.

39. "Navajo rituals work more through reciprocity—I have done this, now you in turn must do that—than by supplication: 'If an economic transfer did not take place, under the laws of reciprocity, the exchange of knowledge would not be complete'" (Parezo 1983: 30).

40. "If a witch says he is one, he will die right away" (Kluckhohn 1967: 214n.220).

41. Navajos call themselves Diné, which translates as People, in the same sense as "We, the people of the United States . . ."

42. That is, to his own clan relatives, to get him away from the area belonging to his wife's clan.

43. Kluckhohn found that "in the distribution of the 'far-off' witches the Chin Lee area is mentioned far more frequently than any other" (1967: 59).

44. This tale, in different words, was published in Kluckhohn, *Navaho Witchcraft* (1967: 200–202n.179), where Kluckhohn credits "the field notes of Drs. A. H. and D. C. Leighton" as his source.

45. The word Yeibitchai is used for the supernatural beings themselves, for the ceremony in which they are represented, and also for the masked humans who represent them.

46. Not because of malice, but rather because supernatural power is dangerous to those unprepared for it.

47. Given to the Navajo people by Changing Woman, it is basic to all ceremonies.

48. "The strength and elasticity of the Navaho basket renders it serviceable as a drum, in other words, *it is turned down* and beaten with a drumstick" (Franciscan Fathers 1968:295). A sketch of a pottery drum and of a drumstick appears on p. 289.

49. Excellent photographs of such masks (and on the facing page, three Yei) appear in Wyman (1983: 540).

50. Photographs of many aspects of Navajo ceremonies that

Lucky talks about appear in Part IV, The Enduring Way, of Laura Gilpin's *The Enduring Navaho* (1968). They were made, for the most part, between 1950 and 1965; they still convey much of the feel of Lucky's time, and I recommend them highly. "Navaho gathering for a Squaw Dance" (p. 227) dates from 1934; the two "Awaiting the night ceremonial" photographs (pp. 242, 243) are classic; and the two-page photograph "The long prayer of the Nightway" (pp. 244–245) shows the Yeibitchai dancing in the hogan.

51. The wooden masks of the Shalako have movable mouth parts, which, when brought sharply together, make a loud crack, as when two boards are clapped smartly together.

52. Their bodies painted the ocher red of the southwestern landscape, naked except for breechcloths and moccasins, and with apparently hairless heads and disfigured faces, the mudheads travel from house to house making grunting and other unintelligible noises and carrying on, sometimes quite scandalously, with each other and with those watching. For representations of them and of the Shalakos, see Wright 1988.

53. Coals, as here, or various gifts as mentioned later, can be thrown "through the roof," the opening in the center of the roof of a traditional hogan, which is more mundanely used by smoke rising from the all-purpose wood fire below.

54. That is, reducing the colored stones and other substances to fine powders to be used to form the various colored elements of the drypainting. See Parezo 1983 for a full treatment of dry- or sandpainting.

55. This ceremony must have occurred some twenty-five or thirty years earlier; Lucky's recall of this detail is noteworthy.

56. Inside a hogan the motion should always be, as here, "sunwise": east to south to west to north. This very movement echoes the being of Changing Woman, who for eternity moves from the youth of the east to the old age of the north and then again through the cycle.

57. Several ethnographers have noted the indifference of at least some Navajos to the pain of animals. In 1942, DCL noted:

> About Aug. 16 Thomas shot a chicken hawk in the wing. Alfred got hold of it somehow and brought it home. He showed it to me with glee and later several times held it by its outstretched wings and pretended to attack the decrepit old broken-legged rooster with it. I don't know its ultimate fate, but probably an uncomfortable death. Today I have seen him kick one of the little kittens about 3 feet, and tie a rope around the neck of a cringing dog, then blindfold him and let him fall

off the roof of the vegetable cellar with great amusement. B finally saw him and told him to stop. He doesn't seem like an especially mean child otherwise. (Aug. 27, 1942:35)

W. W. Hill (1943:13) wrote:

I once observed a man take a cat and dog and knock their heads together until they howled, scratched, barked and bit. This action was considered screamingly funny by all present.

It should be noted, however, that Lucky is equally casual in reporting his own injuries: "I said I had a headache, that was all."

58. Although often heard, the term squaw dance is neither a translation of the Navajo name nor an accurate term for Enemyway. The Navajo name is Anaa'ji, as spelled by the Board of the Medicine Men's Association; the Board suggested a fee of fifty dollars for a two-night ceremony or five hundred dollars for five nights. The latter sum makes the longer Enemyway equally costly as nine-night performances of Mountainway or of Nightway (Yeibichai) (See Frisbie 1987:465n.27).

59. "Although the War Ceremony includes sexual exhibitionism, otherwise rare, the rattlestick, the leading symbol, must be carried by a female virgin. I was told that since girls lose their virginity very young, it is hard to find a virgin who qualifies" (Reichard 1963:136).

60. Such give-aways occur in many Native American ceremonies. They have several functions, one of course being to distribute wealth more evenly throughout the group.

61. Here, as in the case of "washing" the sheep, Lucky is being a good Navajo child in expecting to learn by his own observations rather than through questioning someone verbally.

62. For an introduction to Enemyway (Reichard 1950:357n.1 calls it War Ceremony), of which the riding and shooting that Lucky describes are the beginning, see Haile 1938.

63. Performance of a complete ceremony may be lengthy and expensive, so a small but essential part of it may be performed as a trial (Reichard 1950:102). The blackening rite (Anit'eesh; see Frisbie 1987:465) is such a trial for Enemyway.

64. As described by Reichard (1950:136), "A young man may pay a girl to dance with him exclusively, and stealing away together at this time has public sanction." Bill Sage said:

But the boys and the girls when they dancing there they can talk and they can make appointment and that is what they do and they meet afterward. When the mother goes to sleep or gets busy somewhere afterward, the girl can slip away. That is the way Lucky been doing it (May 2, 1940:30).

65. Also called the Corral Dance, or the Dark Circle of Branches (Frisbie 1987:5).

66. McNitt wrote that, at a later date, the famous trader Lorenzo Hubbell, who neither smoked nor drank, learned of this illegal still and operation, and "angered by what he heard and later saw ... arranged to buy the store and, with equally direct action, smashed the still and dumped out the mash." McNitt's informant recalled that Hubbell bought the store in 1918 and sold it about 1925 (1989: 205–206). (I thank Dave Brugge for bringing this reference to my attention.)

67. Until well into this century it was customary for government agents and other Anglos to refer to Native American males as boys. Lucky and/or Bill have picked up the usage; here, Lucky may indeed have been in his teens, but the word recurs again at the trial in Santa Fe, when older men are involved, and at the Chapter House dedication (at the end of the book), when Lucky was in his thirties. A Southern Ute friend told me that, years later, he still resented that his father and other Ute men had always been called "boys" by the superintendent at the Ignacio, Colorado, agency.

68. Indeed, the architecture of Zuni and of the pueblos visible from this train is identical.

69. Sweatbaths are generic purifiers and, in specific, may be used, as here, to remove the contamination of having been around outsiders or to ward off the evil that may occur because of such contact.

70. Opler wrote (1965:369) that the weak corn beer called *tiswin*

> is considered the most nourishing of the beverages and is often spoken of as a food, because its mild stimulation when taken in moderate quantities has helped many a person withstand the rigors of travel and want.

Considered appropriate to any social occasion, it was the only alcoholic beverage that the Apaches consumed to any extent.

71. This is the first part of the initiation of boys into the Zuni kachina cult. For a full description of the ceremony see Stevenson (1904), Bunzel (1932), and, most recently, Barton Wright (1988).

72. That is, they were from what is called the checkerboard area, the alternate sections of land along the western routes of early trans-

continental railroads that had been deeded to those companies as a government subsidy. Goodman (1982:57) describes the situation:

> Inhabitants of Ramah {as well as those of the Kainti area} live on checkerboard parcels within the simplified boundaries shown on most maps. Most of the continuous areas of this reservation were gained by exchange of land between Navajo and federal, state, or private land holders. Additional property also was purchased with funds provided through public laws. Some of the land was purchased from the Picuris and Pojoaque Indian pueblos. Although parcels of land were held by the Navajos before then, the public laws that provided for the present configuration were enacted in 1956.

73. A strange answer, since the term usually refers to the color of the horse.

74. The clear lesson here is that the cooperating social unit is responsible for the consequences of Lucky's actions, and also that he is part of a social unit rather than an isolated individual; Wood's mother will have to pay Lucky's fine, for example, and the whole group will be blamed if the bull doesn't recover.

75. Since this statement is not factually true, the woman may be emphasizing that, functionally, Lucky has become a child of the Woods.

76. Lucky's question, apparently asked for the first time in his life, is immensely poignant because it comes right after he was told, "You still haven't anybody to help you."

77. If he is not a good worker and good herder, no one will care to have him as a son-in-law.

78. In other words, she was recounting Navajo history.

79. "Plumeway, also called Downway or the Feather Chant, like Nightway represents the Yeis in its sandpaintings and its dances, although in the 1970s it was rarely performed. Also like Nightway, it is used for diseases of the head or other ailments, such as rheumatism; but when these are attributed to infection from game animals, especially deer, such troubles may be called 'deer disease'" (Wyman 1983:546).

80. See Leighton and Leighton 1949:70–71.

81. While one person is the official patient, the "one sung over," the salutary effects of the performance of the ceremony extend outward to those in attendance and, ultimately, to all people everywhere. Selfishness is antisocial, and a selfish performance of a ceremony would lessen, perhaps entirely negate, its beneficial consequences.

82. Lucky does not often put himself down, so this self-pitying

may be occasioned by his earlier description of Mrs. Wood talking to him as if she were his mother.

83. Apparently Talking God, leader of the Yeis; Tohnenili is Water Sprinkler.

84. In contrast to being paid in credit which, of course, could be used only at the issuing store.

85. Thus, a sister or half-sister to Agnes.

86. This is how Lucky was married, not with a ceremony, but rather by acting as a husband.

87. Three of Lucky's eleven children died. Nothing was said about one death, another was a seemingly natural death of an infant, but the third, that of an older son, occurred quite violently when he tried to ride an unbroken yearling and was dragged and/or kicked to death (see below, "Lucky's Son Is Killed").

88. "After his marriage, Lucky worked at the home of his wife. . . . He says these people were 'pretty rich'" (LS 255, 256) (Summary of Subsistence Data 3); and

> it has already been mentioned that Lucky's mother-in-law had property. Apparently she came from a well-to-do family, for we were once told, "George's mother's brother used to be pretty rich, about 2000 head of sheep, 100 or more head of cattle."

The woman he is referring to as George's mother is actually his own mother-in-law, for George is Lucky's wife's brother {and also Don's uncle} (Social Relations 45). Lucky sometimes also refers to her as Big Hail's mother (Social Relations 42).

89. "Bill asked Lucky if he would talk about sex. Lucky said, 'No, not for twenty-five cents an hour.' He thought Bill ought to explain to us how Navahos feel about that subject so that we would not ask questions of that kind. Bill went on to say that this topic is regarded in the same way as some of the songs; it cannot be discussed after the winter is over and the thunder of spring has been heard. This matter here is just like that and that is what Lucky says, 'There is a lota snake crawl out now, I don't want to tell about those things. Main part, I don't like to get bitten by snake,' he says, 'more than I can help.' According to Bill, not only the individual who spoke of these things, but also the members of his family and his livestock would be in danger of snake bite or would be menaced by thunder, bear, or whirlwind. Consequently our data on this subject are far from complete. However, incidents arose and bits of information came our way which indicate that Lucky has had a good many affairs with women (Social Relations 36).

90. Hoofs (Claw) Chant (Akeshghaan'ji) is one of the eighteen ceremonies depicted on the 1984 "Traditional Navajo Ceremonies" chart by Eddie Tso and Lloyd Thompson (Frisbie 1987:432n.5). Frisbie notes (1987:465n.27) that in a 1979 list of ceremonies the spelling is given as Akeshgaanji', with the translation, again, as hoofs (claws).

91. Using these terms of relationship to refer to his mother-in-law is quite possibly a verbal form of mother-in-law avoidance.

92. That is, after the ritual four days of seclusion had ended.

93. Actually Don is the son of Lucky's wife's sister, who died of influenza. Don helped bury his grandfather; Lucky and his wife did not go over at the time (LS 350–351) (Social Relations).

94. No doubt because of his status as a respected elder.

95. That is, he had endangered himself by looking at the corpses.

96. Mutually agreeable resolution of a conflict is the Navajo ideal, in contrast to the punitive nature of Anglo justice.

97. In the official list, inexplicably, the pseudonym of Big Head is given as Big Head; earlier (p. 111) Agnes's father is called Long Hair, a name not on the list of psuedonyms.

98. More frequently the word ashamed is used to characterize the kind of acute embarrassment caused by a breach of proper behavior, in this case a man being near his mother-in-law.

99. The owl is a common harbinger of death in the Southwest.

100. Navajo husbands, having married into the group, are vulnerable to such charges.

101. Sending the medicine bundle, the jish, ahead with the person who has called for the singer is the usual practice.

> The literature and the Ramah Project Notes are full of examples of the practice of sending the jish ahead. {Lucky}, for example (Leighton and Leighton 1940 RPN), mentions an intermediary who returned "with a big load on his horse—the medicine bag and also the buckskin masks." This equipment was followed by the arrival of a Nightway singer two days later (see also Dyk 1938:265, 270–71, 272, 1947:151). The custom is still practiced today, whenever possible. (Frisbie 1987:104)

102. While the great majority of Navajo singers are male, more women than men are diagnosticians. An insightful exploration of this fact, true in many other cultures as well, appears in Kehoe (1973).

103. In Navajo a'tch'a means very specifically hungry-for-meat, for mutton, as compared with hunger for food in general. Bill's daughter Marie laughed and said, after I told her of Lucky's frequent mentions of meat,

All those medicine men eat meat all the time. They get a lot of respect. They're first to get fed, and they get the best meat, usually the ribs (p.c., Dec. 18, 1989).

104. Such a sing serves also to "hang up the shingle" of a new singer—to announce that he now is competent to perform a ceremony.

105. Clearly, the men were cooking for themselves.

106. This is, succinctly, the basis of the Navajo economic-leveling system

107. That is, he is a clan relative younger than she is. In Lucky's story, there is no reason for Agnes to claim Lucky's services other than that she is his clan sister.

108. Later, however (pp. 195–196), Lucky says that he and Ralph were brothers; they had different fathers but the same mother (Social Relations 15).

109. Because he had won so much money, Lucky's life was being threatened by Dave Rope, a threat that he at least took seriously enough to leave for home immediately. Lucky told Ralph where he got the cigarette; perhaps Ralph didn't think Dave's medicine would operate against him, although clearly it did. Lucky believes that witchcraft caused Ralph's death, I think, or otherwise he would not pass it off to the Leightons with a bare "He died two years ago."

110. This is an example of the quite lavish hospitality Phil owes Lucky merely because they are relatives.

111. "If it becomes obvious during a ceremony that the patient is dying, the singer is expected to leave and to remove the jish before death occurs" (Frisbie 1987 : 106).

112. "Sometime after this John became ill. A sing failed to help him and he was taken to the Ft. Defiance hospital where he died" (LS 481) (Social Relations 18).

113. It is hard for me not to believe that, in the Navajo way of thinking and from Lucky's own juxtaposition here, he did not connect his stopping and staying overnight to help Agnes with the death of his son. Remember his references to her as "that woman," his statement that she had come near the hogan where he was living but did not speak, and his conviction that she had continued to be angry with him:

> One day later that woman came back, right near my home. We could see her from the hogan. . . . After that whenever I saw her she wouldn't talk to me, she was mad at me (p. 172, herein).

114. George is the boy's mother's brother and thus of the same clan as the mother and the boy himself. If no outsider is available, then the nearest relatives of the clan of the deceased are most responsible for the task of burial.

115. The term brittle marriage has been used to characterize Navajo marriages; both the social ties and the duties to one's clan relatives are strong enough that marriage ties may prove extremely fragile as, clearly, they did in this instance.

116. Because so many ceremonies have the goal of restoration of wholeness to someone suffering disorder, whether mental or physical, allowance has to be made, as here, for ceremonies to be performed at other than their ritually proper season. As Reichard says,

> Detached rites may be performed also for those too ill to submit to the full chant, or for a person unfortunate enough to need a chant at a forbidden season—the Night Chant in summer, for example (1950:102).

117. Precisely this process, with the addition of an apprenticeship, has been, until very recently, the only way for singers to learn their profession.

118. For each ceremony, a medicine bundle or jish is assembled that contains various substances vital to the performance of that particular sing:

> Kluckhohn . . . states that ritual paraphernalia were still being made in 1950 by Ramah Navajos, although the number of people with the necessary ceremonial knowledge was declining annually (Frisbie 1987:97).

119. "I {AHL?} asked Bill Sage why Lucky went around so much to the sings and he said it was largely due to the medicine men urging him. The medicine men do no work at the sings except singing and so they value a man who is a good helper and they were always telling Lucky to meet them here and there. The more he did it the better he got and the more they wanted him" (Subsistence 9).

120. Knowing the songs involved in a ceremony by rote memory is one thing; here, Lucky acknowledges that, at that time, he had not learned the sacred lore that explains and underlies the ceremonies.

121. It is hard to imagine a more platitudinous ending for Lucky's life story, but then hortatory endings to recountings of certain types seem universal.

Editor's Epilogue

1. New Mexico's Department of Vital Statistics will not divulge the date or cause of Lucky's death. The information about the woman-not-his wife and the violence of his death comes from members of Bill Sage's family, and the April date was given to me by the funeral home that released his body for burial. The Gallup newspaper should have reported his death, but I had searched it twice without finding the story; I think I was successful on the third attempt. The *Independent* (Apr. 22, 1958:1) reported that a man "of this area" had been picked up by the Gallup police early that Sunday morning, April 22, 1958. He had been beaten severely and was wandering about on the north side of town in a dazed condition. He told the police he had been jumped by five males, who took his wallet with eight dollars in it. The police drove the man to St. Mary's Hospital, where he died an hour later. He had an eight-inch cut on the top of his head, at least four cuts on his face, and a one-inch stabwound on the back. He was conscious long enough to give his name, which was recorded as Herbert Anderson. Both these names are as similar to Lucky's first and last names as, say, Johns and Jones; any written identification would have disappeared with his wallet; and it would not be surprising if he slurred his words. In any event, no other April deaths in Gallup fit at all, and no further information about the murder was forthcoming from the police since there were no leads to pursue.

REFERENCES CITED

PERSONAL COMMUNICATIONS
Bill's Daughter 1989 (November 9, December 18)
Leighton, Alexander H. 1990 (April 18)
Leighton, Dorothea C. 1982 (March 10, 11), 1984 (June 20)

PUBLISHED WORKS
Begay, Shirley M.
1983 Kinaaldá: A Navajo Puberty Ceremony. Revised ed. Rough Rock, Arizona: Rough Rock Demonstration School.
Bennett, Kay
1964 Kaibah: Recollection of a Navajo Girlhood. Los Angeles, California: Westernlore Press.
Blanchard, Kendall A.
1971 The Ramah Navajos: A Growing Sense of Community in Historical Perspective. Navajo Historical Publications 1. A Publication of the Research Section, Navajo Parks and Recreation. Window Rock, Arizona: The Navajo Tribe.
1975 Changing Sex Roles and Protestantism Among The Navajo Women in Ramah. Journal for the Scientific Study of Religion 14(1): 43–50.
Brough, Rosemary Joy
1953 Lucky, the Opportunist. A Psychobiological Personality Study

of a Navajo Singer. M.A. thesis, Department of Sociology, Cornell University.

Bunzel, Ruth
1932 Introduction to Zuni Ceremonialism. Smithsonian Institution, Bureau of American Ethnology Annual Report 47. Pt. 3. Pp. 467–544. Washington, D.C.: U.S. Government Printing Office.

Clifford, James
1986 Introduction: Partial Truths. In Writing Culture: The Poetics and Politics of Ethnography. James Clifford and George E. Marcus, eds. Pp. 1–26. Berkeley: University of California Press.

Dyk, Walter
1938 Son of Old Man Hat: A Navaho Autobiography. Lincoln: University of Nebraska Press.

Dyk, Walter and Ruth Dyk
1980 Left Handed: A Navajo Autobiography. (Sequel to Son of Old Man Hat.) New York: Columbia University Press.

Franciscan Fathers
1968 An Ethnologic Dictionary of the Navajo Language. Saint Michaels, Arizona: Saint Michael's Press. (Originally published in 1910.)

Frisbie, Charlotte J.
1967 Kinaaldá: A Study of the Navajo Girl's Puberty Ceremony. Middletown, Connecticut: Wesleyan University Press.
1987 Navajo Medicine Bundles or *Jish*: Acquisition, Transmission, and Disposition in the Past and Present. Albuquerque: University of New Mexico Press.

Frisbie, Charlotte J., and David P. McAllester, eds.
1978 Navajo Blessingway Singer: The Autobiography of Frank Mitchell, 1881–1967. Tucson: University of Arizona Press.

Geertz, Clifford
1988 Works and Lives: The Anthropologist as Author. Stanford, California: Stanford University Press.

Gilpin, Laura
1968 The Enduring Navaho. Austin: University of Texas Press.

Goodman, James M.
1982 The Navajo Atlas: Environments, Resources, People, and History of the Diné Bikeyah. Norman: University of Oklahoma Press.

Griffen, Joyce
1980 Navajo Funerals, Anglo-Style. Museum of Northern Arizona Research Paper 18. Flagstaff, Arizona.
1988 Dorothea Cross Leighton. In Women Anthropologists: A Bio-

graphical Dictionary. Ute Gacs, Aisha Khan, Jerrie McIntyre and Ruth Weinberg, eds. Pp. 231–237. New York: Greenwood Press.

Haile, Father Berard O.F.M.

1938 Origin Legend of the Navaho Enemy Way. Yale University Publications in Anthropology 17. New Haven, Connecticut: Yale University Press.

Hill, Willard Williams

1935 The Hand Trembling Ceremony of the Navaho. El Palacio 38(12-13-14):65–68.

1938 Navajo Use of Jimsonweed. New Mexico Anthropologist III(2): 19–21.

1943 Navaho Humor. General Series in Anthropology 9. Menasha, Wisconsin: George Banta Publishing Company.

Jett, Stephen C., and Virginia E. Spencer

1981 Navajo Architecture: Forms, History, Distributions. Tucson: University of Arizona Press.

Kehoe, Alice B.

1973 The Metonymic Pole and Social Roles. Journal of Anthropological Research 29(4):266–274.

Kennedy, John G.

1973 Cultural Psychiatry. In Handbook of Social and Cultural Anthropology. John J. Honigmann, ed. Pp. 1119–1198. Chicago: Rand McNally and Company.

Kluckhohn, Clyde

1927 To the Foot of the Rainbow: A Tale of Twenty–five Hundred Miles of Wandering on Horseback Through the Southwest Enchanted Land. New York: The Century Company. (Reprinted 1992, Albuquerque: University of New Mexico Press.)

1949 The Ramah Project: In Gregorio, the Hand–Trembler: A Psychobiological Personality Study of a Navaho Indian. Alexander H. Leighton and Dorothea C. Leighton. Papers of the Peabody Museum of American Archaeology and Ethnology, Harvard University 40(1):v–vi.

1956 A Navaho Personal Document with a Brief Paretian Analysis. In Personality and Cultural Milieu. Douglas Gilbert Haring, ed. Pp. 513–531. Syracuse, New York: Syracuse University Press. (Originally published in 1945.)

1970 Navaho Witchcraft. Boston: Beacon Press. (Originally published in 1944.)

Langness, L. L. and Gelya Frank

1981 Lives: An Anthropological Approach to Biography. Novato, California: Chandler & Sharp Publishers, Inc.

Leighton, Alexander H.

1984 Then and Now: Some Notes on the Interaction of Person and Social Environment. Human Organization 43(3):189–197.

Leighton, Alexander H. and Dorothea C. Leighton

1949 Gregorio, the Hand-Trembler: A Psychobiological Personality Study of a Navaho Indian. Papers of the Peabody Museum of American Archaeology and Ethnology, Harvard University 40(1).

León-Portilla, Miguel

1975 Aztecs and Navajos: A Reflection on the Right of Not Being Engulfed. An Occasional Paper of The Weatherhead Foundation. New York: The Weatherhead Foundation.

Lidz, Theodore, M.D.

1966 Adolf Meyer and the Development of American Psychiatry. American Journal of Psychiatry. Special Section: Adolf Meyer: 1866–1950. 123(3):318–332.

Marcus, George E.

1986 Contemporary Problems of Ethnography in the Modern World System. In Writing Culture: The Poetics and Politics of Ethnography. James Clifford and George E. Marcus, eds. Pp. 165–193. Berkeley: University of California Press.

McNitt, Frank

1989 The Indian Traders. Norman: University of Oklahoma Press. (Originally published in 1962.)

Opler, Morris Edward

1965 An Apache Life-Way: The Economic, Social and Religious Institutions of the Chiricahua Indians. Chicago: The University of Chicago Press. (Originally published in 1941.)

Parezo, Nancy J.

1983 Navajo Sandpainting: From Religious Act To Commercial Art. Tucson: University of Arizona Press.

Ramah Project Notes

n.d. On file at the Laboratory of Anthropology, Museum of New Mexico, Santa Fe.

Reichard, Gladys A.

1963 Navaho Religion: A Study of Symbolism. (First published in 2 vols., 1950). Princeton, New Jersey: Princeton University Press.

Shufeldt, R. W.

1891 Mortuary Customs of the Navajo Indians. American Naturalist 25:303–307.

Stevenson, Matilda (Coxe)

1904 The Zuni Indians: Their Mythology, Esoteric Fraternities, and

Ceremonies. Smithsonian Institution, Bureau of American Ethnology Annual Report 23. Pp. 3–634. Washington, D.C.: U.S. Government Printing Office.

Stewart, Irene
1980 A Voice in Her Tribe: A Navajo Woman's Own Story. Socorro, New Mexico: Ballena Press.

Telling, Irving
n.d. A Preliminary Study of the History of Ramah New Mexico. Unpublished manuscript, Special Collections Library. Albuquerque: University of New Mexico. [Written in 1939?]

White, Richard
1983 The Roots of Dependency: Subsistence, Environment, and Social Change among the Choctaws, Pawnees, and Navajos. Lincoln: University of Nebraska Press.

Wright, Barton
1988 Patterns and Sources of Zuni Kachinas. No place of publication given: Harmsen Publishing Company.

Wyman, Leland C.
1983 Navajo Ceremonial System. In Handbook of North American Indians 10: Southwest. Alfonso Ortiz, ed. Pp. 536–557. Washington, D.C.: Smithsonian Institution.

Wyman, Leland C., Willard Williams Hill, and Iva Ósanai
1942 Navajo Eschatology. University of New Mexico Bulletin 377, Anthropological Series 4(1).

INDEX

accidents: bites, 44, 148, 149; horses, 64, 81, 130, 158; injuries, 43, 93, 104, 113, 149, 158, 197, 200–201; jumping from a train, 91; near-drowning, 66; near-hanging, 83; near-shooting, 44

Agnes, daughter of Big Head, of Long Hair, 111, 143–45, 170–72, 190, 223 n.107; father of, 222 n.97; grandfather of, 112; sister or half-sister of, 221 n.85

Albuquerque, 86, 89, 144

alfalfa, 182, 184

Andy Day, 67

Anglos. *See* white persons

Apache, 45, 87, 93, 219 n.70

Apache Wind Way, 41, 61, 83, 157, 195, 196, 199

Arnold, 83, 91, 107; brother of, 91

Aspen Spring, 95, 193, 202

Aspera, 180, 181, 202

automobiles, 72, 82, 84, 120, 132, 143, 153, 196, 201; road and, 165

Badger Scratch, 178

Bad Water, 125, 129

Bare-headed, 68, 110

Barney, 14, 57–59, 104, 133, 180

basket, 35, 36, 37, 56, 64, 76, 80, 109, 169, 216 n.48; basket wedding, 11, 168–70

beads. *See* jewelry. *See* trade goods

beer, tiswin, 93, 219 n.70

Bending Tree Woman. *See* Wood's mother

Benito, 158; daughter of, 106

Bert, 41, 140, 173, 177, 195

Big Ears, 68

Big Fred, married Lucky's mother's sister, 41, 81, 109, 114, 157–59, 198, 211 n.3, 215 n.28

Big Hail, 90, 107, 108, 118, 136, 137, 138, 139, 146, 150, 168, 169, 170; mother of, 134, 221 n.88

Big Head, 107, 144, 145, 222 n.97

Big Mountain, home of Tinlei, 48

Big Singer, 38, 49, 50, 51

Black Horse, 37–41, 139, 213 n.20, 214 n.24; daughter of, 40–41

Black Mountain, 57, 94, 95, 97, 104, 117

blackening a patient, 75, 162, 186, 198, 199, 218 n.63

blanket, saddle blanket, 37, 38, 53, 56, 59, 61, 64, 91, 96, 108, 117, 124, 130,

references, 227–31
rich people, 40, 58, 113, 118, 221 n.88
Roan Horse, oldest son of Big Hail, 112,
    116, 118, 137, 145, 147, 180, 181,
    200; oldest son of, 110; son of, 115,
    116; wife of, as hand-trembler, 152,
    191
Robert, brother of Ernest, 83, 116, 119,
    163, 197
Rope, Dave, 176–79, 223 n.109
Rudolpho, 211 n.7
Runner, singer, 112

saddle, 40, 45, 46, 52, 58, 59, 71, 75, 77,
    78, 79, 84, 95, 96, 97, 98, 99, 101,
    106, 109, 115, 120, 122, 123, 124–25,
    130, 131, 132, 134, 138, 156, 160,
    190, 191, 198, 200
saddle blanket. See blanket
Sage, Bill, the interpreter, 1, 2, 14, 15,
    57, 58, 106, 113, 122, 144, 145, 146,
    150, 179, 198, 215 n.28, 218 n.64,
    221 n.89, 224 n.119; brother of, 159;
    Chester and, 107; Clinton and, 12;
    daughters of, 214 n.24, 222 n.103;
    Ellen, Bill's wife and, 2, 12, 111;
    family of, 41, 206, 225 n.1; Harold
    and, 12–13; Jack's wife and, 196;
    mother-in-law of, see Agnes; Old Man
    and, 35, 157, 158; Ted and, 113, 115,
    120, 193, 194, 195, 196; Ted's wife,
    daughter of Long Hair, and, 152, 193,
    196; Tom and, 107
Salamon, 189
Salazar, 176
Salt Lake, New Mexico, 104, 180
salt, trip to gather, 180. See also trade
    goods
sandpainting, dry painting, 43, 61, 64,
    65, 108, 109, 162, 193, 194, 215 n.30,
    217 n.54
Sandy Hill, 104
Sandy. See Lucky's father
Santa Fe, 214 n.24; prison in, 40–41,
    105, 139; trial of bootlegger in, 84,
    86–89, 106
sawmill, 92, 165
Scout, Old, 196, 198
seclusion, following a death, 35, 42, 150,
    222 n.92
Seth, 176
sex, 91, 122, 176, 218 n.59, 221 n.89

shade. See brush hogan
Shady Lake, 100
Shalako, 58–60, 167, 217 n.51
sheep, 37, 39, 41, 45, 46, 60, 78, 82,
    89, 90, 91, 94, 95, 97, 98, 99, 100,
    101, 102, 103, 104, 105, 111, 115,
    117, 118, 120, 127, 128, 129, 135,
    136, 139, 140, 143, 144, 145, 146,
    148, 159, 160, 166, 169, 182–90, 194,
    195, 202, 221 n.88; dipping of, 68–70;
    herding of, 36, 38, 41, 42, 43, 51, 91,
    106, 113, 138, 147, 162, 168, 174;
    lambing of, 61
Shiprock, 57, 104, 176, 181, 182
Short Hair, 168; wife of, 168
sickness. See illness; accident
sing, 34, 35, 36, 38, 41, 42, 43, 48, 49,
    51, 53–57, 58, 61–65, 68, 70–81, 83,
    94, 103, 107–10, 112, 113, 114, 115,
    117, 125, 126, 129, 130, 132, 133,
    134, 142, 144, 146, 152, 153, 157,
    158–59, 160, 162, 163, 164, 183, 184,
    185, 186, 192–94, 195, 196, 197, 198,
    199, 200, 212 n.8, 223 n.104,
    224 n.116. See also names of specific
    ceremonies
singer, 33, 34, 36, 38, 41, 43, 46, 49,
    55–57, 58, 61–65, 76, 79, 83, 90,
    107–10, 112, 113, 114, 129, 130,
    146, 152, 160, 162, 164, 186, 193,
    196, 198, 199–200, 201, 205, 211 n.1,
    213 n.14, 222 n.102, 223 n.104,
    224 n.117
Slim, 160, 161, 162, 163
sling, leather, 43
Smith, Sam, married Lucky's mother's
    sister, 41, 42, 44, 61, 81, 82, 83, 93,
    107, 123, 133, 141, 142, 146; mother
    of, 41; sister of, 42, 43; wife of, 61–
    62, 141
snow, and snowstorms, 42, 44, 45, 92,
    141, 142, 146, 168; Big Snow of 1931,
    201–2
Sombrero, shot by Lucky's father, 106
spring. See water
"Squaw Dance." See Enemy Way
squirrel, 147–48, 164
St. Michaels, 81, 95, 103, 164, 202; Press
    of, 213 n.19; school of, 37
Stanley, 137–38, 146, 160, 180, 181,
    190; wife of, 137, 139
Star Way, 112